"STAND BY YA BEDS!"

Life as a 1970s Police Cadet

By

Steve Woodward

© Copyright 2020 Steve Woodward

All rights reserved

This book shall not, by way of trade or otherwise, be lent, re-sold, hired out, or otherwise circulated without the prior consent of the copyright holder or the publisher in any form of binding or cover other than that in which it is published and without a similar condition including this condition being imposed on the subsequent purchaser. The use of its contents in any other media is also subject to the same conditions.

ISBN: 978-1-913839-03-1

MMXX

A CIP catalogue record for this book
is available from the British Library

Published by
ShieldCrest Publishing Ltd.,
Aylesbury, Buckinghamshire,
HP18 0TF England
Tel: +44 (0) 333 8000 890
www.shieldcrest.co.uk

ACKNOWLEDGEMENTS.

My sincere thanks go to the following people whose memories, anecdotes, photos and encouragement have all helped to make this book possible; Stef King, John Gunner, Duncan Warry, Phil Travers, Richard Smith, Chris Gosden, Paul Rowsell, Ian Heath, Russ Bramley, Paul Williams, Adrian Prangnell, Laurie Parsonage, Martin Gibson, Matt Coumbe, Wayne Colebrook, Alan Robertson, Chris Cox, Mick and Beverley Dodds, Andy Reed, Shaun Terry, Andy Worship, Dave Brown, Andy Williams, Alan Dabbs, Kevin Emblen, Mick Streeter, Kev Mason, Gary O'Flaherty, Pete Kerley, Tony Astill, Eric Greenall, Peter Stoddard, Fred Masters, Charlie Lovegrove, Derek Stevens, Paul Stickler, Gerry Hopkins, David Harfitt, Davina Smith and Trish Woodward.

History of the Priory, Bishops Waltham by Peter Finn, published by Hedera Books.

CONTENTS

Foreword	I
Dedication	IV
Prologue	VII
Cadet memories – various contributors	XXI
History of The Priory	LV
Chapter 1. Piglets	1
Chapter 2. Welcome to Bishops Waltham	12
Chapter 3. Brockenhurst Camp	55
Chapter 4. Fareham Tech and the Oily's	78
Chapter 5. First Expedition	87
Chapter 6. Dartmoor	99
Chapter 7. Broccoli and Bromide	110
Chapter 8. Lima Papa	165
Chapter 9. Our Last Year	186
House Names	228
Books by Steve Woodward	231

"Stand By Ya Beds"

FOREWORD

"Stand By Ya Beds" is far more than an account by the author, Steve Woodward, of his experiences as a Police Cadet in the Hampshire Constabulary. It represents an historical account of a period, which for many of us saw the transition from school to entry into the regular force. Whilst some who never undertook those three years, often commented that cadets failed to experience a wider life, Steve manages to capture the breadth of activities that welded cadets together on a physical, cultural, community and friendship basis. For those of us who were there, it will bring back great memories of early uniform life, especially at Bishops Waltham Cadet Training School. Not only the disciplined regime, police officer trainers and characters, but also the huge opportunities we were given to participate in other activities. These ranged from Further Education, Community Service, Duke of Edinburgh Award, Outward Bound, Brockenhurst Camp, swimming qualifications, Voluntary Service Overseas, sports of all types, rock climbing and police attachments. The list goes on, and it will refresh many memories for the reader. Unbelievably we actually got paid for doing this!

Friendships and camaraderie were welded during this time, and for many have lasted to date. What is also interesting is that most cadets stayed to perform thirty years' service in the Hampshire Constabulary. As an investment, it secured regular staff who wanted the career of a Police Officer, not a transitional work experience which today sees so many leave the service after only a few years.

Steve Woodward

Brockenhurst Camp 1972 with from left to right Cadets Ian Readhead, Philip Elliott, Adrian Noye

At one stage, ex-Police Cadets represented 17% of the Force Establishment.

Hampshire Constabulary Cadet intake 1972

"Stand By Ya Beds"

This book will bring back wonderful memories and perhaps a few challenging ones to the reader. I enjoyed every page and laughed at many of Steve's experiences which mirrored my own. In writing "Stand By Ya Beds", Steve has authored a book which will bring much pleasure, and records an important period in the history of the Hampshire Constabulary.

I salute him.

Ian Readhead OBE, QPM, LL.B (Hons)
Deputy Chief Constable
Hampshire Constabulary
1972 – 2008

III

Steve Woodward

DEDICATION

Sadly, less than three weeks after writing the Foreword, Ian Readhead passed away. He had the Hampshire Constabulary running through his veins and genuinely regarded the force and those who served within it as his second family.

When the news of his death was announced there was an outpouring of grief on Police social media groups, the likes of which I don't think any of us had ever witnessed before. A common thread developed throughout the hundreds of tributes from those who worked with him or under him. Firm but fair, a true leader, a coppers copper, a great boss, the like of which we will never see again.

Although we served at almost the exact same time, I didn't actually ever work with him, although at major events during our time he always seemed to be there, leading from the front, directing the troops and ensuring we were all fed and watered. As a result, he commanded huge respect from us all.

However, I did 'work' with Ian at Families Day at Netley over many years. It was a day he held dear because it gave him the opportunity to meet current and former colleagues in a relaxed family atmosphere and I believe it was one of the highlights of every year for him. My wife and I have organised the classic police vehicle side of the event since 1995 and he would always go out of his way to come and thank us for doing so and would often talk to the car owners, many of whom had travelled from all corners of the UK to attend the event. He was particularly pleased to meet a contingent of French Police officers I'd invited in 2007, who had brought along a 1960s Renault 4-CV from the Paris Police museum collection. He was fascinated by it and actually took it for a drive.

"Stand By Ya Beds"

Later that day he hijacked me, following my appearances on the BBC TV series Traffic Cops and placed a sash over my head whilst at the same time whispering in my ear "Smile ya bastard" as Jan Brayley, the force photographer, took photos. He then shook my hand and thanked me most sincerely for representing the Hampshire Constabulary in a professional manner. He didn't have to do that, and I will never forget it.

Ian Readhead gets to grips with a little French Police car
Photo Jan Brayley

Whilst writing this book I knew right from the start that I would approach Ian and ask if he would do me the honour of writing the Foreword for it, given that he was and will now always remain the Hampshire Constabulary's highest-ranking former Cadet. However, I waited until I had just about finished writing it before asking him so that he had the opportunity to read it in full.

He emailed me back stating that he was currently in hospital but would be discharged within a couple of days and would be delighted to write the Foreword once he was home. Despite his serious health condition (which I wasn't fully aware of) he kept his promise and within days had written the foreword for me.

Ian Readhead ambushed Steve Woodward at Families Day
Photo Jan Brayley

Ian Readhead was proud to have been a Hampshire Police Cadet and like so many of his colleagues I am proud to have known him. I would therefore like to dedicate this book in his memory.

Sir, I salute you.

Steve Woodward

PROLOGUE

History of the Police Cadet scheme nationally and within Hampshire

Whilst writing and researching the material for this book I was astonished at the complete lack of available historic records on the Police Cadet scheme both nationally and locally within Hampshire. It made the writing of the book all the more important to me. Although the main body of the book is a look back upon my own personal experiences and those of my colleagues back in 1975, I felt I had to include the history of the Cadets that came before us to give the reader some idea of the changes that took place prior to us joining. Due to the almost complete lack of historical records I've had to rely, for the most part, on the memories of those young men who came before us and I am grateful for their input.

Pre-amalgamation in April 1967 there were of course a lot more city and borough forces around the UK and as in just about every aspect of policing, each force tended to do things "their way" rather than there being any national protocols, other than enforcing the law of the land of course. Certainly, Hampshire County, Portsmouth City and Southampton Borough/City had their own uniformed Cadet schemes but they weren't residential and the educational side of things seems to have been rather sporadic. But the idea of having Cadets goes way back to the war years and in some forces before that.

So where did it all start and why? It's proved impossible to pin a date on it or a person responsible, but the West Riding Constabulary had boy clerks as far back as 1929 with Nottingham City Police not far behind them. The first such boy clerks in the

Metropolitan Police started in 1934. Prior to the outbreak of WWII most forces it seems had some kind of system to employ boys as young as 15, which then was the school leaving age of course, as "messenger boys". This is a very broad term as I have learned that typically, each force had a variety of names or titles for these young lads, ranging from "Boy Clerks" to "Junior Clerks", from "Messenger Boys" to "Cadet Clerks".

Their responsibilities varied from force to force but most of their duties consisted of answering telephone switch boards, writing out messages from the public or other officers to be passed onto the right department, some menial admin tasks, oh and making the tea no doubt. Most, if not all, wore civilian clothing.

At the outbreak of war there appears to have been a move towards a more organised and uniform approach on a national basis with the formation of the Police Auxiliary Messenger Service or PAMS as they were called.

The Police needed messengers and from 1940 they took on lads below the age of 18, with their own bikes, (some forces recruited at the age of 15, others at 16). The PAMS were to act as messengers during and after air raids. They were issued with uniforms – army surplus dyed black - and wore berets, or tin helmets during raids. They were employed full-time although it is thought that some Police Authorities also took on volunteer PAMS who only worked when the sirens went off.

As usual there does seem to have been a wide variation in standards of dress and equipment. In Guildford and Reigate Borough Constabulary the lads were issued with blue dungarees, a steel helmet and wore an arm band with "Police Messenger" embroidered on it. In Birmingham City though the PAMS were issued with very smart Police uniforms, complete with peaked cap

VIII

plus a steel helmet. There appears to have been a rank structure looking at the below photo.

Birmingham City Police Auxiliary Messenger Service look really smart. Their shoulder flashes state 'Police Auxiliary Messenger'

PAMS were generally recognised because most wore a PAMS patch somewhere on their uniform. Certainly, in Southampton Borough Police (see Gerry Hopkins story elsewhere here) the patch was worn on the left pocket of his tunic and he wore a peaked cap.

PAMS were given basic training in first aid and in the use of stirrup pumps. They had to know where all the civil defence and Police out-stations were – they would often be riding their bikes at night in the black out and would not always be able to see street signs; during or after an air raid streets could be blocked with rubble and debris.

A Birmingham City PAM hands over his message to a Sgt

From the first-hand account of those who served as PAMS it seems that in some areas where there was little enemy bombing, e.g. Oxfordshire, that PAMS were used as extra pairs of hands to make up for the lack of manpower particularly in the headquarters offices. In areas targeted by the enemy the PAMS filled their primary role of taking messages during air raids but would also help the rescue services when needed. This was clearly the case in

"Stand By Ya Beds"

Coventry where PAMS proved their worth during the heavy bombing raids.

George Frederick Barratt of the Coventry PAMS was awarded a British Empire Medal in June 1941 – his citation reads:

"Police Messenger Barratt, who was in the lower corridor of a building when it received a direct hit from a high explosive bomb, was blown by the blast for some distance. When he recovered, he immediately made his way to report to the Main A.R.P. Control Centre and was sent out with a message. On the way he was blown off his cycle by another blast. He remounted and continued his journey but ran into some broken telephone wires and sustained injuries to his neck. He delivered the message and returned with the reply. First aid treatment was obtained for him and although he was badly shaken again, he went out through the rain of falling bombs to deliver other vital messages."

Another Coventry PAMS' citation for the British Empire Medal reads:

"Howard George Miles, Police Messenger, Police Auxiliary Messenger Service, Coventry. During a severe enemy air attack Police Messenger Miles rendered great assistance by delivering urgent and important messages. He dealt with many incendiary bombs and, at grave risk to himself, helped to rescue a baby who was trapped in the wreckage of a house. Miles showed courage and devotion to duty."

Meanwhile the Southampton Borough Police also recruited a dozen young lads as PAMS and based them at the Special Constables HQ at 78A The Avenue. Initially they were issued with military great coats and a tin hat to afford them some protection during air raids which of course were frequent in Southampton and Portsmouth. It's ironic when you read further on in this book that only a few miles away at The Priory, which later became the Cadet Training School, that the young lads housed there as trainee missionaries during the war would watch the air raids on both cities, whilst these other young messenger boys ran all over the city delivering their vital information. As in Coventry there were some extraordinary acts of bravery from the PAMS, including Leonard Natt who was awarded the British Empire Medal for his brave conduct.

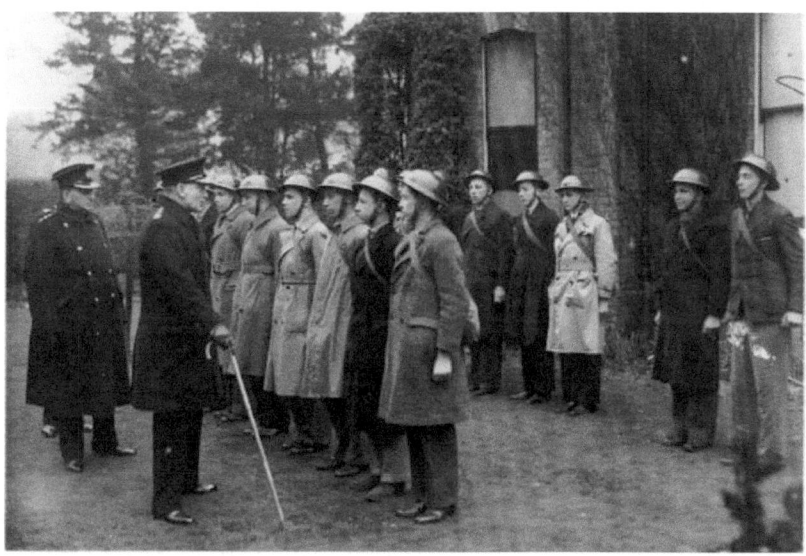

The Southampton Borough Police Auxiliary Messengers are inspected for the first time. Leonard Natt BEM is in the rear rank on the right.
Photo Hampshire Constabulary

Other Southampton PAMS included Norman Brown, Harold Ingram and Gordon Meacher. As each lad reached 18 so they were drafted into the military and not all of them returned. But those who continued with their duties in Southampton came up with an ingenious method to boast morale by producing their own magazine every month. These magazines would cover their exploits during air raids, some of it quite humorous obviously and if there was news of one of their former colleagues from abroad then this would also be reported on. Copies of the magazine were produced on the copy machine at the Civic Centre HQ.

"Stand By Ya Beds"

On 20th July 1945 the PAMS nationally was disbanded and all those still serving were rebranded as Police Cadets. So, in essence we do have a start date for the name Police Cadet. However, the Metropolitan Police were several years behind county forces and didn't form what they called their Police Cadet Corps until 1951.

Immediately after the war there was a major shortage of manpower for obvious reasons and although a good number of former police officers returned to their pre-war occupations it was younger men that forces were keen to recruit and a modicum of success was achieved until the National Service Act 1948 snatched large numbers of young men away from the service again. Any young lads of 16 joining the Police Cadets would be conscripted into the military for two years after their 17th birthday. National Service didn't end until 1960 and between 1948 and 1960 there were conflicts in Malaya, Korea, Cyprus and Kenya where British troops were involved and sadly many of those former Cadets were killed in action.

During this same period there is a rather large gap in the historical information available so I have had to rely on the memories of those who joined up as Police Cadets, as you will see further along in this book. Despite the fact that the examples quoted come from three forces within the county of Hampshire, there were quite similar structures to them all, with uniform, drill, physical training, first aid training, expeditions and Outward Bound Courses all falling within the curriculum.

Then Section 17 of the Police Act 1964 gave Police Cadets statutory recognition;

Section 17, Police Act 1964
Police Cadets

The chief officer of police of any police force may, in accordance with regulations under Part II of this Act and subject to the approval of the police authority as to numbers, appoint persons as police cadets to undergo training with a view to becoming members of that police force.

(2) Subject to such regulations as aforesaid, all police cadets (including persons appointed as such before the commencement of this Act) shall be under the control of, and subject to dismissal by, the chief officer of police.

(3) Without prejudice to subsection (2) above, the police authority by whom a police force is maintained shall, for the purposes of any enactment relating to the functions of employers and of any rule of law with respect to the vicarious liability of employers, be treated as the employer of any police cadets undergoing training with that force.

(4) In the application of this section to the metropolitan police, for the reference in subsection (3) to the police authority there shall be substituted a reference to the Receiver for the Metropolitan Police District.

The January 1966 edition of the Police Journal carried the following report on Police Cadets. Sadly, the full version of the report is not available.

Police Journal report
1st January 1966

Police Cadets are now a firmly established part of the Police Service, with a history going back to days long before the Second World War, when boy clerks, messengers and other youthful employees in forces were serving as the pioneers of what has become a prime source of recruitment. Some of them are now in high places in the Service, and many of their successors, the regular Cadets of more recent times, have already reached senior rank and in some cases hold chief officer appointments.

Orthodox opinion among the majority of older Police officers has tended to look askance at the men who have come in after Cadet Service. Scepticism of their police quality has been based upon the feeling that no-one should be sworn in as a Constable without a modicum of experience as a member of the public. To some extent this view has hardened since the suspension of the two year period of national service; it is felt that a young man who has been in the Police enclave since his school days has too little idea of how the layman thinks and is thus inclined to be intolerant and "police minded".

This way of regarding the Cadet-to-Constable does not by any means command universal agreement; some would say that the boy who goes into the academic world, into an office, or a factory, is going to have far less opportunity of broadening his mind than a boy who goes into the Police Service, because Police duty is a great educator. Be this as it may, the recruitment of youngsters of good quality has been immensely facilitated by the Cadet system and Cadet training today is very much better than in times, not so long ago, when the Cadet was employed as nothing more than a tea boy and nothing more than an office factotum. Moreover, in modern times, young people of the calibre required are infinitely less likely to go into the kind of employment which they will relinquish by the time they are 20 or shortly afterwards, as they did before the war, and purely from the recruiting viewpoint the Cadet system has become virtually indispensable.

END

The following year after the Portsmouth City Police and the Southampton City Police amalgamated with the Hampshire and Isle of Wight Constabulary the new force commenced its search for a suitable training school for an estimated 100 new Cadet recruits per year. You can read the full story on the acquisition of the premises at Bishops Waltham in the Chapter entitled History of The Priory.

Elsewhere in the country similar Police Cadet schemes were up and running but yet again there were differences, some of them quite significant. For example, the Manchester City Police taught some of their Cadets to ride motorcycles or drive cars. In typical police fashion they were trained way beyond what was required to pass the standard driving test, with written exams on the Highway Code, Roadcraft, basic mechanics, plus a very strict manoeuvring test that was far harder than the standard test. If you failed just one aspect you failed the entire five-week course! The instructors were authorised to pass or fail their students on their basic civilian test. It didn't mean their Cadets were then entitled to drive or ride Police vehicles but it must have saved them a small fortune in tuition fees. Manchester City weren't the only force to do this though, with the likes of Merseyside and West Midlands having similar schemes whilst in Hertfordshire they went one step further by allowing those Cadets who had passed their light weight bike test (up to 250cc) to ride bikes like the Velocette LE's, BSA 250s or Francis Barnett 200s from the station to the force workshops when the bikes required service or other maintenance. After the bike had been serviced the Cadet rode it back again. In 1964 Cadets in Worcestershire were tested to ride motorcycles and once passed they were allowed to ride Ariel Leaders and were used as Divisional Messengers, so very similar I suppose to the PAMS on their bicycles during the war. Meanwhile in the old York and North East Yorkshire force Cadets could take a variety of motor related courses, including cars and motorcycles. Believe it or not there was even the opportunity to do a two-week attachment to the Mounted Division so you could learn how to ride a horse! But when you understand the thinking behind their approach it does make a lot of sense. Having Cadets pass all these courses meant that come the time they became PC's they weren't

XVI

abstracted from their station strength for four or five weeks at a time to undertake such courses because they'd already done them. Wiltshire Police operated a similar scheme with five week driving courses for some of their Cadets.

Manchester City Police Cadet under instruction on a Velocette LE200
Photo Greater Manchester Police

Meanwhile back in Hampshire the new Cadet Training School at Bishops Waltham welcomed its first intake of Cadets in 1971 with Chief Inspector Mike Harland as the officer in charge with Chief Inspector Ken Ward taking over in 1972.

A national recruiting campaign aimed at enticing 16-year olds to join the Cadets came about around this time and a colourful four-page brochure was produced by the Home Office, with the majority of photos featuring Hampshire Cadets, officers, cars and buildings. Called "A Flying Start As A Police Cadet" these brochures were distributed to schools, colleges and libraries throughout the UK in an effort to boost recruitment into the

Police at a time when numbers were dropping dramatically, due mostly to the awful pay. The brochure these days is a bit of a collector's item.

Hampshire's first residents at Bishops Waltham in 1971 with Ch/Insp Mike Harland in the centre. Three of the instructors include Sgt Keith Middleton, Sgt Gerry Todd and PC Pete Manns

"Stand By Ya Beds"

The last residential intake for Hampshire was in September 1978 and by 1980 the Cadet scheme in Hampshire and most other forces was being phased out, due in part to the fact that recruiting officers straight into the role as PC's was no longer a problem. There was also the cost of maintaining a large old building like The Priory together with the cost of equipment and staffing. Budget cuts were another factor of course and cutting the Cadet budget was an obvious target. The very last Cadet in Hampshire, by virtue of the fact that he was the youngest in his group when he joined, was Phil Marsh. Ironically, I took him out on patrol with me when I was a PC at Southsea.

The Cadet scheme does live on into the 21st Century but its not an organisation that many of us ex-Cadets would recognise. The Volunteer Cadet Scheme (VCS) is aimed at young people aged 13 – 17, although there are schemes available for kids as young as 8. It's a national scheme, but obviously force dependant and within each force the Cadets meet up for around two hours per week. They obviously don't get paid but during their meetings learn first aid skills, how to use radios and get visits from the likes of Dog Section, Traffic (RPU), ARV etc. They are encouraged to take part in the Duke of Edinburgh Award scheme and assist at things like Force Families Day, New Forest Show and other major events. They get a uniform consisting of trousers and shirt with a tie, a fleece and a peaked cap with blue band of course or a beret. The idea behind it is as old as the name itself; to grab their interest whilst they are young and enthusiastic.

Did the old Police Cadet scheme work? Without a doubt. For those of us who survived and went on to become Police officers I think the values of self-discipline, fortitude, stamina, a sense of humour, oh and the ability to make a really good cup of tea were skills that stayed with us throughout our careers. Most of my Cadet intake from 1975 have remained in contact with each other throughout the years and we have held a couple of reunions. This is not unique to my intake either. Having spoken to a good many other ex-Cadets whilst researching this book, it became apparent that other intakes do the same, no matter what their era. There is a unique bond between us all, which I hope comes through when you read of our experiences.

Steve Woodward
Hampshire Constabulary
1975 - 2008

"Stand By Ya Beds"

CADET MEMORIES

Southampton Borough Police Cadet memories from 1946 to 1947

By Gerry Hopkins

I joined the Southampton Borough Police in 1946 as Cadet Clerk CC3 Hopkins. I was issued with a very nice uniform which was very similar in style to a senior officer's uniform in that it had a tunic with a shirt and tie, rather than the buttoned-up dog collar tunics that PCs and Sgts had to wear. This did cause a bit of friction between the PCs and us Cadet Clerks because our uniforms were a lot more comfortable and looked smarter. However, the first thing I had to do when I was issued with it was to remove the old PAMS badge from the tunic, so it was clearly second hand.

Our main duties at the Civic Centre HQ were basic admin duties; taking the overnight hand written charge sheets up to the typists, then getting copies made on the old duplicating machine, before distributing those copies to the Chief Constable, the CID office or the Courts.

I had to give evidence in court once after witnessing an accident immediately outside the Police Station. I was looking out of an upstairs window when I saw a gentleman park his cycle against the kerb and come into the station. A few seconds later the bicycle fell over into the road. I then saw a car drive over it, causing a lot of damage. I clocked the registration number as it drove off and gave it to a Police officer who traced the car owner. He denied the incident and pleaded not guilty in court, so I was summoned to give evidence and the driver was convicted. I was feeling quite pleased with myself until the Superintendent demanded to know why I had been wasting my time staring out of a window when I should have been working.

Once a year the Southampton Borough Police hosted a major fund-raising event at the Regent Cinema (now the Mayflower Theatre) where famous actors, actresses, singers and other entertainers would put on performances to paying guests with all the profits going towards the Police Widows and Orphan's Fund. As Cadet Clerks our job was to act as ushers to guide people to their seats. I managed to speak to a lot of the famous performers and got their autographs, which I still have today.

On March 22nd 1947 I was called up for National Service and so had to leave Southampton Borough Police. I joined the RAF and after basic training managed to get myself into the RAF Police, which took me all over the world for the next few years.

Cadet Clerk Gerry Hopkins Southampton Borough Police

"Stand By Ya Beds"

Southampton Borough Police Cadet memories from 1952 to 1954

By David Harfitt

Cadet David Harfitt Southampton Borough Police

My ambition had always been to become a Policeman. My father took me to see a Superintendent of Police at Shirley Police. He had known my father for many years – I think they lodged together as single men. Anyway, he recommended the Police Force as a career and I applied to become a Cadet. I had to pass an entrance examination and a strict medical. I had to be over 5' 10" too. This was for Southampton Borough Police Force.

Southampton was not a city in those days. Each Force had different criteria. In the City of London each applicant had to be 6' tall for example. Anyway, I passed everything and less than one month after my 15th birthday, in April 1952, I became a Police Cadet in Southampton. The uniform was very smart and we wore a forage cap rather than the standard peaked cap. It was the main identifying feature that we were Cadets and not PCs.

For the first few months, every Cadet had to work in the Control Room at Police Headquarters in the Civic Centre. We worked three shifts – 6am – 2pm, 9am -5pm, and 2pm – 10pm. We learned how to man the main telephone switchboard. This was the entire telephone connection system for the building. Three telephonists worked it during the day from 8am – 6pm, but the cadets and policeman ran it at other times. Calls would come in and the operator would connect them to the person they wanted. There were also internal calls between all the Police Stations in Southampton as well as the 999 emergency system which had recently started. It was very complicated and entailed pulling out cords, feeding them into sockets, and then ringing the telephone bell of the person required. Internal calls would have to be connected to an outside line before they could dial the number they wanted. It was very easy to make a mistake and pull the wrong cable out and so cut someone off. If it was a superior officer, you certainly knew about it! When a call ended, a light would come up on the line and it could be disconnected, but it was always wise to listen in on the line first, to make sure they were not still speaking. Nothing was secure obviously.

Every incoming 999 call, or Police enquiry, had to be recorded by typing a transcript of the call on a message pad. These were kept and where action had to be taken, the result was also typed or written on the message. Everyone and anyone up to the Chief Constable could see the 'message file' as it was called. There was an open front office in the complex and members of the public would come in to report things. These reports were treated in the same way. We also had radio connections with patrol vehicles and where a 999 call or other incoming message had to be relayed to a vehicle for action and a result, all this had to be recorded on the 'message file'. Calls to the other Police Stations and their responses were the same. As a Cadet, I took a fair share in all this organisation, but we were not allowed to take the 999 calls! Our most important job was the 'communications' desk. Policemen went out on the Beat with a whistle and a truncheon in those days. The only method of communicating with the Station was by telephone.

I remember being on duty one evening when a school teacher made a 999 call. She was preparing to do a school play based on the story of Snow White and the Seven Dwarfs. She could only remember the names of six of the dwarfs, and dialled 999 to ask if any of the friendly policemen could give her the name of the seventh. The Information Room staff did try to help. In those days, we only took a few 999 calls every day, and most of those came from telephone call boxes.

Throughout the entire town situated on street corners, were Police Pillars with a telephone and a public loudspeaker system fitted. There were also a few boxes – these were old brick Warden offices with a table and telephone, built during the War. They also had the public telephone/loudspeaker units outside, so that the public could call the Police Station. Each Beat had one, two, or three of these Pillars or boxes. Most were on Beat boundaries, so that they could be used by several officers. When the men were paraded at the start of their duty, they were given a 'ringing in time' – Beat 1 ringing on the hour, Beat 2 ringing at 12 minutes past and so on. They then called in each hour to report. If they didn't ring in, something was wrong and a search was commenced. The Cadets had a copy of the Sergeant's 'ringing in' record and would monitor everything, If a Constable had to go to Court, or take his meal break, or had an appointment elsewhere, he had to notify the Cadet. The Cadet would then inform the Sergeant.

At this point one has to realise that most of the Policemen at that time had been in the War. They were hard men – Guardsmen, Marines, Commandos, Bomber Pilots, and so on. It was bad enough having to report in to a 'kid' without telling them when they were going off somewhere! The Sergeants were even harder, and the times my ears rang, when a Sergeant would ask, where was PC 245? I would say, "Sorry Sergeant, I think he's gone to Court." "You THINK he's gone to Court. Don't you know? He could be down in East Street with a bloody knife in his chest and you don't KNOW. FIND OUT, that's your job." When one looks back, the responsibility placed on such young shoulders was quite high. We got to know every Policeman, every Sergeant and where all the Beats were. We knew every vehicle call sign. Through the telephone system we got to know what everyone did and who they were. It was a thorough grounding in basic Police work and I never forget it, or the people I worked with. One of the Sergeants lived in New Milton long after his retirement, and we became quite good friends.

After a few months, during which time David Stanford also became a Cadet, and worked with me in the Information Room, I was posted to the Headquarters General Office in the Civic centre. There were 16 cadets and they worked in a variety of offices. The Criminal Records Office had the most, followed by the General Office, Warrants and Summons's, and the Lost Property Office. One Cadet worked in the Photographic Office, and there was one Cadet in some of the Police Stations around the Town. We did not move between offices because our time there was fairly short. Most started when they were sixteen and started their military service on 'call up' soon after their eighteenth birthday. I was an exception to this because I joined within weeks of my fifteenth birthday and stayed until I was almost nineteen.

"Stand By Ya Beds"

Southampton Borough Police Cadets 1953
Cadet David Harfitt is front row on the left
Sgt Bill Kinchington was the drill instructor

It seems difficult to believe now, but almost every office was manned by policemen. The only civilians were female telephone operators, who worked during the day, and secretaries who typed all the letters. The General Office was responsible for Pay, Aliens (foreign nationals), Firearms, Post, both internal and external, Force Records, and obtaining Stores and Stationery. The Chief Constable, Charles Box, and the Deputy Chief Constable, Alfred Cullen, also had their offices nearby and were in frequent contact. PC's Bob Lamb and John Fitzpatrick were in charge of Pay and they did everything – taxes – superannuation – sick pay and so on. They calculated everyone's pay, and each Thursday, went to the Bank under escort to draw the cash, and then divide it out for each individual and separate it into sections to be forwarded to different Police Stations and offices to be paid out. Everyman reported to his office or station at 2pm on a Friday for a formal

Pay Day Parade. They would line up and when their names were called, would march forward, salute the Officer and receive their pay, sign the Pay Sheet, salute again, and march away. Those on leave or short term sick leave would collect their pay when they returned to duty. Those who were away on courses or long term sickness, would have a Post Office Postal Order sent to them. The Cadets would get these from the Post Office. Very few people had bank accounts and certainly not in the police service.

There were also Savings and Insurance payments stopped at source. One was the Widows and Orphans Fund where everyone paid so much a week. If an Officer died on duty, his widow would receive a lump sum, but if no one died, there would be a pay out at Christmas, plus interest. The fund rolled over year after year, so that one usually got back everything at Christmas, plus a bonus. The Cadets would pay this money into Banks at the same time as going to the Post Office. One must realise that my pay at this time was about £2 a week – a senior Constable would receive about £10 - £12. There were no computers like today. The only calculator available was a big mechanical machine about the size of a big typewriter. It had keys and a large handle which was pulled for each calculation. We only had one in the office, and it was very noisy, and sounded throughout the office for most of the day. Almost every day a crisis took place, because Bob and John could not balance the books! Can you believe that two old policemen were responsible for the pay of every policeman, from the Chief Constable down, and every civilian in the police force. Not only pay, but pension contributions, National Insurance, Tax, and savings were all done by Bob and John.

An old policeman called Ian Gilbert ran the Firearms section. He had been a Special Constable during the war. He was a lovely man, who would always give advice and guidance. He never spoke for the sake of speaking. He was an object or ridicule because it was suspected he was 'gay', but I knew nothing of these matters then. He was a kind man who was always cool and calm, and he did nothing to upset me. There were a lot of firearm holders in Southampton. People who belonged to gun clubs, sporting types, and many who held weapons after the war as sentimental belongings – an Army Officer's .45 pistol that had been carried throughout the war, for example. PC Ray Paice was the Aliens Officer. He dealt with foreigners who were in the UK on a visa and had to report to the Police, or wanted to extend their visas. Finally, there was PC Harry Oliver who was 'Jack of all Trades' and the friend of everyone. He taught me quite a lot about the ways of the world and about the 'birds and the bees'. My father never spoke about such things and the school certainly didn't – as far as magazines went, I only got as far as the Beano and the Dandy Comics! Harry never went into great depth, but I knew how a girl could get pregnant! Inspector Minet ran the Office, and Sergeant White, who was a real father figure, was his deputy. The person overall was Chief Inspector Pearce who had an office next door.

Each Cadet had certain responsibilities but we all shared some jobs. I recall writing in an Occurrence Book each day. We would read through the Message Files from the Information Room and find details of unusual calls to the Police. Fire calls, missing persons, mental health matters, and so on. We would cross reference them for future information. We had to answer all the office telephones, and run messages. We used to collect the stores and stationery from the Council Offices each Monday morning and then distribute them to all the offices and Stations. We collected mail and typed envelopes for it to be posted off. I would like a pound for every time I typed 'The Commissioner of Police of the Metropolis, New Scotland Yard, Whitehall, SW1'. A large envelope went off to him every night. This was before teleprinters or fax machines – everything was handwritten or typed, and went by post. Criminal records, disqualification details, fingerprints for checking nationally, and for records. It all went by post.

Soon after I arrived in the Office, I was made the 'personal cadet' for the Deputy Chief Constable. If he wanted his weekly purchase of cigarettes collected from the tobacconists, I went. If he wanted his shirts from the Chinese laundry, I went. If he had papers for someone, I delivered them. Letters to Solicitors by hand – it was me. Each morning I would go to the Information Room to collect the 'In Messages' and take them up to the Deputy's office, where I would wait outside for him to come in. He would usually arrive about 9.30am whereupon I would follow him into his office. I would give him the messages to read and then hang up his hat and coat. I would stand by his desk until he read something of particular interest, and then he would say; "Get me Superintendent so and so". I would pick up the phone and of course the telephonist would be very prim and proper until she heard my voice! She would put me through to the Station concerned and then the Superintendent would answer and I would say; "I have the Deputy Chief Constable for you, Sir." At this stage I would give Mr.Cullen the telephone and I would leave the office and wait outside until he called me back in. I really felt like the 'bee's knees'. Sometimes he would want something from one of the offices and I would run and get it. When he had finished at about 10am, I would take the messages to the Chief Constable, who had just come in. He was far less trouble – his shirts and cigarettes were delivered! He would call for me when he had finished reading the messages, and I would return them.

I had three embarrassing moments taking the 'in message' files around over the years. I was with the Deputy Chief Constable one morning when he asked me to get a Superintendent on the phone. I got through and passed the telephone to my boss. I then turned around briskly and marched off towards the door, followed by the telephone, its heavy stand, a table lamp, and an early type of dictaphone. They all smashed to the floor, breaking into a dozen pieces. The boss's hand was still at his ear – a voice was coming from the phone on the floor -

XXX

"Stand By Ya Beds"

"Hello Sir! - are you all right – what is happening?" My foot had caught in the wires running down from the desk top, and as I walked away, I pulled it all behind me. I think the Superintendent thought there had been an assassination attempt. I apologised profusely and attempted to pick up all the pieces, but Mr. Cullen could not have been more kind. He collected the phone and told the Superintendent that he would call him back, and then he got down with me to pick up what he could. I had to go and get a dustpan and brush of course, but Mr. Cullen was a gentleman throughout.

My next faux pas involved the Chief Constable. As I approached his door there was a Policeman waiting outside to be interviewed. Mr. Box called the Policeman in and told me to follow him in with the 'in messages'. By the time I entered, he had told the man to sit, and the policeman was sat there to full attention with his helmet under his arm. I strode in, placed the message file on the desk in front of the Chief Constable, about turned, and marched out. Just before the door, I slipped on the highly polished floor, and fell forward, grabbing a coat stand which crashed down too. The Chief Constable was dressed formally that day, and had placed his bowler hat on the top of the stand. It fell off and rolled across the floor finishing up in front of the desk. Like a subjugated Black Adder figure, I crept across the room to retrieve the hat. The Policeman could not conceal his mirth and tried covering his face with his hands. The Chief Constable was certainly not amused nor as conciliatory as his Deputy and said; "Come on – pick it all up and get out!". I picked up the stand, replaced the hat, and got out while I still had a job. The office floor was highly polished marquetry woodwork, with a large carpet square in the middle. New leather soled shoes sealed my fate.

Sometime after that I was in the canteen with a lad called Michael Hooper discussing the Chief Constable's cigarette

XXXI

ordering system. The cigarettes would come in from the supplier and they would be taken in by one of the senior members of the office. Just after I got back into the office, the telephone rang and I answered it. The voice on the other end said; "Chief Constable here – come in and see me." This had never happened before – if he wanted something, he would ring Inspector Minet. I thought immediately 'this is Mike Hooper – it's a practical joke!', so I said; "OK Mike – what do you want, I'm busy". The voice said again; "Come in and see me." I said; "I'm not falling for that – if you don't stop buggering about, I'm putting the phone down." The voice then said; "Who is that? Give me Inspector Minet – I'm not having you talk to me like that!" Oh! Dear – it IS the Chief Constable, I thought, so I put him through to the Inspector and waited for the 'bollocking'. Actually, it went down well and everyone except the Chief Constable thought it was funny.

On another occasion I made it into the National Press. On this day I was the Cadet chosen to do the 'Bank Run'. I had various envelopes containing hundreds of pounds to go around the town to the Post Office and various banks. I was on my bicycle and to keep the money separate, I put some of envelopes in my saddle bag. I propped my bike up on the kerb outside of the Post Office and went in to get Postal Orders. As I was standing in the queue, a person came in and shouted out, "Does anyone have a bike out here – the wind has blown it over, and pound notes are blowing all over the place." I ran outside to see the funniest sight ever. A major traffic light controlled cross roads in the centre of Southampton, with almost all the traffic stopped for people running about in the road picking up pound notes. Other people were standing on the side, and people were giving them money, thinking they were the owners! I was in uniform of course, and I went around collecting the money from people. Most of the money had stayed in the saddle bag, but about £110 in £1 notes had come out, and as it was quite windy, had scattered everywhere.

XXXII

"Stand By Ya Beds"

When I counted it, there was only about £5 missing! Of that, another £3 was handed in to the Police Station the following day.

When I returned to the Office it was like a Spanish Inquisition. First, I had to tell Sergeant White, then Inspector Minet, then Chief Inspector Pearce and finally the Deputy. I then realised that their Police minds suspected me of taking the money. No one would leave money in a saddle bag and it certainly would not blow about. As for people being honest and collecting it, that would not happen. A little later, the Press were on the scene, and it all became clear: it had happened! What were they doing – giving a 16 year old, hundreds of pounds to transport about the town on a bicycle? It was front page news the next day in all the National Papers – 'IT RAINED POUND NOTES IN SOUTHAMPTON YESTERDAY' read the headlines. Strangely, cadets never did the 'bank run' again.

Each Wednesday afternoon, we would all go to the Speedway/Dog Tracks off Archers Road, where we had drill under Sergeant Kinchington, an ex-Guardsman Drill Instructor. We would march up and down, about turn, salute on the march, march time and do all the things which soldiers did. This went on for the whole afternoon. Policemen marched regularly in those days – Remembrance Day parades, Church Parades, Funerals for departed officers and so on. They marched out to their Beats from the Police Station with the Sergeant who would fall each man out when they reached his beat. In Southampton it was not uncommon for 10 – 14 men to march out on night duty. Even the Policeman's helmet is based on the headgear worn by soldiers in the 19th century.

Around 1954/55 we started further education for one day a week. We went to Southampton College for further education in St.Mary's Street. There we learned shorthand and typing, English language, and geography. I remember that was the first time we had contact with girls. The shorthand was a waste because one could not use it legally for recording conversations with a suspect.

My proudest moment came in July 1954. The Queen's Coronation took place in 1953 and to thank the Police for all the work done then, she decided to have a Royal Review of all the Forces in the UK, including the Ulster Constabulary. There would be over ten thousand policemen on parade in Hyde Park, and she would review them all from her special Land Rover. Policeman, Policewomen, Dog Handlers, Special Constables and Cadets. One Cadet would come from Southampton and parade with about sixty other representatives. There was a lot of conjecture and after some of my 'clangers' I didn't have much hope. Finally, the Daily Order for the parade came out, and there was my name – Cadet 16 David Harfitt. We had several small-scale parades to learn the order of the parade, because it was so large, that they had to use bugles to sound for each movement. The bugles were on loudspeakers. Come the day, Wednesday, 14th July 1954, we all left Southampton in special coaches, all dressed in immaculate uniforms, to go to London. Relatives and friends could also come to a special visitor stand where they could see the Parade. My Dad, Nellie and Aunt Trix came. Once there, I was separated from the others and joined other Cadets from all over the country.

We were all in large squared groups and the Queen came by slowly in her Land Rover. We then had to form up and march past the rostrum where she took the salute. There were so many of us, I hardly got to see her. On the way home, we stopped at a pub in Hartley Witney on the A.30 London Road, (there was no motorway), and everyone one had a drink – or two. I can remember one or two Policeman going out onto the main road and stopping traffic for the fun of it! Most embarrassing for me when we returned to Southampton, was the fact that my relatives had got left in London! After the Parade, Dad had taken them off to show them the sights of London, but didn't allow enough time

XXXIV

to get back! They returned later that night by train. I still have all the photographs, special Orders, newspaper cuttings and other details of this special day. I never had to parade before the Queen again, but I did attend two Royal Visits where I performed crowd control in front of her – one in Newport on the Isle of Wight, and one in the New Forest.

Southampton Borough Police officers ready for their trip to Hyde Park, London for the Royal Inspection from HM Queen Elizabeth II. Cadet David Harfitt is second row centre. Deputy Chief Constable Alfred Cullen front row centre

Steve Woodward

Hampshire and Isle of Wight Constabulary Cadet memories from 1958 to 1960

By Fred Masters

In 1958 all applicants for the Hampshire and Isle of Wight Constabulary Cadets were required to be at least 5 feet 8 inches tall (to attain 5 feet 9 inches by age 19 years) be aged between 16 and 19 years, and to be no less than a certain weight. Your application had to include last year's school report.

I was later required to report to Winchester Headquarters for interview by the Chief Constable Mr R.D Lemon and the ACC Mr Gill. There were some medical questions but no formal medical examination.

We were told on the day of the interview that we had been appointed and then told where we were to serve and simply told to report to that police station at 9 am on the date of appointment, in my case 7th January 1959. This was later confirmed in writing. There was no uniform issued at this point. We were also told that lodgings would be found for us, except for those posted to Winchester, who would live in a dormitory at Police Headquarters (this was the old house which was then HQ).

I reported to Andover Police Station in civvies where an existing Cadet was told to walk me to my lodgings. The first few days I was shown around but mainly told to sit by the switchboard and learn how to use that, as Cadets would be required to frequently man the telephones. So, the initial time was mainly telephone duties. A cord board which included private lines to PHQ and Salisbury 999 calls for both Police and Fire were separate phones - Police black - Fire Red. Fire calls were quite interesting as it required sounding the siren and bells in retained firemen's houses.

"Stand By Ya Beds"

After about a week I was taken to HQ where I was issued with my uniform which did not include a mac but an overcoat, a cape and leggings. The blue shoulder flashes read Hampshire and Isle of Wight Police Cadet.

There were three Cadets at Andover and one of the three Sergeants was given the job of looking after Cadets. Duties for Cadets were mainly day shifts Monday to Friday and Saturday morning. We did three months uniform patrol, three months CID (in the office in uniform) and three months Admin. Uniform duties were definitely the best as you went on patrol with beat officers. CID and Admin were mainly clerical. Sometimes when on uniform patrol we worked 0600 - 1400 or 1400 - 2200.

The Wolseley traffic car was the only vehicle fitted with a radio but if you helped to wash the car you might get a ride.

Once a month all Cadets from Hampshire and Isle of Wight had to report to Winchester HQ for one afternoon of training. The first hour was an inspection parade followed by marching up and down. The training officers were Sgt Rowe and Chief Inspector Kitch. We spent some time in the classroom - but we were not taught law. I can't remember what we were taught though.

Once a year Cadets were required to attend HQ for a two-week residential course which included obtaining a First Aid Certificate and Life Saving qualification. We used to march to the outdoors Winchester Lido for Life Saving with our towels and trunks neatly rolled under our left arm. A marching body of Cadets with Sgt Rowe complete with swagger stick at the front. Another course we attended was for Civil Defence which took place mainly at Civil Defence HQ in Andover Road, Winchester.

Hampshire and Isle of Wight Constabulary Cadet course 1960 Cadet Fred Masters is in the front row, second in from the right

Some Cadets were randomly selected to go on Outward Bound Courses and some including myself were sent to the Training Ship Foudroyant which was then anchored in Portsmouth Harbour. This included sailing right around the Isle of Wight.

Hampshire and Isle of Wight Constabulary Cadet memories from 1961 to 1963

By Peter Stoddard

I joined the force as a uniform Cadet at the age of 16, in 1961. Previously to the uniform Cadet scheme the force recruited Police station Boy Clerks who wore civvies. In the years leading up to 1960s the force had problems recruiting Constables because it was at a time of full employment and low Police pay. They realised that if they could recruit Cadets straight from school at that early

"Stand By Ya Beds"

age, there was a possibility that they would go on to join the force when they reached 19 years. We were issued with a Cadet uniform on joining - there were no female recruits. Our initial training was at the old 19th Century Police Headquarters at West Hill, Winchester.

The 1961 intake of Cadets into the Hampshire and Isle of Wight Constabulary.
Cadet Peter Stoddard is front row, third in from the right

There was accommodation above the main front building, nicknamed 'The Brothel' due to its dull Dickensian interior. I think there was a full-size snooker table there. This upper floor dormitory area would have been used to accommodate new Constable recruits from the very early times of the force in the 1840s. There was another accommodation block a short distance away above a newer building. We were trained in a classroom, a wooden annexe building at the rear. The recruiting sergeant was Sergeant Laurie Fielder. After about a month of the book work we were posted in our two's and three's to Police stations all over the county.

I was posted to Fareham, divisional headquarters in Osborne Road. The building is still there now and used as the Registrar's office. Fareham division stretched from Emsworth, including Havant, to Gosport, across to Bursledon and up to West Meon. The Chief Superintendent was George Hatcher.

On my first day I was joined by two other Cadets, Paul Turner later Inspector, and Graham Tarrant, later Det. Superintendent. They have both sadly died due to cancer. Paul lived at Waterlooville and cycled to Fareham every day along the top of Portsdown Hill. Graham lived in the Cowplain area and he had a Norton 350 cc motorcycle and travelled to work at Fareham on that. I had a Raleigh 50cc moped which I rode to work from my home in Gosport. Strangely I can never remember being cold or wet on my commute.

At Fareham a schedule was worked out where we were separated and each spent three months in different working areas of the Police station. For instance, one of us would go to Divisional CID admin doing simple admin work with crime reports and chatting to the friendly typist. I still keep in touch with them to this day.

Another of us would go to the divisional admin office upstairs. This was staffed by the formidable Mrs Denham-Jones, Jim, a retired Met PC and Eileen, the Bench Office clerk. The Divisional Admin Officer was a Chief Inspector. The third Cadet would join the station duty PC in the front office. On other days we went out on foot patrol accompanying the regular town beat PC. One such officer, who I still see today was Jim Jupe. This duty showed us how to make hourly, ten minute 'points' at

XL

"Stand By Ya Beds"

telephone kiosks - in case we were needed. No radios or mobile phones then.

I did an early turn once. After the parade I walked with my tutor for the day to the old fire station in West Street. On entering the building I could see the night duty firemen asleep on camp beds. My colleague filled and lit a large kettle so that when the fireman awoke shortly afterwards, they were greeted with a fresh pot of tea. It could be a good thing when attending a fire to know the fire crews personally.

Getting a call in the day was a rare event but one day we were sent to a house in the town centre where the elderly occupant had not been seen by neighbours. There was no reply to our knocking and it was decided to force an entry. An insecure window was found at the rear and as it needed someone who was agile I was nominated to climb in through the window. I let the others in and we found the occupant, alive but ill in bed, unable to move. Conditions in the house were 'poor.'

The station admin work was at its lowest level, filing and typing up of reports. We were all sent to night school to learn touch typing. The station office in the first few months I was there, was heated by a coal fire.

Our role was to shadow the station PC to learn how he dealt with the public and also to take hand written messages. This was in the days of no email, fax machines or teleprinters and so all crime circulation messages were handwritten. The headquarters switchboard would phone us hourly it seemed, to get us to write down reports of burglaries, stolen cars etc., from throughout the county. We in turn would then phone the sub division station officers at Gosport and Havant and repeat the messages for them to write down. These messages were put on a daily information bulletin board, to be read by Senior Officers, CID staff and by the sergeant at the shift briefings.

Occasionally we were allowed to act as the 'observer' in the traffic patrol cars. A hand written log sheet was kept of all radio messages sent and received. The cars were black Wolseley's fitted with a lovely bell. Such a nice civilised way to stop people who had been speeding. If I remember rightly, at the end of my time as a Cadet, Fareham Traffic had just been issued with a Volvo Amazon estate car (which the force History Society still owns). I was an observer in it one day with the driver, PC Ron Harris and we were sent to a serious accident. He had a skilful habit of a rolling a handmade cigarette with one hand – whilst on a high-speed run - which he lit just as we stopped at the scene.

The next part of our Cadet training plan was for all of us to go back to school and take more GCE exams. Most of us had passed some of these when we left state school but headquarters wanted us to gain more or retake those that we had failed. The plan was that all the Cadets from around the county would attend Eastleigh Technical College (now Barton Peverill) which then was a sixth form college, capable of teaching us to do these exams. We were not the best attentive pupils, having left school, thinking we had finished exams and having started to see how life was outside school.

The plan was that we were to be accommodated at the YMCA Fairthorne Manor at Botley from where we would catch the train into Eastleigh every day. None of us had cars at that time although some had motorbikes. After a year or two, there had been so many accidents involving Cadets on motorbikes, breaking legs, that they were banned for a while.

At Fairthorne Manor, a large rambling Victorian place, we were accommodated in dormitories. Apart from day one, when

"Stand By Ya Beds"

the training Sgt would be there to show us around the accommodation, we were left completely unsupervised except for the Manor's civilian catering staff. In winter we played table tennis all evening - we were the only residents.

In the summer Fairthorne was idyllic. We used to ask the staff to borrow canoes and we would canoe down the River Hamble as far as the Jolly Sailor pub at Bursledon. If you got the tide right you will go downstream with the ebbing tide, and after a couple of pints would canoe back to the Fairthorne with a rising tide. Health and Safety did not exist back then and of course we had no life jackets.

Towards the end of my Cadet service we heard about a surprise visit paid one morning by HQ Training staff to Fairthorne. They were shocked to see how badly we lived in the dormitory - leaving behind in the morning unmade beds and a general mess everywhere. It was after this inspection we heard rumours of a plan for more disciplined Cadet training in future years. Bishops Waltham here we come!

Years later I spoke to Cadets involved in the new scheme at Bishops Waltham and I was shocked to hear of their disciplined lifestyle and lack of after work freedom. When we returned from college each day we had complete freedom to take part in our own outdoor activities or to go to the pubs in Botley.

The Duke of Edinburgh Award scheme was founded in 1956. The object was to get young people to take part in sporting activities and camping expeditions for which you could earn medals, bronze, silver or gold depending on how well you did. Shortly after it started headquarters must have realised that this scheme was ideal for Cadet training, to fill in time and to improve our fitness etc, prior to joining the job.

Steve Woodward

The highlight of the scheme was a three-day hike and map reading exercise, sleeping rough at night. Day one was 15 miles, day two was 20 miles and day three was 15 miles long. In order to prepare for this three-day hike someone at HQ came up with the idea of a summer Cadet Training Camp.

These were held at a County Council field (Tile Barn) at Brockenhurst. Our intake of Cadets must've been one at of the very early camps which was run by Sergeant Fred Hodgson and Sergeant Alan Kemish. They were such good leaders and organisers, being ex-military, that they were both quickly promoted after each successive camp, and at the end of their service were both Chief Superintendents.

The field where the camps took place in the early days had no facilities whatsoever and our first task was to dig latrines and a cesspit. We then had to erect our own tents and gather firewood for cooking fires. They were like a Scout camp but with more physical activities.

There was an early start each morning at 0615. Each tent was allocated a large pit prop log which we had to carry around the running track and perform gymnastics with, just to get us started for the day. We kept the pit props in the tent at night to keep them dry and therefore lighter. Next day we were set to build an assault course, the highlight of which was two wires stretched across trees for us to step across.

One year I was with a group of about four, starting our three-day hike as part of the Duke of Edinburgh Award scheme. Fred Hodgeson had to draw up a plan for each days walk and where we were to stop overnight. As a check on us we had to write down wording copied on a few check points, to prove we had been there.

On this occasion he did the route plan in a bit of a rush and it wasn't until the end of the first day that we realised he'd made a mistake with the distance of the walk on the following day. It was supposed to be a 20 mile walk but he had given us nearly double that. He was not a man you could easily point out his mistakes to, so we studied the map and worked out how we could do a 20 mile walk and, using information in local tourist maps and guide books, answered the questions about the landmarks at the distant points, we didn't plan to go to.

On the night of the second day Fred turned up at our camp site, conveniently near the Royal Oak pub, Fritham, with a worried look and admitted that he realised that day two of our walk was far too long. He had no way of contacting us apart from our pre-set night stop. We all put on the appearance of looking completely worn out and he took pity on us. He looked at our next day's route and altered the walk to a simple five mile one instead of the expected 15 miles. If he ever found out what we had done he would not have been a happy man! He then left us and we made for the Royal Oak!

During our training as Cadets, we all attended a month-long Outward-Bound course at various centres around the country. Mine was at Aberdovey.

Southampton Borough Police Cadet memories from 1964 to 1967

By Richard Duffin

In 1964 when I joined, the Cadets numbered 16. As each member attained the age of 19 and was sworn in as a Constable his place would be taken by a new Cadet. I can best describe the job by giving a weekly diary of our tasks. Each Cadet was assigned a posting which would be rotated as and when. These postings always commenced at the outset with a period of about three months on the "Communications" telephone in the switchboard room. You would receive incoming calls from officers on the beat who would ring in at appointed times from the pillars on their respective beats. These calls would be noted on a large sheet and should they miss a call a senior officer would be notified as the officer could well be in trouble.

The call would always follow the following course "134 (Officers number) from 2 (pillar number) at say 3 (minutes past the hour) next one at 2 (pillar number) at 3 (minutes past the next hour)". So, this one would go "134 from 2 at 3 next 2 at 3"

As a fresh nervous young 16 year old a certain PC phoned in and in his brusque efficient manner announced "111 from 1 at 1 next one from 1 at 1" The phone then went dead and all I could do was to ring his pillar back and when he answered say "And now in English please". I have forgotten most of my service but that incident in June 1964 will be with me forever.

Other postings would follow. One Cadet would be posted to Bitterne, Portswood, Shirley and Traffic. Others to Photography, General Admin Office, Lost Property, Bench Office, CRO. The final three months Cadet service would be served on the beat, usually at Central attached to various beat officers, learning the trade as it were. By 1966 heavy personal radios had been introduced. Guess who usually had to wear it?

The weekly diary was as follows;

Monday am, PE under the instruction of a PC or Sgt Bob Shergold. If the latter turned up you were in for a hard and strict session. Then back to posting duties.
Monday pm, Posting duties.

Tuesday am, Rest day.
Tuesday pm, Tech College.
Weds am, Swimming.
Weds pm, Posting duties.
Thursday all day, Tech College.
Friday am, PE then back to posting duties.
Friday pm, First Aid, Life Saving and Drill.
Alternate Saturdays delivering the Dealers sheets, detailing all stolen property in the city over the previous week.

As you can see there was emphasis on fitness and education. Upon amalgamation I think the Southampton Cadet numbers had swelled to about 18 and those serving on that date were incorporated into the new Hampshire force.

Portsmouth City Police Cadet memories from 1965 to 1967

By Bob Parker

I joined the Portsmouth City Police Cadets on 10th February 1965.

One memorable attachment saw me at Southsea Police Station in Albert Road on Christmas morning 1965. I was on early turn (6am-2pm) and, as nothing happens on Christmas Day, particularly in the morning, I was left in sole charge of the police station whilst all those on duty were up in the canteen enjoying their big Christmas fry-ups. The front counter was open to the public but no one was coming in and so I sat myself in the switchboard room just off the main office and close to the counter in case anyone did come in. The switchboard was an old fashioned affair with lots of long cords which you stuck into holes corresponding to the telephone needing the call. Alongside the switchboard was the panel which controlled all of the police boxes in the Southsea and Eastney areas.

Steve Woodward

The Police boxes were situated all over the city and could be used by both the public and Police officers to make contact with the police station. The public side had an unlocked door on a fearsome spring which deterred kids from opening them and being a nuisance and, if they did, they invariably got their fingers trapped. Serves 'em right! The police side had a locked door and every police officer in the city was issued with a key. Every key opened every police box. I was quite familiar with using this panel. A light would display on the panel under the location of the box and if it was red then it was the public side being used and if it was orange then it was the police side. Simples. No police officer used nor needed to use the public side did they?

I was minding my own business with my brain in neutral (usual state of affairs) especially having got up at 5am and because it was Christmas Day. Out of the corner of my eye I noticed a red light illuminate under the Outram Road box. What the heck? A member of the public calling for help on Christmas Day. I pressed the switch to connect and using the telephone handset I used the standard response "Hello box. How can I help you?" A man's voice said "It's the Assistant Chief Constable here. Send a Traffic car to pick me up". This was a prank, right? Very funny. So, I replied "And I'm Father Christmas. You've clearly had one too many. Shut the box and go on your way". I then disconnected the call. No one is going to get one over on me when I'm in charge of the police station.

What happened next occurred in very quick time. I could hardly keep up with the speed of events in my head. I heard the front door crash back against the wall and in a split second the front counter flap flipped 180 degrees crashing back onto the counter. We must be under attack from Special Forces. Another split second and a huge frame filled the door to the switchboard room. Standing before me, quivering with rage and with a face as red as beetroot was Brian Morrissey – the Assistant Chief

"Stand By Ya Beds"

Constable. It turns out that he lives in a house right by the Outram Road police box. How was I to know? By now the troops upstairs in the canteen had been alerted by the crashing and banging and came pouring down the stairs to repel the intruders. I was the first to be told my fortune followed by the Inspector and the Sergeants for leaving me in charge and for not training me properly!

As an afterthought I've recently dug out the letter I received in January 1965 with my joining instructions and look who signed it…….Brian Morrissey, who was a Supt then!

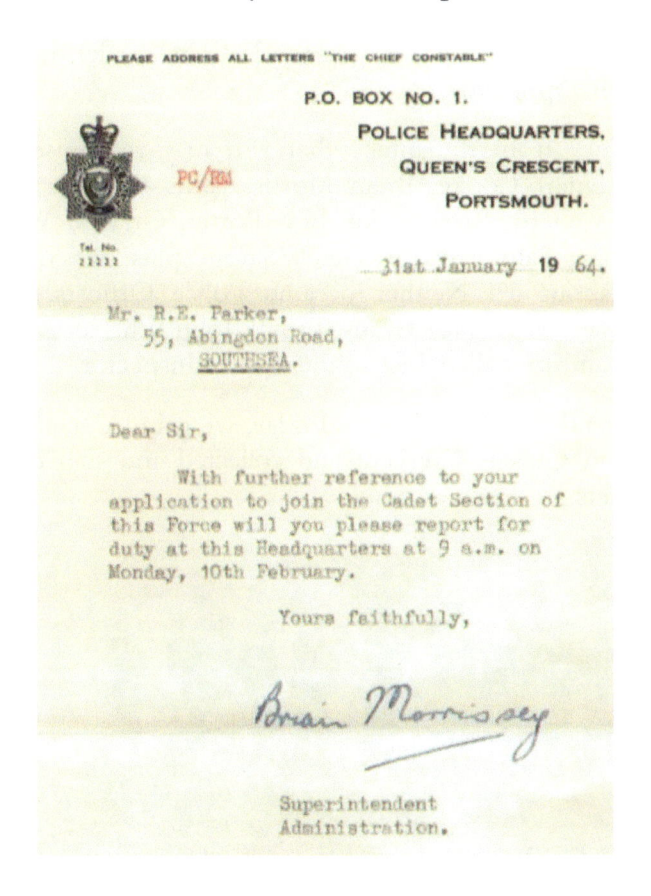

```
PLEASE ADDRESS ALL LETTERS "THE CHIEF CONSTABLE"

                            P.O. BOX NO. 1.
                            POLICE HEADQUARTERS,
           PC/RM             QUEEN'S CRESCENT,
                            PORTSMOUTH.
Tel. No.
22222                       31st January 19 64.

Mr. R.E. Parker,
    55, Abingdon Road,
       SOUTHSEA.

Dear Sir,

        With further reference to your
application to join the Cadet Section of
this Force will you please report for
duty at this Headquarters at 9 a.m. on
Monday, 10th February.

            Yours faithfully,

            Brian Morrissey

            Superintendent
            Administration.
```

XLIX

Portsmouth City Police Cadet memories from 1967 to 1968
By Charlie Lovegrove

I'm not sure how far back Cadets were part of the Portsmouth City Police. I think they had 'cadets' prior to 1939, but not in the way we think of Cadets today. Southampton City Police also had Cadets.

I joined the Portsmouth City Police Cadets on the 12th September 1966. At the time I believe there were about 15 -20 of us, differing in ages from 16 to 19. Those nearing 19 were obviously were ready to go to Sandgate District Training College as PCs. My claim to fame is I was the last City Cadet, before amalgamation in April 1967.

Some names from my intake that you may recognise are Shaun Eade, Stuart Cooke, Brian Morris, Chris O'Neill, Alan Griffiths, Barry Gard, Russ Parke, Bob Porter, Graham Wells, Keith Ackerman, Sam Browne, Derek Savage plus two others who left in about 67. Neither became Police Officers. Our Instructor was PS 57 Horace Evans. I think John Wheeler was in overall charge and I recollect he had the rank of Inspector.

We were paid weekly and every Friday, we paraded at Police Headquarters in Queens Crescent and collected and signed for our wage packets.

Portsmouth City Police Cadets on parade for an HMI inspection

"Stand By Ya Beds"

Our programme was as follows;

Week 1. Monday and Tuesday at Highbury Technical College, where we did typing, British Constitution and other subjects. To be honest I cannot remember what they were, it was 50 years ago. Wednesday, Thursday and Friday, we went to the Royal Naval Gymnasium in the mornings and practised drill and physical exercises. In the afternoons we went to Naval or Marine swimming baths and trained in Life Saving, which resulted in ALL of us obtaining Life Saving Awards of various levels. There was a Cadet Team, which were entered into various Life Saving events in the South of England.

Week 2. Monday and Tuesday, the same as week 1. However, the rest of the week we were at a Police station within the city. To be honest we were used as Telephone Operators and tea boys. (there were no female cadets). Apart from our own observations we were not taught any Police procedures at all.

We were also expected to take part in the Duke of Edinburgh Award Scheme at Silver and Gold level. We had to do Judo as our physical section of the Award. Needlessly to say most of us obtained the Gold Award.

After amalgamation, the system of training changed and we were integrated into the Hampshire Constabulary system.

I believe that up to the summer of 1967 and possibly the autumn of 1967, some of the Hampshire Cadets, (those in the photos) were enrolled in the Highbury Tech College course. Because as far as I recall, sometime in late 1967, the 'Senior' Cadets, myself included were given station postings and a Training Programme, which included attachments to various departments like Traffic, CID, Station Duty and at least two weeks at

Headquarters, West Hill, Winchester where again we went around the different departments.

Portsmouth City Cadets and Hampshire Cadets on a hike in Sussex, led by a lecturer from Highbury College.
Left to right; Unknown, Brian Morris, Mr Carter from Highbury, Steve Moyce, Charlie Lovegrove, Unknown, Terry Templeman and Stuart Cooke (crouching)

In the summer of 1967, we took part in a Cadet camp, held in the New Forest, (the infamous Brockenhurst Camp) led by Inspector Kemmish, accompanied by his staff, two or three Sgts, plus 4 or 5 PC'S, all of whom were very fit and encouraging. In April 1968 there was a camp held at Abercrave in the Brecon Beacons. We were also encouraged to take part in exercises held jointly with the Army (Escape and Evasion).

"Stand By Ya Beds"

Hampshire Cadets in 1967
Left to right; Terry Templeton, Unknown, Brian Morris, Unknown, Charlie Lovegrove, Steve Moyce, Derek Savage and Stuart Cooke.

At some stage the Cadets started to reside at Fairthorne Manor, Botley and that is when I think they were transported to Fareham Technical College. I did help Sgt Graham Lewis in some of the activities he did with the 'junior' cadets at Fairthorne Manor, usually judo. I'm not sure how long this building was used.

In the early summer of 1968, I went to an Outward Bound Course in the Lake District, at Eskdale. Again, most of us went on these courses, but to different centres. We were also expected to complete a period of C.S.V. (Community Service Volunteers). This usually lasted about 12 weeks and could be anywhere in the

UK. Mine was in Norwich, in July and August of 1968; a community programme run by the Y.M.C.A. Some more fortunate than me, were put forward for V.S.O. (Voluntary Service Overseas). This I think could be 6 months to a year.

Obviously after October 1968, my time as Cadet was complete. I did enjoy my time as a Cadet, although I did get fed up with swimming every week and occasionally the camps were hard going.

However, I made some good friends, sadly some have passed away and those remaining I do not see regularly, partly because of where I presently live, and this is why the Facebook page Hantspol Retired is excellent for keeping in touch.

HISTORY OF THE PRIORY

The history of The Priory is perhaps not as old as you might think, its somewhat Gothic façade belies its age and it has led a fascinating life. But who built it and why?

Sir Arthur Helps KCB, 1813 – 1875 was a gentleman of wealth who moved within political and influential circles and was Private Secretary to Thomas Spring Rice, Chancellor of the Exchequer. In 1860 he was appointed Clerk of the Privy Council. This appointment brought him into regular contact with HM Queen Victoria and Prince Albert the Prince Consort, who held Arthur in very high regard. In 1861 he purchased the Vernon Hill estate in Bishops Waltham and the income he earned from that allowed him to fulfil his writing ambitions.

Sir Arthur Helps

In 1862 he established the Bishops Waltham Clay Company for the manufacture of bricks and terracotta. He was also involved with the Bishops Waltham Railway Company, set up to link the brickworks and the town with the main London - Southampton line. However, profits were small and he faced competition from the Staffordshire Potteries. Helps also financed the Coke and Gas works which lit the town from 1864.

In the early 1860s a wave of compassion for the country's poor and infirm swept the nation and a large number of infirmary's, hospitals and workhouses or poor houses were built. Sir Arthur Helps donated a slice of the Vernon Hill estate to the local community for the building of an infirmary, dedicating it to the memory of Prince Albert who had recently passed away (Dec 1861). On August 4th 1864, Prince Leopold, the 11 year old son of Queen Victoria and Prince Albert performed his very first public duty by laying the foundation stone for the building, which was named the Royal Albert Infirmary. A painting of the occasion is now housed at the National Portrait Gallery.

Prince Leopold lays the foundation stone to the Royal Albert Infirmary. Note the number of dignitaries present and the raised viewing platform far right. Picture; London Illustrated News

"Stand By Ya Beds"

The building was designed by Mr Robert Critchlow and built at a cost of £2661. The opening ceremony took place on 7th November 1865. It was again attended by Royalty with Prince Arthur and Princess Helena and Princess Louisa performing the unveiling of the Royal Standard that revealed a statue of their father Prince Albert above the portico of the front entrance. Either side of the statue in shallow niches were the armorial bearings of the Queen and the Prince Consort cast in stone. The ceremony was witnessed by a huge number of dignitaries including MPs, the Mayors of Portsmouth, Southampton and Winchester, the Bishop of Winchester and other members of the Clergy, senior military officers, Parish councillors and many others. The two approach roads were later named Victoria Road and Albert Road, with other side roads called Leopold Drive and Princess Close.

The opening of the Royal Albert Infirmary by Prince Arthur, Princess Helena and Princess Louisa in 1865.
Picture; London Illustrated News

The Infirmary was a charitable organisation and relied totally on public donations and sadly the promised funds didn't materialise enough to actually open the hospital properly and it therefore remained empty for several years. Within a month of Sir Arthur Helps death in 1875 the statue of Prince Albert had been removed and gifted to Southampton Borough Council. In 1877 the building and its grounds were put up for sale and described as follows;

A desirable property consisting of a superior freehold building intended for use as an infirmary. Most substantially built of best red brick, standing in its own terraced grounds and commanding extensive views.

The description continued;

A capacious building of modern design with red brick exterior; and adequately adapted and suitably situated for an infirmary; the interior arrangements having ample accommodation, with four large Wards, nurse's and matrons rooms, surgery and operating rooms, bath rooms, lavatories and well-arranged offices; rendering it most complete as an infirmary or convalescent hospital. The ground floor is completed with the exception of a few fittings and the first floor remains unplastered and unceiled but the whole might be completed, fit for use, at a comparatively small cost.

Then in 1884 it was purchased by a Mr Hurley as a private residence and he renamed it Albert House. Mr Hurley was a miller and corn merchant who lived in Albert House with his wife, six children, a governess and domestic servants.

By 1889 the building had been sold again to Dr Jacob Kalff and renamed The Priory although no-one knows why. In 1902 it was sold to Arthur Robson and by 1908 was back on the market again, this time by auction and was described as follows;

A gentleman's exceptionally well built and substantial residence in a fine position with local amenities that include hunting, shooting and fishing. There are ten lofty bed and dressing rooms, five substantial reception rooms, domestic

"Stand By Ya Beds"

offices, including a large servants sitting room, extensive lawns and meadow, a tennis court, coach house and capital stabling.

It is believed the asking price was around £4000 but it didn't sell and at the time of Arthur Robson's death in 1911 he and his family were still living there. His widow then placed the property back onto the market and in 1912 it was purchased by the Society of Missionaries of Africa, a Roman Catholic Missionary organisation known as the White Fathers, led by Father Pierre Travers. The organisations aim was to train teenage boys as missionaries and then send them out to Africa to undertake God's work. As the number of boys increased so The Priory needed to be extended with further accommodation and so in 1913 Father Travers employed architects to extend the rear of the original building and by the end of the year a fine three storey building was erected parallel to the main building and connected the two buildings with a two storey structure, all in terracotta brick in keeping with the original building, all at a cost of £5735 and completed in just four months! From above the buildings looked like a capital H.

The new rear and centre sections joined the front section of the house. Note the students playing crochet on the grassed lawn and that large tree

Steve Woodward

Side elevation in between the two main sections of The Priory

Aerial view of The Priory showing its H style

During the main building works, in October 1913, a new statue of Our Lady with the Child Jesus in her arms was commissioned in white stone and installed in the niche above the front entrance where Prince Alberts statue once stood. The new dining room also doubled as the school chapel with a raised high alter placed at the far end beneath its three stone arches.

This is the earliest known photo of the front of the original building complete with its new statue in place above the front door

By 1914 a number of the older boys and some of the staff, including Father Travers who were French nationals, were conscripted into the French army. The school was then run by Father John Forbes. As the war embroiled British troops the school was ironically turned into a temporary hospital and convalescent home. In mid-1915 on the advice of the Police, the staff were advised to ensure that all windows were blacked out at night for fear of German attacks from the air. The very next night two Zeppelins passed overhead and one evening a fighter plane skimmed over the top of the school and landed on the fields, before refuelling from a can and taking off again!

The Priory between the war years

By the end of the war the school was left with no pupils at all as all of them had been conscripted on reaching the age of 18. It struggled to rebuild itself and had just about recovered fully when the Second World War broke out in 1939 and for three years the school closed to new pupils and again it lost a good number to military service. In late 1943 the school was requisitioned by the military and housed American servicemen in preparation for D Day in June 1944. The school and grounds were occupied by large numbers of troops, military vehicles and equipment.

There were still 12 boy's residing at the school during this period and they were housed on the top floor dormitory. When the air raid sirens went off, they would make a dash for the windows to watch the bombing raids on Portsmouth and Southampton. It is recorded that on one occasion, whilst watching events outside from their darkened room, that the mattress and bed linen from one boys' bed was completely removed and hidden. As Father Kinseller approached to ensure they were all in

"Stand By Ya Beds"

bed, a huge cry of pain could be heard as the boy landed, at high speed, on nothing but the wire bedstead, to howls of laughter from his roommates!

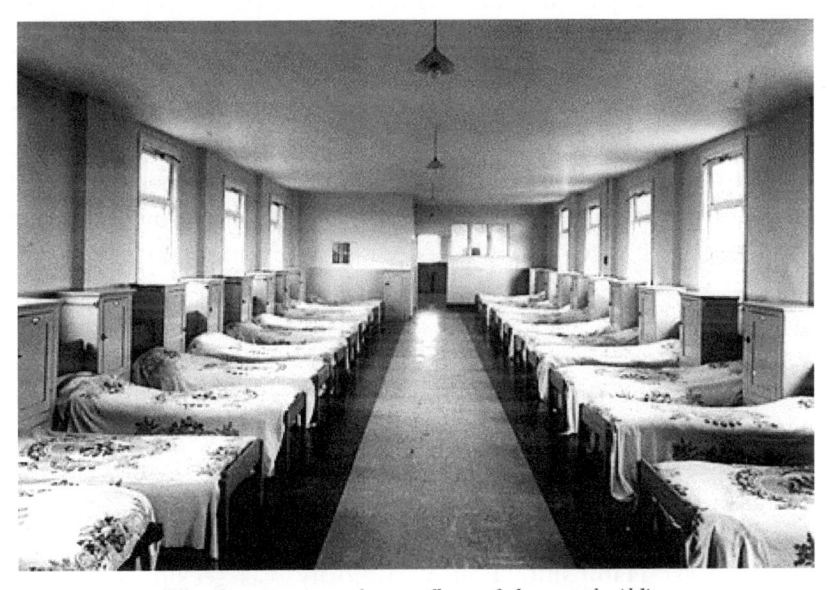

The dormitory on the top floor of the rear building

By May 1944 there were 350 men accommodated in the main building with hundreds more in tents erected on the fields and of course by the first week in June they had all left. But that wasn't the end of The Priory's war time experiences because by now the Germans had invented the V-1 flying bomb or the 'doodlebug' as it got nicknamed here and the boys and staff had a number of very near misses with one of the bombs crashing so close it shook the entire building. There were several other near misses throughout June and July 1944. Shortly after the war the Royal Engineers returned to The Priory to repair the badly damaged entrance road and the area known as the Quadrangle (in between the two main buildings), as they had been ripped up by heavy military vehicles. They dug up the concrete and the rubble formed the base for new tennis courts built in the grounds. Further war records report that from 1945 to 1947 some 75 Italian and German prisoners of war, captured at Tobruk and El Alamein were brought to the The Priory every week from nearby prison camps to take part in Mass within the chapel. Afterwards they often played football with the boys.

By September 1946 the school was up and running again with almost 80 student priests in residence and the numbers rose steadily thereafter and the school flourished as originally intended throughout the 1950s and into the early 1960s. However there were major changes taking place within the Catholic Church and around standards of teaching for A level students and the elder boys were being shipped out to St. Johns College in Southsea, itself a Catholic school run by the De La Salle Brothers and by 1966 were now boarding at the college and not The Priory. By June 1967 The Priory was closed and offered for sale. At some point the statue above the front door disappeared, never to be seen again.

In 1967 Hampshire Police Authority was seeking a suitable property for use as a Cadet Training School and the Hampshire Chronicle reported that 'enquiries by the Chief Constable Mr Douglas Osmond resulted in information of the impending sale of The Priory being obtained'. Lord Ashburton, the Chairman of the Police Authority considered the building was easily adaptable and perfectly sound and a sub-committee of the Authority was appointed to consider proposals for acquiring the premises report that 'The property was excellently situated for the purpose in the centre of the Police area'.

A number of additions and adaptations were required to accommodate the proposed 100 Cadets and the costs for this work, in addition to the sale price of £50,000 was estimated to be £100,000 and this was the figure submitted to the Home Office. However, considerable extensions and modifications to the buildings were required (transforming the dormitories into separate rooms, D Block, the Pavilion and Games Area) together with extensive renovation works required to the Long Field into additional playing fields cost a lot more than anticipated. The first 74 Cadets moved in on the 25th April 1971, although they had been billeted elsewhere since the previous September. The first full term of Cadets was admitted in September 1971. One of the first Cadets there was Eric Martin who recalled having to clear the large attic space during which they found a voodoo doll and an upside down cross, which spooked them somewhat because they knew it had been some kind of monastery.

When the Cadet Training School (CTS) opened its doors for public viewing for the first time in February 1972 the Hampshire Chronicle reported that 'The school, which is residential, has cost the county's rate payers nearly £200,000'.

On 18th October 1980 Hampshire Police Authority approved the proposal to move the school to the former Royal Victoria Hospital at Netley, where it would form part of the new Hampshire Constabulary Support and Training Headquarters. Due to a number of factors that move wasn't completed until early 1988. In July 1988 the old site at Bishops Waltham was offered for sale and bids were invited.

The building lay empty for several years with no interest shown by purchases except property developers whose proposals did not satisfy Hampshire County Council who owned the site. After a poll of local electors by the Bishops Waltham Parish Council in 1991, the parish approached the County Council with an offer of £175,000 to purchase the 21 acres of playing fields for use as a recreation area. The parish had by this time secured grants totalling £23,500 towards the cost of bringing the fields, which had been neglected since the police departed, into good working order. About the same time an offer was accepted from a house building company for the school buildings and part of the elementary school site on Victoria Road, which together totalled 4 ½ acres. At the end of March 1993 all negotiations were completed. The housing site was sold to Wainhomes (Southern) Ltd who demolished the The Priory buildings in mid 1993 and replaced them with an estate of 42 houses.

FOR SALE BY PRIVATE TREATY

in 3 lots

THE FORMER BISHOPS WALTHAM INFANT SCHOOL

and

THE PRIORY POLICE TRAINING COLLEGE

Bishops Waltham, Hampshire

Totalling
25.12 acres (3.14 proposed housing)
32800 sq.ft suitable for institutional uses

Fox & Sons
LAND DEPARTMENT

The Priory up for sale for the last time

"Stand By Ya Beds"

A sad end to a once proud building as it is demolished in 1993
Photos Russ Bramley

Steve Woodward

The extensive playing fields were sold to the parish for £119,477 which was considerably less than they had been prepared to pay. The fields were enhanced to provide a recreation area with unusually fine amenities (including the Pavilion which is still in use) with the fields being used for football, rugby, cricket, bowls, children's play area and walking. It is appropriately named Priory Park.

CHAPTER 1

Piglets

I knocked on the door.

"Come in, sit down" sighed Mr Starky the school careers officer as he puffed on his cigarette, shuffled wads of paperwork, before sitting back, looking over his specs towards me and wearily asking me the question.

"So, do you have any idea what you want to do when you leave school?" he asked as he swept a pile of fag ash from his desk and onto the floor.

"Yes sir" I replied confidently.

His eye brows rose slightly and he sat forward, leaning on the leather elbow patches attached to his grubby pea green corduroy jacket. Just for a second he looked quite pleased that he had a pupil who'd given him a straight answer rather than having to persuade me to take up an apprenticeship at Plessey Radar or British Hovercraft Corporation, both mainstay employers on the Isle of Wight. Then the furrows on his forehead deepened significantly. Surely, I was winding him up?

"Oh let me guess, you want to be an Apollo astronaut or fly Concorde is that it?" he said sarcastically.

"No, I want to join the Police" I squawked.

"Oh………..really? OK then" he replied with a genuine element of surprise in his voice. He quickly stubbed his fag out in the already over full ash tray.

He then asked if I had actually done anything about it and when I said I'd already sent my application form off to join the Hampshire Constabulary's Cadet scheme he was even more astonished.

"Well you seem to be completely sorted then, not much I can do for you is there. One question though; why do you want to join the Police?"

"I've no idea, I just know that's what I want to do" I replied, feeling a little bit stupid that I didn't have a more concrete answer for him.

That was probably the shortest career interview he'd ever conducted. But he did have a point; just why did I want to join up? I mean none of my family had ever been in the police so there was no heritage to live up to and I'd had very little interaction with the Old Bill during my youth. In fact, I can only think of three occasions when I did.

Living on the island during the early 1970s was an interesting period in history, especially if you lived anywhere near the islands three prisons at Parkhurst, Albany and Camphill. My father was a prison officer at Parkhurst and we lived on the prison estate opposite and I'd gone to the nearby Parkhurst junior school before moving up to Cowes High School. A large number of convicted IRA prisoners were incarcerated at Albany and Parkhurst and in October 1970 many of them rioted in Parkhurst. Tensions grew during 1971 and 72 when some IRA prisoners went on hunger strike resulting in one of them dying. There was public outcry when IRA sympathisers, dressed in black berets and dark sun glasses escorted the hearse from Parkhurst to the ferry at Fishbourne.

From my bedroom I would often hear major disorder going on inside the prisons at night and on several occasions saw the flames from the fires they had set ripping through the roof of the buildings. I think it was the summer of 1971 when we were subjected to what was basically a night time curfew on the estate. Serious threats had been made against the families of prison staff, all our houses were linked with alarm bells that seemed to go off with monotonous regularity and cars were banned from parking on the estate unless they had a small Dyno-tape security number stuck to the back of the rear view mirror. Police cars patrolled the area every half an hour or so and we had policemen in our school almost constantly. For us kids it was great, we loved it, but for the parents and others it must have been of great concern. So, I got quite used to seeing a lot of police activity for a while but didn't actually have any close interaction with them.

The second, more personal situation came when I was about 13 or 14 and I was cycling up Northwood Road on my bike when a car came around the bend in front of me and collided with a parked car, sending the passenger straight out through the windscreen and onto the pavement. I was completely traumatised and had obviously never seen anything like it before. One of the police officers who attended chucked my bike into the back of his van and drove me home to Parkhurst where he took a written statement from me. I learned later that the young man had sadly died.

The third occasion was more of a brief encounter and it took place a few months later. I was on my bike coming home from band practice and cycling passed Albany prison. As was my habit at the time I was happily cycling along with both my hands down by my sides rather than on the handlebars when I suddenly heard

3

a booming voice behind me on a loud speaker system bellow out the words;

"*God gave you hands, bloody well use them*" and as the police car over took me I swear I could hear the two coppers inside the car laughing out loud as I wobbled from side to side desperately trying to grab the handlebars!

A few weeks before my 16th birthday and having submitted my application I got a home visit from Sgt John Wavell who was responsible for recruiting on the island. He was a very upright, almost stiff in posture type of man whose eyes were slightly crossed beneath his somewhat bushy eye brows. He was rather stern and forth right in his questioning and I was quite nervous in his presence.

He asked me all about my education at Cowes High School and whether or not I'd pass all my O Levels and CSE exams in a few weeks' time. I sort of shrugged my shoulders and grimaced at the thought of something that actually I hadn't thought much about. Until now that is.

I got grilled about being in the Scouts and all the badges I'd gained, the expeditions I'd been on and most important of all, my experiences with the renowned marching band I was a member of. The 1st Newport Scout Band at that time was rated as one of the top marching bands in the UK and we'd won a large number of trophies and tournaments up and down the country. I'd played snare drum with the band for more than five years now and I'd loved every minute of it. Sgt Wavell said that the sustained discipline and the marching skills would definitely come in handy if my Cadet application was to be accepted. I felt a little more confident all of a sudden.

"One last question" he said "Why do you want to join the Police?"

"Erm……..I don't know really, I just know that's what I want to do" I replied somewhat nervous again.

"Well young Stephen you'll have to come up with a much better answer than that come the time of your interview" he said "So you'll need to work on that".

Before he left he said he'd approve my application and that the next step would be the entrance exam in a few weeks' time. He shook me firmly by the hand, wished me luck and left.

A few weeks later I was talking to my mate Ken in class. He was joining the Royal Navy and we were comparing notes about our futures when another lad called Alan Robertson came across because he'd overheard our conversation.

"Are you joining the Police Cadets Woody?" he asked.

"If I get through the entrance exam in a couple of weeks' time yes" I replied.

"That's amazing mate so am I and Wayne Colebrook is joining up as well" he said with a huge smile on his face.

Both Alan and Wayne were in my year at school and although they weren't in my peer group, I did know them well enough to be more than happy that they might be joining up with me. And a couple of weeks later the three of us boarded the hovercraft at Ryde and made the 8 minute trip across The Solent to Southsea, where we walked across Southsea Common, resplendent in our best clobber to Byculla House in Queens Crescent. This fabulous old building was once the headquarters of the Portsmouth City Police before it amalgamated with the Hampshire and Isle of Wight Constabulary in 1967.

We were greeted at the reception desk by a Sgt who took us up a creaking wooden stair case to a class room where there were several other 16 year old lads all looking as nervous as I was. We all sat there in silence as a few more candidates entered the room and took their seats. Two Sgts then entered and handed out the exam papers. There were three; English, maths and a problem solving paper and we had two hours to complete them. I was good at English but crap at maths so I wasn't looking forward to that paper, but got stuck in as best I could.

Once the two hours was up we adjourned outside for a fag. Al, Wayne and I compared notes which is never a good idea because it makes you doubt the answers that you gave. After an hour or so we were ushered back into the class room. The two Sgts were ashen faced as they called out the names of about 8 or 9 lads and they were taken away by one of the Sgts. As soon as the door was closed our Sgt stood in front of the dozen of us who were left.

"They are the lucky ones" he said.
My heart sank and my stomach turned over several times.
"They all failed the exam and have had a lucky escape. You lot all passed and subject to your interview and medical you will be accepted into the Hampshire Constabulary. God help us" he said with a smile.

My second taste of Police humour was I suppose as black as the incident on my bike but actually I quite liked it. Alan and Wayne had passed as well and we all breathed a sigh of relief. One by one we were taken to another room for our formal interviews with a Chief Inspector.

I was now shaking like a leaf as I sat before him. Just like my home visit from Sgt Wavell I got asked all the usual questions about my education, the Scouts and the band. And then it came.

"So why do you want to join the Police then young man?" he asked.

"It's something I have always wanted to do and I like helping people and I think this is probably the best way to do that" I replied, sounding like a contestant from the Miss World tournament although I refrained from telling him that I loved animals and prayed for world peace.

He showed no emotion whatsoever and told me to go back to the class room. No sooner had I got back there I was taken to yet another room for my medical. I had to strip down to my underpants and stand in the middle of the room, all 8 stone of skinny whiteness. I was weighed, measured for height, had my temperature taken, then he looked in my ears, my eyes, down my throat and yes, he then grabbed my balls and told me to cough. Doing an eye test in your pants is a weirdly vulnerable experience as well.

Then it was back to the classroom to wait with the others until we were all done. The Chief Inspector and the two Sgts returned and one of our class was called out and taken away. My heart was pounding once more. But I needn't have worried because the rest of us had got through and we would receive our joining instructions in the post.

The three of us travelled back to the island feeling ten feet tall. It was a surreal feeling and all of a sudden I felt like an adult and not a school boy. But it was back to school for all three of us the next day, we had exams coming up after all. A couple of weeks later a rather formal letter arrived, addressed to my father, confirming my appointment, together with a start date in September.

"Stand By Ya Beds"

HAMPSHIRE CONSTABULARY

Tel. No. Winchester 68133
Telex Nos. 47361/2

Our Ref. P/CTS/KEO/C.104/75
Your Ref.

CHIEF CONSTABLE'S OFFICE,
HEADQUARTERS,
WINCHESTER.
SO22 5DB

11th August, 1975.

Dear Sir,

I am directed by the Chief Constable to refer to your son's interview at this office, and I am pleased to confirm that he has been accepted for appointment to this Force as a Police Cadet.

I should be obliged if you would arrange for your son to report to the Cadet Training School, Albert Road, Bishop's Waltham, not later than 2.30 p.m. on Sunday, 7th September, 1975. He will attend a residential Training Course for new Cadets and, unless required for duty at the School, he will be allowed home leave from 5.30 p.m. on Friday, 12th September to 10.00 p.m. on Sunday, 14th September, 1975.

Both you and your wife are also invited to attend the Cadet Training School when your son reports on Sunday, 7th September, 1975. This invitation also applies to the guardians of those Cadets who are unable to bring their parents to the School on this occasion.

It is intended that whilst your son is being allocated accommodation, etc., the Officer-in-Charge will address you briefly about your son's training programme during the ensuing months. You will then be given the opportunity of looking over the premises and meeting some of the staff at the School. It is anticipated that this will be concluded about 4.30 p.m. when we will have to ask parents to leave the School.

May I draw your attention to the information contained in the enclosed joining instructions.

Would you please confirm that your son will be able to join this Force on Sunday, 7th September, 1975.

Yours faithfully,

Assistant Chief Constable
Personnel Department

A few days later I was walking towards my class room when I saw my younger brother and three of his mates coming along the corridor. As they passed me so they started laughing and once they were a further ten yards or so down the corridor so they started shouting out "Piglet" and "Steve's going to be a piglet" as they then ran off laughing and hollering. And every time from then on, they'd shout it out as soon as they saw me. It was never done when I was close enough to grab one of them by the throat and I suppose it's just something I'm going to have to get used to.

8

Piglets

Exams over it was time to leave school, which was a weird experience. Saying good bye to friends you'd been close to for several years knowing that you would probably never see them again as we all took our separate paths was quite emotional. It would be another three months or so before I went back to the mainland to start my training and so I spent much of the summer working on a farm. I cycled the 7 or 8 miles each way to Calbourne and had to be there by 6am or else! The farmer was a hard task master and didn't suffer fools. The days were long and hard as we were hay bailing most of the time. It was hard physical labour in the warm summer sun, loading the hay bales onto the deck of a flatbed lorry, stacking it as high as we dare, then driving it back to the farm to unload onto a conveyor belt and stack the bales even higher inside the barn. The hay got into every orifice on your body. And I do mean everywhere! There was a particular technique for lifting and moving bales of hay. With up turned palms, you'd slip your fingers under the two strands of twine, lift the bale onto your right knee, twist it towards your chest and as it hit your upper torso so you pushed it hard upwards with your arms, turning it forwards and onto the stack, all in one movement. I think weight lifters call it the snatch and jerk, which has other connotations I know but I'm sure you get my drift! My hands got quite badly blistered but as the weeks went by and we started bringing in the straw bales as well so my muscle tone increased, which was something I knew I was going to need plenty of at training school. And I learned to drive on the farm too, albeit in an old British Hovercraft Corporation flatbed truck!

The dreaded big brown envelope arrived in the post. The exam results were out. I really wasn't very confident about things and with good reason because I just hadn't tried that hard, I couldn't be bothered frankly. My parents stood there as I opened the envelope. My O Level results consisted of a B in English Language, B in Design Technology, B in Technical Drawing and a D in English Literature. My CSE results were even worse; C in

Maths, C in Geography, D in Biology, D in Physics and an E in German. They were barely enough to get me into the Cadets. My parents were far from happy with me but then that wasn't unusual and I couldn't wait to get off the island and away from my domineering mother in particular.

I had a bit of a transportation problem though. There was no train station in the village of Bishops Waltham or anywhere near where the training school was and certainly no regular bus service back to Portsmouth some 15 miles away from where I'd catch the ferry back to the Isle of Wight at weekends or whenever. My father decided that I needed a motor bike and so off we went to the local motorcycle dealer; Dave Death Motorcycles at Carisbrooke, such a quaint name for a bike dealer! I have to admit to being rather excited about getting a motor bike. A couple of slightly older school mates already had theirs and I'd read a fair bit about one or two models. This was the era of the sports moped and the model of choice was the Yamaha FS1E or the Fizzy as it was affectionately referred to, preferably in Popsicle purple. But my father wasn't impressed with old man Dave Death, he didn't like his attitude for some reason and so we headed across to the only other bike shop on the island where they sold pedal cycles and something called a Puch moped. I'd never heard of them before now but rather liked the look of the Puch Grand Prix Sport with its sleek looks, alloy wheels and fancy graphics. But that one was far too expensive and so I had to settle for the Puch M50 Sport in bright red.

All I had to do now was learn how to ride the thing. My father sat me on the back as he rode it to a quiet spot just off Forest Road. There he taught me the basics but I couldn't get my head around the clutch and that I had to pull the clutch lever in whenever I stopped otherwise the bike would stall. He got really angry with me at one point but I got there in the end. Over the next few days, I rode it along the quiet roads on the island trying to master this new form of transport and I had to learn quickly because my first proper trip on it would be on the mainland as I headed towards training school.

CHAPTER 2

Welcome to Bishops Waltham

At last the day had arrived; Sunday 7th September 1975. My father drove the car onto the ferry and we took the 45 minute trip across The Solent to Portsmouth. We sat in the passenger lounge, which was engulfed in the stench of diesel fumes emanating from the engine room below deck. I so wanted a cigarette but as my mother still didn't know that her eldest son had been smoking since he was 15, I thought it best for now that I kept them in my pocket. I'm sure she must have known but the mere thought of telling her didn't bare thinking about. I also felt uncomfortable in my best clothes which I'd last worn to my cousins wedding earlier in the year and which consisted of a cream coloured blazer, a brown shirt with huge butterfly collar, even bigger blue and white patterned kipper tie, brown Oxford Bags trousers and black and white brogue shoes! Well it was the mid 1970's!

My heart was pounding as we drove through the entrance and into the Hampshire Constabulary's Cadet Training School. We were stopped by a Police officer at the monolithic looking main building and he then directed us to the car park and then where to report once we had entered a fair sized wooden building called The Pavilion. After booking in we were given a cup of tea and then sat down with lots of other nervous looking, smartly dressed 16 year olds with their respective parents. I saw Wayne and then Alan and we sort of nodded to each other. It was comforting to see a couple of familiar faces. Within half an hour the room was full, there seemed to be hundreds of people crammed in with

Welcome to Bishops Waltham

many of them having to stand around the outside edge of the room because there simply weren't enough chairs.

First look at the Cadet Training School as we drove through the gate
Photo Hampshire Constabulary

The room fell silent as a number of uniformed Police officers entered and stood at the front facing us. They all looked very stern and I wondered just what was going through their minds as they cast their eyes over us. To my left was a lectern and Chief Inspector John Harrison welcomed us all to Bishops Waltham, our home for the next 10 months. He reassured our parents that we would be well looked after but that we would be made to work hard and that physically we would be beaten into the best shape of our lives because the physical training side of being a Police Cadet was at the fore front of their objectives, together with improving our educational needs. This would see us attending Fareham

"Stand By Ya Beds"

Technical College four out of five days a week. Then in a year's time we would be sent home so that we could then work at the Police Station nearest to our home address until we reached 18 years of age and then if successful would then be accepted into the force as a Police Constable. Well that all seems simple enough and after the parents were given a quick guided tour of the school and its facilities, they were all invited to vacate the premises and leave their off spring at the school gates!

After they'd gone, we were ordered back to The Pavilion where we got the proper welcome lecture from Chief Inspector Harrison. He had a granite face and a very authoritive manner about him. He told us in no uncertain terms what the school rules were, how he demanded that we work hard and play hard and……….

"Am I boring you young man?" he bellowed.
He was looking slightly to my left.
"Yes you in the brown suit, blue tie, STAND UP"
We all turned to look.
Oh shit its Al.
"Are you tired sonny?"
"No sir" he replied
"Then why are you yawning?" he shouted.

Before Al had a chance to answer Mr Harrison turned to one of the instructors and directed him to take Alan outside and introduce him to the sports field. A beetroot faced Alan was led out of the Pavilion and down onto the sports fields which consisted of at least three full sized football pitches and was made to run around the perimeter in his best suit!! The rest of us could be seen shuffling backwards in our chairs and sitting bolt upright.

Mr Harrison continued to lay down the school rules and told us that we were the largest intake of Cadets the force had ever taken in with 65 of us on the course rather than the usual 45 to 50.

Welcome to Bishops Waltham

He then introduced us to his staff; his deputy was Inspector Raymond Chadwick, there were two Sgts in Keith Middleton and Gerry Todd with four PC's as the main instructors. They were Pete Kerley, Russ Parke (himself a former Portsmouth City Police Cadet), Tony Astill and Pete Manns. There was a resident Matron to look after our medical needs in Mrs Snodden who was affectionately known as Snoddy.

Chief Inspector John Harrison and Inspector Raymond Chadwick

"Stand By Ya Beds"

Sgt Gerry Todd and Sgt Keith Middleton

16

Welcome to Bishops Waltham

PC instructors Russ Parke and Pete Manns

"Stand By Ya Beds"

PC instructors Pete Kerley and Tony Astill

Welcome to Bishops Waltham

Alan came back into the room, huffing and puffing like Thomas the Tank Engine! He looked absolutely knackered. No sooner had he taken his seat, Mr Harrison stood down from the lectern and handed proceedings over to Sgt Middleton. The Chief Inspector and his Deputy then left. We were then split up into four groups or 'houses' and introduced to our House Instructor. I was in Rowan House, whose colours were red and our instructor was Pete Kerley, a man in his early 30's I think with a full beard. He seemed friendly enough. To my great surprise both Alan and Wayne were also in my house which was great. Alan was still breathing heavily and clutching his chest.

There were 14 of us in Rowan House and Pete Kerley took us out from the Pavilion and into the car park to begin the grand tour of the school. To our left and down a steep embankment were the playing fields, which consisted of two full sized football pitches, a hockey pitch and two rugby pitches. To our right are the tennis courts which can double up as basketball courts and behind the Pavilion is the assault course which we were told we would become very familiar with!

We walked up the car park towards the main building. To our left was a large shed with a tractor inside and lots of heavy duty lawn mowers and other equipment belonging to the head grounds man 'Mad Mick' and just past that was D Block or sick bay. This was a modern single storey annexe to the main building.

"Stand By Ya Beds"

Walking up from the car park towards the rear of CTS with D Block in the fore ground
Photo Hampshire Constabulary

To our right were two more wooden buildings that we were told were class rooms.

Welcome to Bishops Waltham

The wooden classroom buildings
Photo Hampshire Constabulary

Then we entered the main building and into a single storey extension that was called the Games Area. Placed strategically around the outer walls were various items of weight lifting equipment, crash mats, wooden PT benches, a pummel horse, table tennis tables and boxing gloves. This would also be the place we had to report to each morning at 0600 sharp to commence the morning run! Oh great, a morning run.

"Stand By Ya Beds"

*The Games Area and the stairs that lead to the dining room and lounge area
Photo Hampshire Constabulary*

From the Games Area we were taken down a narrow hallway to the oldest part of the main building, which was the main reception area for visitors to report to and where the Chief Inspector and all his staff had their offices. There was a library and a separate reading room and all the walls were decorated with framed photographs of previous courses, former instructors and senior officers. In the middle of the reception area was an old wooden spiral stair case painted in white that creaked loudly as soon as anyone stepped on it. And there were two telephone booths with pay phones attached to silver painted peg boards surmounted by a Perspex bubble to afford a modicum of privacy as you talked.

Welcome to Bishops Waltham

The reception area
Photo Hampshire Constabulary

Then it was back down the hall way, through the Games Area, up half a dozen stairs where we turned right and into a large dining hall. The polished wooden parquet flooring gave the room an air of sophistication. At the far end beneath three stone arches was a slightly raised floor with the top table mounted on it. This was where the instructors sat at meal times. The rest of the tables were arranged in four long rows, one for each 'house'. At this end of the dining room was a huge gilt framed portrait of HM Queen. To the right was the kitchen and the serving hatch and we were told that the head of the kitchen staff, Mrs Haysom would be responsible for feeding us morning, noon and night.

"Stand By Ya Beds"

The large Dining Room that was once the chapel
Photo Hampshire Constabulary

Grubs up! The large kitchen at CTS
Photo Hampshire Constabulary

Then it was about turn, out of the dining room and along the hall way to the 'Small Lounge' which just had a number of chairs placed around the outer walls and a record player in one corner. No smoking was allowed in this lounge. On the wall outside the small lounge was the Pigeon Hole, an old wooden letter rack split into alphabetical cubby holes where we could collect our post from home. Then we entered the main lounge area which was huge and split into two halves. At the far end was a big colour TV with loads of two seater and single seat chairs, which were all very modern affairs with wooden frames and either bright orange or lime green cushions. At this end of the lounge was a battered table football table, a bar billiards table and a dart board. There were a number of those pillar type ash trays with the chrome push-down tops that swallowed your fag butts into the bowels of the receptacle and made that rather satisfying swooshing noise as it did so. There were a few more chairs scattered around and in the corner was a separate small room with a metal roller shutter window and this was the tuck shop where we could purchase all manner of chocolate, crisps and sweets together with pints of draught Coke, lemonade or limeade! We would be expected to man the shop from time to time.

View of the Big Lounge taken from the dining room end

"Stand By Ya Beds"

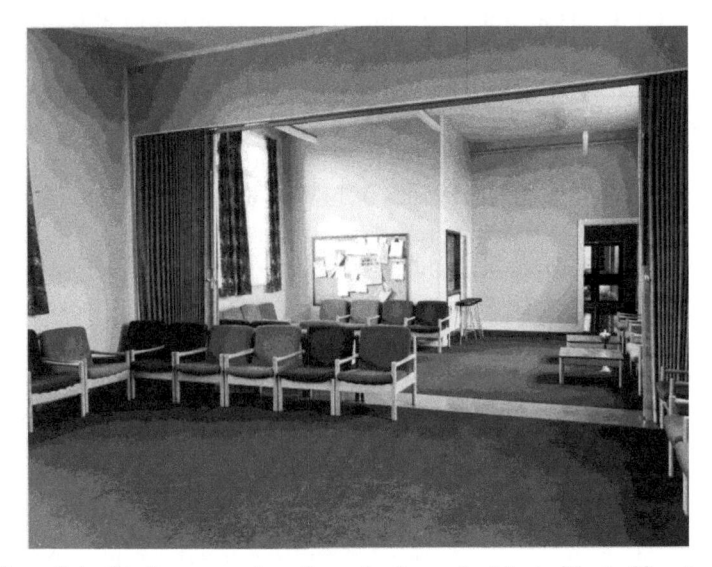

View of the Big Lounge taken from the far end with the Tuck Shop in the far left corner

We went through the lounge and out the far door to a concrete stair well. We were marched up the stairs to the first floor. To our right were the showers and the toilets and to the left were Rowan House rooms. Pete Kerley consulted his clipboard;

"Cadets Bramley, Gibson, Mason and RD Smith, in this room here" which he then opened and ushered them in.

"Cadets Woodward and Goward in this one here. I hope you two are nice and cosy as you have the only two man room on this floor" he smiled.

In the room next door to us were Cadets Warry, Howsego, Pucket and Gosden, followed by Cadets Sexton, O'Flaherty and French and in the last room Cadets Colebrook, Robertson, Sewell and Murphy. We were told to collect our belongings from the Pavilion, settle in and report to the dining room in an hour.

Welcome to Bishops Waltham

My new roommate shook my hand and said his name was Andy. The first thing that struck me about him was his hair because he had a lot of grey in it which made him look older than his years. He said his father was a police officer and rode bikes and I got the distinct impression that he was slightly in awe of him. We exchanged a bit of small talk before heading back down to the Pavilion to collect our stuff and then spent another ten minutes trying to find our room again!

Our room was situated at the rear of the building and over looked part of the playing fields and the roof of D Block. It was a rather spartan room with just two single beds, two single sized wardrobes, a bedside cabinet each and a chair and desk each. The orange curtains matched the beds counter pane but clashed somewhat with the dark red carpet. As we started to put our stuff away into the wardrobes there seemed to be a lot of laughter coming from the room next door which we could clearly hear through the very thin walls.

My bedroom for the next 10 months

"Stand By Ya Beds"

Then it was back down to the dining room where we were instructed to sit at our respective house tables as the instructors took up their places at the top table. We could smell dinner being prepared from behind the metal roller shutters in the kitchen and it smelt just like school dinners always did.

Inspector Chadwick then addressed us for the first time. He wasn't a humorous man and appeared to be the disciplinarian for the establishment. He insisted that we call all the instructors Sir and we had to stand if any of them entered a room where we were sat. He started off by telling us that uniform fitting would take place tomorrow, along with haircuts for everyone, that interviews to assess our educational needs would take place later next week and that lights out was at 2230, no ifs, no buts, if you are caught out then you will be punished accordingly. School discipline would be rigorously enforced and starting right now our self-discipline was something that we would have to learn more of. The morning run would commence at 0600 every week day morning and consisted of one lap around the entire perimeter of CTS which worked out at approximately 2 miles.

Then it was time for dinner and up went the roller shutter to reveal a large kitchen with a number of smiling ladies behind the counter. We were introduced to Mrs Haysom, a small lady in her 50's with the most ginger of ginger hair I'd ever seen. We were told in no uncertain terms that if we ever had any complaints about the food which was "highly unlikely" then we were NOT to complain to the kitchen staff but to speak to one of the instructors. And so we lined up with a tray each and collected our food before returning to our respective tables. It was the first chance we'd all had to get to know each other within our groups. We were joined by Alan Spiers who was a Phase 3 Cadet. As the 'newbies' we were referred to as Phase 1 Cadets. Amongst our intake were half a dozen Phase 2 Cadets. These guys were a year older than the rest of us and would only be with us for a few weeks before going out to their home stations and wouldn't have to go to Fareham Tech. The Phase 3 Cadets had done their 12 months training at CTS and had volunteered to remain on at the school to help mentor the next batch, i.e. us! Part of their role was to assist the PC Instructors and to ensure the aforementioned school discipline was fully adhered to.

After dinner we were given free rein to explore the school further but most of us seemed to congregate in the big lounge where we played table football or bar billiards whilst sipping pints of coke from the tuck shop. Everyone seemed friendly enough but as the evening wore on we were reminded more than once that lights out was at 2230 sharp. It had been a rather long and taxing day and it wasn't long before I went and found my room again. Andy was already there and as we compared notes on the evenings activities so there was a shout from the far end of the corridor "Lights Out".

At 0530 my alarm clock went off and I got straight into my PE kit and made my way down to the Games Area where we were ordered into our house groups before a register was called to ensure that we were all present. Our duty Instructor for the day was PC Tony Astill who bore an uncanny resemblance to Freddy Mercury complete with moustache. He was dressed in a dark blue track suit and he would lead us on the morning run to show us the route.

"I think Cadet Robertson already knows the route though don't you" he smirked.

We all laughed as Al just sort of winced and said "Well at least I'm dressed the part this morning Sir" which was probably the right thing to say.

I'm not a great runner, never have been. I can sprint a couple of hundred yards but anything more than that and I lose interest, as well as stamina. And so out the door we went with PC Astill shouting out enthusiastically.

"Stand By Ya Beds"

"C'mon you blokes".

We passed D Block towards the car park, but then it was down the steep embankment to the first football pitch, down the full length of that, turn left at the end by the hedge, then along the bottom of both football pitches, the hockey pitch, both rugby pitches, then down the length of the last rugby field, along the top of both rugby pitches, turn right and across the rear of The Pavilion, past the assault course, through an area of rough grass and weeds, then turn left up the side of the tennis courts and back to the Games Area. It was knackering and we were told we'd be doing it every morning no matter what the weather was like. After a quick shower it was time for breakfast. Now I've always liked my breakfast and the choice here was amazing, full English, cereals, toast, pints and pints of milk, tea, coffee etc etc, in fact I think I'll just stay here all day and eat.

As soon as breakfast was over it was time for haircuts and uniform fitting. The buzz was palpable. To get the uniform was obviously a big step for all of us. We were split into two groups with one group going off to get their uniforms sorted whilst the rest of us lined up to get our hair cut. Mine was already reasonably short or so I thought. I sat in the chair as PC Russ Parke got to work with the electric shears and a pair of scissors. He seemed really friendly and pleasant as we chatted away. It was just like being in your local barber shop.

"Do you want to keep your side burns?" he asked politely.
"Yes please" I replied.

Two snips later and both my side burns were dropped into my lap.

"There you are" he said "You can keep them now"

I wonder how many others fell for that one? Having very short hair wasn't the fashion for young males in mid 1970s Britain.

Welcome to Bishops Waltham

Having very short hair was normally the reserve of skin heads that didn't have the best of reputations at the time whilst the rest of the male populous were happy to have collar length hair with a feather cut. I guess it's something we'll have to get used to.

Then it was time to get the uniform. We were measured top to toe and handed two tunics, two pairs of trousers, three blue shirts, two black clip-on ties, a Police cap with blue band and a brand new pair of boots. Additional items included a Gannex rain coat, black gloves, a torch and a white plastic name badge with your name stuck on with a length of Dyno tape. This was to be worn at all times whilst on CTS premises, on duty or off duty.

Cadets Shaun Terry, Mick Streeter and Russ Bramley

"Stand By Ya Beds"

*Fresh out of the box, top left Steve Woodward
Top right Russ Bramley,
Bottom left Phil Travers,
Centre Alan Robertson,
Bottom right Stef King*

Welcome to Bishops Waltham

Gary O'Flaherty, Duncan Warry and Adrian Prangnell

The last item was a pocket note book, a hard backed blue book that we had to write in every half an hour, detailing what we were doing. It had to be very neat and all the headings had to be underlined. This was to get us used to the idea of religiously filling it in when on patrol and for gathering evidence.

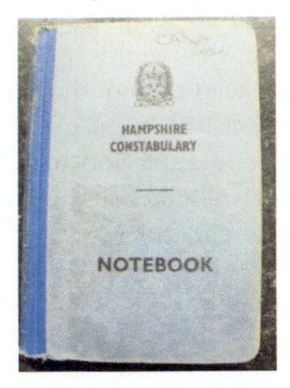

First pocket notebook

"Stand By Ya Beds"

I took the whole lot up to my room and looked in the mirror. It looked great and I think I grew another couple of inches. Then it was back downstairs where we were given instruction on caring for our uniforms. This included ironing lessons! We were told not to put an iron directly onto the fabric because it would melt the upper surface of the material and it would become very hard and shiny. Instead you had to place brown parcel paper, shiny side up, onto the item of uniform and iron on top of that. There was an alternative to the brown paper system and that was to use a damp tea towel and the choice was ours, whichever suited us best. Trousers were to be pressed to ensure that the creases were razor sharp with no parallel lines. Tunic sleeves were to be treated the same way and to ensure that the front crease was perfectly positioned so that when standing to attention both creases could be seen running perfectly vertical. Shirts had to be ironed all over but sleeves also had to have razor sharp creases in the appropriate places. Boots had to be polished all over but the toe caps and the area around the heel had to be bulled to a mirror finish. We were given instruction in how to accomplish this. You had to take a tin of black Kiwi boot polish and a well-used yellow duster type cloth. Don't use a new one because it will leave lots of little yellow hairs all over your boots. Take the cloth, place it over your right index finger, lick the end and then dab it into the polish. Once you have a decent amount of polish on the cloth place your finger onto the area to be polished and apply the polish using a very small circular motion. Continue doing this whilst spitting onto the same area every now and then to keep the polish fairly fluid. You will soon build up a coating of polish that will give a mirror like finish. Be warned though that if you apply too much polish it might look good for a while but it will crack and fall off in big chunks and you will have to start all over again.

It sounded easy enough for those of us with standard boots with a proper toe cap. But these were only available to those of us with size 10 feet or under. If you had bigger than size 10's you were issued with a different type of boot which had a textured

Welcome to Bishops Waltham

covering that looked like spots, including the toe cap area. Those with such boots, which included Andy, were instructed to heat the back of a tea spoon with a lighter and when it was hot enough to run the spoon over the toe cap to melt the leather and smooth it into a better surface on which to commence the spit and polish routine.

After lunch it was time for some basic drill. Sgt Middleton was our drill instructor and we started with the very basics like standing to attention, at ease, then standing in height order, in line front to back, side to side, before learning about open order march, right dress, eyes front etc. We even had to learn how to salute. It was all very basic and fairly easy. But then it was time to march. Well having come from a back ground with the band I found marching very easy, I'd been doing it almost daily since I was ten years old. Wayne was the same having been a member of the Combined Cadet Force band at school. Others weren't so lucky. Sgt Middleton was a patient man but he was being severely tested right now. There were some who had absolutely no coordination at all and somehow ended up marching right arm and right leg together then left arm, left leg. What made it even funnier was that they knew it was wrong but couldn't change it. There was a lot of laughter going on especially when Sgt Middleton started to lose his patience.

"Cadet French what the fuck are you doing?" he screamed.
"Cadet Goward you look like a chimpanzee, keep your arms straight"
"Cadet Dwyer have you shit yourself?" he screamed.
"No Sir" he yelled back.
"Well stop marching as if you have then"
And so it went on all afternoon. It was more tiring than the morning run! After dinner the entire evening was spent preparing our uniforms for our first inspection tomorrow morning. The ironing room on our floor was little more than a cupboard with two irons and a work top to facilitate the pressing of uniforms.

We took it in turns as best we could and the mixture of damp tea towels, steam and burning brown paper produced a uniquely pungent smell that I doubt I will ever forget. Every now and then you'd hear an agonised scream where someone had either burned themselves or worse had managed to iron a neat set of tram lines into their trousers!

In every room there were fresh faced Cadets eagerly bulling their boots, spitting copious amounts of phlegm onto the toe caps before furiously polishing around the cap in tiny circles like some demented ice skater making swirling patterns on the ice. Bulling boots was either something you could do or it wasn't. There didn't seem to be anything in between. Wayne Colebrook and Martin Gibson were brilliant at it and let's be honest darn right smug about it. And it wasn't long before others started offering them money or fags to bull theirs. Personally, I fell into the middle ground of reasonably OK but no-where-near-as-good-as-Colebrook's boots and no matter how hard I tried I just couldn't quite get that mirror finish. Andy was having even more problems with his speckled boots because no matter what he did with the hot spoon or the polish all he got was a matt black finish more reminiscent to that found on the bonnet of a 1970s Ford Capri.

Before we knew it, it was lights out time. I was asleep in seconds but was rudely awakened at 0130 by the sound of the fire alarm. We had been warned earlier in the day that it may go off at some time as a practice run but even so it scared the crap out of me at first and reminded me of the prison alarms at our house. So, it was on with the PE kit and we ran downstairs shouting and hollering to ensure that everyone was up and out of bed. We assembled in our houses outside the Games Area and it was bloody freezing. A register was called and once they were satisfied that everyone was there, they very kindly let us go back to bed.

Getting back to sleep wasn't easy and 0530 came around even quicker. We all gathered in the Games Area for the morning run, which now I knew how far it was I was dreading even more.

Welcome to Bishops Waltham

There were a couple of the lads that looked like professional runners and spent 10 minutes limbering up whilst the rest of us were still trying to prise our eye lids apart. We set off again and by the time we got to the second football pitch I was about three quarters of the way back down the pack. I certainly wasn't the slowest but I needed to up my game somewhat. I came back into the Games Area huffing and puffing with my hands on my hips gasping for air. But it seemed like most of the others were doing the same so at least I wasn't suffering alone. At breakfast we were told that one of our in-take had resigned already because he thought the physical side of things was too tough! I don't think we've even started yet.

After breakfast we assembled in the car park with our respective instructors for our first inspection from Mr Chadwick. We formed up, did a few drill manoeuvres before waiting our turn for him to inspect Rowan House. I was in the front row and unfortunately for me was placed next to Wayne who looked like he'd been groomed by the fucking Grenadier Guards; he was immaculate and his boots were so well bulled that if he'd stuck his right foot underneath the skirt of a passing female you'd have been able to see what colour knickers she was wearing. My only saving grace was that the Inspector would get to me before he looked at Wayne and not the other way around otherwise I wouldn't stand a chance. I had butterflies in my stomach as he stood in front of me and looked me up and down. He then walked around behind me before returning and looking me straight in the eye.

"Cadet Woodward your boots are a disgrace, you definitely need more practice with the iron because you haven't got creases in your trousers, they're more like folds and put your bloody name badge on straight" he growled. With that he moved next door to Wayne and after a few minutes I heard him say.
"Excellent standard Cadet Colebrook, you could teach Woodward here a thing or two".

"Stand By Ya Beds"

"Yes Sir, thank you Sir" replied Wayne who I knew was looking smug. I didn't need to look at him to know that.

After that initial inspection we were told that as tomorrow was Wednesday we would be inspected again as we will be every Wednesday from now on and that would include a full room inspection after breakfast. Well that was something to look forward to. We spent the rest of the day being interviewed by Sgt Middleton or Inspector Chadwick together with a number of tutors from the nearby Fareham Technical College to assess what courses we would undertake once we started there in two weeks' time.

After some debate it was decided that I would redo my technical drawing course because I was good at that and it was hoped I could upgrade from my C Grade O Level to an A. I also fancied doing O Level Law, although this would be civil law and not criminal law which I thought was a little bit short sighted but was hardly in a position to argue. I also had to do maths and French, both of which I hated. The very thought of having to go back to school was something I just wasn't interested in doing frankly, I thought I'd left all that shit behind but I got reminded by Mr Chadwick that my school grades were average at best and that here at CTS it was expected that I would get my head down, work hard and obtain better results. There were a few within our group who were brainy enough to commence A Levels which I thought was even worse until I found out they'd be missing the all-day Wednesday physicals that the rest of us would be doing on our only day off from tech.

And to get us in the mood for studying we were set some homework to complete by next week. Each of our 'houses' were named after famous Police leaders and instigators in Rowan, Peel, Mayne and Fielding. Our homework was to research those names and write an essay on the impact they'd had on policing and the only way to do this was to access the books from the CTS library.

Welcome to Bishops Waltham

PEEL HOUSE; Sir Robert Peel (1788 – 1850) twice served as Prime Minister and twice as Home Secretary. He is regarded as the father of the modern Police force, having founded the Metropolitan Police in 1829 and based them at Scotland Yard. The names 'Bobbies' or 'Peelers' quickly followed.

MAYNE HOUSE; Sir Richard Mayne (1796 – 1868) was a barrister and the joint first Commissioner of the Metropolitan Police and served that post for 39 years, the longest incumbent in the force's history. In 1829 Mayne wrote "The primary object of an efficient police is the prevention of crime: the next that of detection and punishment of offenders if crime is committed. To these ends all the efforts of police must be directed. The protection of life and property, the preservation of public tranquillity, and the absence of crime, will alone prove whether those efforts have been successful and whether the objects for which the police were appointed have been attained." This later formed the basis of the Police oath.

ROWAN HOUSE; Lieutenant Colonel Sir Charles Rowan (1782 – 1852) was an officer in the British army and served at the Battle of Waterloo. Along with Sir Richard Mayne he became the first joint Commissioner of the Metropolitan Police. The two Commissioners were almost entirely responsible for the organisation of the new force. In twelve weeks, they managed to recruit, train, organise, equip and deploy a force of nearly one thousand men. They drew up regulations and pay scales, designed and ordered uniforms and equipment, and found, purchased and furnished station houses.

FIELDING HOUSE; Sir John Fielding (1721 – 1780) was a notable Magistrate and social reformer. Together with his brother Henry Fielding they formed the first professional police force, the Bow Street Runners. Through the regular circulation of a police gazette containing descriptions of known criminals, Fielding also

"Stand By Ya Beds"

established the basis for the first police criminal records department.

So, the pressure was starting to build; we had ironing to master, boots to bull, rooms to ready for inspection, pocket books to write up and now homework to research.

Our rooms were very simple; a bed, a bed side cabinet (which contained a Gideon's Bible) and a wardrobe each. Nothing was allowed to be left out on show and even the manner in which we placed our personal effects inside the wardrobe was strictly controlled. But the worst bit centred on our bedding. Every morning we had to strip the bed and make up a bed pack. We were each issued with two white sheets, three cream coloured blankets and an orange/red, blue, green or yellow counter pane (House colours). To make up a bed pack you had to fold all three blankets and the sheets in exactly the same shape and size. And I do mean exactly.

Cadets Andy Crawford, Mick Streeter, Stef King, Phil Travers, Pete LeGros, Nathan Johnson and others receive instruction from PC Russ Parke
Photo Hampshire Telegraph

40

Welcome to Bishops Waltham

Then you'd place one blanket down first, then place a folded sheet on top of that, then another blanket, then the second sheet followed by the third blanket, so you ended up with a perfectly shaped block. You then folded your counter pane length ways three times so you ended up with a long, thin counter pane exactly the same width as your block and then you wrapped the block in the counter pane and placed the whole thing at the end of your bed, with your pillows placed on top. No creases, no straggly bits, no curved ends were allowed; it had to be perfectly square. It was all very military like and was designed to help out with that self-discipline thing that we were lectured about on day one.

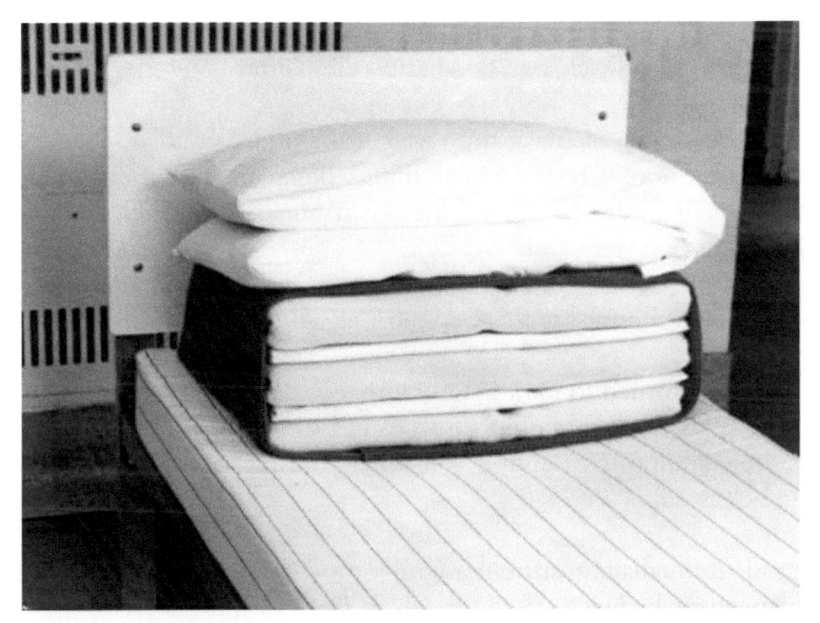

Bed packs would become the bane of everyone's life at CTS

Wednesday morning arrived and we gathered in the Games Area just before 0600 for the morning run. It was only the third day but I already hated this aspect. I don't do running. And it seemed I was getting slower and slower at it too and almost came in last. After a quick shower it was down stairs to an even quicker

"Stand By Ya Beds"

breakfast before bombing back up to our rooms in preparation for our first room inspection. Andy and I thought we had got everything just about right when we heard a voice bellowing out at the far end of the corridor.

"STAND BY YA BEDS"

My heart rate doubled. Our instructions were that upon hearing this order we were to stand at ease next to our respective bed and as the door opened and the officers entered your room you were to stand to attention as they inspected you and your kit. We could hear them next door and they were in there for ages. Then our door opened and Andy and I snapped to attention. Inspector Chadwick, Sgt Todd and Pete Kerley entered.

They were silent as they walked behind us and opened our wardrobe doors. I could hear things being moved about before they opened our bed side cabinets as if on a prison cell lock down looking for contraband.

"What the fuck is this bed pack about Cadet Goward?" asked Sgt Todd.
Andy turned to look behind him.
"Who said you could turn around Goward, you're supposed to be standing to attention, get down and give me 20 press ups" he bellowed.

I immediately stiffened and stood as still as I could as Inspector Chadwick stood directly in front of me.

"Have you shaved this morning Cadet Woodward?"
"Yes Sir" I replied.
"I think you need new blades then, make sure you have another shave before the next inspection" he continued.
"Yes Sir" I said just as Andy got back to his feet.

Welcome to Bishops Waltham

We were given some advice about the manner in which to place certain items like boots, tunics, shirts, cap and personal clothes within the wardrobe with the underlying warning that by next Wednesday such misdemeanours would not go unpunished.

"And sort that fucking bed pack out Goward" snarled Sgt Todd as they left our room to go onto the next one. Andy and I breathed a huge sigh of relief with Andy looking at his bed pack and asking just what was wrong with it? I looked in the mirror and couldn't see anything like a six o'clock shadow, not even a touch of bum fluff but shot off to the shower block armed with my razor to give my face the once over again.

Then it was out to the car park for drill and full uniform inspection from Mr Chadwick again. He looked me up and down, said nothing and walked off. No sooner had we finished our drill and inspection session it was straight back up to our rooms, get changed into PE kit and our first introduction to the assault course. I quite fancied the idea of this for some reason.

You started off by swinging along on the monkey bars for about 15 feet before dropping back down and running up a triangular log frame which was very damp and slippery before climbing up and over a 12 foot high wooden wall, dropping down the other side and then crawling on your belly underneath a rope net. Then you had to climb up a 20 foot rope to a platform where you then placed your hands into a couple of wrist straps before sliding down the aerial runway or death slide as it was termed and into the catch net at the bottom. Once free from that you ran around to the pit which was basically a five-foot-deep trench filled with muddy water. Somewhere at the bottom was a plastic sewer type pipe that ran uphill to the surface and freedom. All we had to do was find the pipe and swim through it and back to the surface!

"Stand By Ya Beds"

The assault course was something we would get to know rather well
Photo Hampshire Telegraph

It all looked fairly easy apart from that water pipe thing at the end. So, one by one we took our turn with some finding it easier than others. Personally, I loved it until I got to the pipe. I stood above the trench looking down into that swirling muddy water for a minute or so until I was shouted at by one of the instructors to get in and stop being such a poof about it. So, in I went. The water was freezing cold and my testicles migrated north to my throat. That was the easy bit. I fished around the bottom with my foot trying to find the pipe. I found it and kept my foot there not daring to lose it. But I had to let go of it if I was going to actually

44

go down there and swim through it. Oh God this is awful. Deep breath, eyes shut and down I went, desperately trying to find the entrance with my hands. I found it and pushed myself inside. The pipe was corrugated and to my surprise was steeper than I had envisaged. I pushed as hard as I could with my legs and pulled with my arms, panic stricken that I would surely drown. But within about three seconds I'd popped out of the top of the pipe, gasped some clean air, wiped my face and eyes and stumbled out onto the grass absolutely covered in liquid shite.

Once everyone had completed the assault course it was time for a quick cuppa and a fag before we lined up in the car park ready to commence our cross-country run. Like I said I don't do running and hated the course I had to do at school which wasn't in the country at all and was basically a road run from the school down a very steep hill onto Cowes sea front, which when the tide was high and the wind was blowing ensured we got covered in freezing cold salt water from the waves, then past the Royal Yacht Squadron and then back up the hill via the notorious zig-zag foot path that would have tested the endurance of Mo Farrah!

Our resident racing snakes Andy Worship and Steve Matcham were almost salivating at the prospect of another run as they limbered up in their best running gear. The rest of us were dreading it. Tony Astill and Pete Manns strolled down to the car park and laid down the ground rules for this two-legged torture, which would take us through a couple of farms and private fields. And before I knew it we were running down the embankment and along the side of the first football pitch towards the hedgerow at the school perimeter where we encountered a traffic jam as we queued to climb over the style that led over the fence and into the first farmer's field. A couple of hundred yards further on and we turned left out onto Tangier Lane, a single-track country lane where we all had to keep to the right. About half a mile later we turned right and ran through a farm yard, up a muddy track to the next field which ran uphill for another half mile where we turned left and ran along the tree lined field, before gradually running downhill towards another farm. It got really muddy here and I spent most of my time dodging strategically placed cow pats that splattered up the backs of my legs. At the end of the lane we had to vault over a gate before coming back out onto Tangier Lane, back into the field, over the style and into the grounds at CTS, up that embankment to the Games Area door. Total distance was about five miles although it felt so much further. I really don't do running!

Time for a very hot shower and as the steam cleared so it was replaced by the great smell of Brut 33 as we splashed it all over before getting back into our uniforms to go and grab some lunch. Then straight after lunch it was back into games kit and we had a choice of football, rugby or hockey. I chose football which we played for about two hours at the end of which I was almost on my knees; it had been a very physical day. And it was something we were going to have to get used to because this was to be our routine every Wednesday for the next 10 months! That evening most of us set about ironing or bulling boots before spending an hour or so watching TV in the lounge armed with a pint of Coke and a Curly Wurly!

About 1015 Andy and I almost had to crawl up the stairs to our room. The day's activities had caught up with the muscles in my legs and I could barely move. After sorting out a few bits and pieces I walked to the end of the corridor to go to the toilet. As I stood there I heard the shout "Lights Out" from the far end of the corridor. Within a minute I was heading back to my room but it was too late because there were three Phase 3 Cadets heading straight towards me; Clive Grace, Steve Mote and Paul Underwood, all three of whom we were already fearful of. They stopped me just as I was about to enter my room.

"What are you doing out after lights out?" demanded Clive Grace.

"I've just been to the loo" I replied.

My excuse wasn't good enough and I was told to get into my PE kit immediately and report to the Games Area. I really wasn't happy about it and was arguing the toss with them when Andy opened the door to see what all the noise was about.

"What are you doing out of bed Cadet Goward?" shouted Steve Mote.

"Just wondering what all the noise was about" he said innocently.

He was then told to get into his PE kit and get down to the Games Area immediately. We were down there within two minutes and within seconds we were joined by another 7 or 8 others who'd also been caught out. The duty instructor was Russ Parke who didn't look too impressed and told us to run down to the car park where he would meet us in five minutes time. I was really pissed off about this, it seemed very petty. We were all moaning about it still when Russ Parke arrived in one of the CTS Transit mini buses and positioned it at the top of the embankment with the head lights looking across one of the football pitches and they illuminated the goal posts at the far end. Our punishment was to run down the embankment, run the length of the pitch, touch the far goal posts, run back up the embankment, touch the Transit six times! So, 12 lengths of the football pitch. And just to ensure we didn't treat this as some kind of leisurely stroll the last one back would get an extra length! Christ I can hardly move as it is.

Down the embankment we went, all of us moaning and bitching about the whole stupid fucking idea and just how much we hated Grace, Mote and Underwood, the bastards. But by the time we'd reached the far end for the first time we'd stopped talking because we all needed the energy for other things. By the time we had done five out of the six Andy and I were half a football pitch length behind the others. We were crap at running! So, here's the picture. The main group are heading towards us on their last length. Andy and I were heading the wrong way towards the far goal as we all passed each other on the half way line. It goes without saying that they all took the piss out of us as they went by. I continued my weary trudge towards the goal, touched the post and turned back towards the car park. To my horror I was completely on my own. Andy had turned at the half way line and joined the rear of the main group. My heart sank. You bastard!

I literally crawled back up the embankment and hit the bonnet of the Transit with my hand. I was dead and the thought of having to do another lap just didn't bear thinking about.

"You're shit Woodward, what are you?" shouted Russ Parke.
"I'm......shit......Sir" I spluttered.
"Yes you are but at least you didn't cheat like Goward did" he continued "and for that Goward you can do another two laps, away you go".

There is a God after all.

We were all instructed to go and get another shower and get to bed. I fell into my pit completely and utterly exhausted but managed to summon up enough energy to mock Andy as he crawled back into our room.

Getting out of bed the next morning with the prospect of yet more running almost brought me to tears. I could hardly move; my body was on the verge of going on strike. To make matters worse it was pissing down with rain. I trudged back into the Games Area second to last.

Breakfast seemed a little more leisurely this morning with no rushing back upstairs to get changed into PE kit and no room inspection. After a briefer than normal personal inspection we were ushered into the Pavilion where Sgt Middleton and Russ Parke introduced us to something called Impromptu Lecturettes. The idea was that they would call an individual to come and stand out in front of everyone else and talk for five minutes on a subject they were handed as soon as their name was called. So, no time to think about it, no time for any form of research and if you cocked it up expect to get the piss taken out of you mercilessly by both the instructors and your contemporaries. The idea was to get us thinking on our feet because as Sgt Middleton informed us so succinctly.

"As you'll find out one day Police work is 10% knowledge and 90% bullshit"

And so, one by one some of us got dragged out the front to talk about such diverse subjects as the chair I was sitting on, the curtains, a ping pong ball, the war in Vietnam, the physical benefits of doing press ups and a whole host of other random subjects. It wasn't easy and acutely embarrassing if you dried up.

After lunch Rowan and Fielding House were kept behind as the other two Houses were taken out to the Games Area. Inspector Chadwick then informed us that we would be taking part in a Hampshire Police tradition this weekend in that we would be going to Brockenhurst Camp for two nights and three days camping. That sounds like fun I thought, did plenty of that in the Scouts, and it should be a doddle for me. We were then directed to the store room where Pete Kerley would issue us with a few more items of essential kit that were ours for the duration of our stay at CTS. One by one we lined up to receive armfuls of clobber including a pair of very sturdy walking boots, a bright orange two-piece Heli-Hanson water proof suit, four pairs of thick woollen walking socks, water proof spats, a ruck sack and a tin of Dubbin grease to help keep our boots from leaking.

The boots were said to be multi-purpose walking, climbing and ski-ing boots. The uppers were an incredibly thick brown leather like substance with yellow laces whilst the soles were solid plastic that had no 'give' in them at all. It was like having two planks of wood tied to your feet. We were also 'encouraged' to purchase a 'House' track suit and a Heli Hanson fleece to help keep us warm whilst on various expeditions. Rowan House colours were red whilst Fielding House was yellow, Mayne House was blue and Peel House was green.

That evening we were instructed to meet in the Games Area to take part in a number of physical activities. These included weight lifting, gym exercises, boxing and circuit training. We got split up into random groups and I got boxing! I've never done boxing before and to date had only ever had one fist fight and that was with my best mate at school and lasted less than 10 seconds! Our referee for tonight's bouts was Pete Manns, himself rather athletic in build with a very wry sense of humour. He dragged out pairs of us, fitted us with proper boxing gloves and refereed each fight, most of which only lasted a round or two. I don't think I was alone in being a boxing virgin.

And then it was my turn. I stepped onto the mat and looked across at my opponent. His name was Mick Dodds and he didn't smile. At all. He looked like a 16 year old version of Vladimir Putin and tended to look out of the top of his head with steely blue eyes. As my gloves were being laced up I did what all boxers seem to do and tried to outstare my opponent. Then Pete Manns called to us both to meet in the centre of the mat. He held our gloved hands together, said "Box" and took two steps backwards. I saw Mick flinch and woke up on my back a couple of seconds later with a numb face! I didn't even see him move. I felt weak and worthless as my skinny body sent messages to my brain demanding to know what the fuck I was doing to myself. The gloves were taken off me and I was told to go and sit back on the side lines as the next two got prepared. I was a bit dazed to be honest, not in pain as such but definitely not the full ticket.

After the next bout two more lads were called out. One of them was Nathan Johnson, a black youth with a lot of attitude. He was wearing a pair of blue and gold silk karate shoes and had a matching gown. He started doing all these warm up moves and slow motion chopping motions with his arms. We all sat there with various expressions on our faces.

"Oi, Grass Hopper" shouted Pete Manns "What the fuck are you doing?"

"Just warming up Sir" he replied as he did a quick Mohammed Ali type shoe shuffle.

His opponent was George Barker a sort of chisel faced individual who also had a bit of an attitude and just stood there nonchalantly chewing an imaginary piece of gum.

"You've got five seconds Johnson" growled Pete Manns "And take those granny slippers off".

By now the rest of us were both amused and intrigued. This lad Johnson must surely be an amateur boxer at least and clearly fancies his chances. They came together on the mat and Pete Manns told them to box. Johnson then literally danced around George Barker for almost a minute, doing shadow punches and making some rather bizarre grunting noises. And then George threw a proper punch that connected perfectly with Nathan Johnson's jaw and down he went like a sack of spuds. It was hilarious.

"Well I'm more than a little disappointed Mr Johnson, I was expecting you to go at least 12 rounds" smirked Pete Manns.

"I would have done but you never gave me the chance to warm up properly and……."

"Sit down Johnson you're starting to bore me now, right next two"

Sometime later John Gunner was picked to box Andy Reed who already had a reputation for being a bit of a nutter. (think Animal from the Muppets). Pete Manns said to John as he was 'gloving up'

"If you are to have any chance, get the first punch in".

So, as they were told to "touch gloves" at the start, instead of touching gloves, John followed the advice and threw the first punch instead, hitting Andy square on the nose. The room went deafly quiet as everyone held their breath, staring in disbelief and then, seconds later, Andy lived up to his reputation and pummelled John to the ground with flailing arms like a demented dervish. The instructor stepped in to stop the bloodshed and hauled John out of the ring and sent in Tony Hastings, who was a keen boxer to sort the 'animal' out. John never boxed again but gained the nick name of "One Slug Gunner".

And so the evening went on with us also having a go at weight lifting which I was equally as inept at. I was told I needed to gain some weight and that I would be placed upon a special diet which entitled me to a whole pint of full fat milk every morning. That sort of reminded me of the one-third bottles of luke warm milk we were compelled to drink every day in junior school for much the same reason.

Friday morning arrived and I was starting to flag a bit. The morning run seemed to get longer and longer every day and our inspections seemed to get pettier by the minute. But today promised to be a little different although still physically testing. Today we are learning to abseil. So, after breakfast Rowan House climbed the fire escape up onto the roof of the main building overlooking the fields. It was quite a view from the top of this old three storey building. Pete Kerley seemed to revel in this sort of thing. He was a thoroughly nice guy and I reckon Rowan House had fallen on its feet getting him as our instructor.

He laid out all the safety rules, explained how the kit worked and then with the help of one of the Phase 3 Cadets who'd obviously done it before, he lowered him from the roof and safely down to the ground some 60 feet below. I'm not sure if the flimsy cork lined helmet we had to wear would have saved any of us from serious injury had we done our best Humpty Dumpty impression though. It certainly didn't look like it would. Now I'm not scared of heights but there is something about abseiling that is just plain lunacy and that's the very first step out over the edge of the roof or wherever it is you happen to be abseiling from, because you have to reverse out backwards and it's a totally alien feeling. It's a trust thing I suppose. Trust in your equipment. Trust in the person holding onto the other end of the rope. Trust in yourself that you are going to do it right and trust in that helmet. Well maybe not the helmet!

A couple of brave souls who coughed to having done it previously were the first volunteers quickly followed by myself. For some reason I thought it would be fairly easy and that I wouldn't have any issues with it. Pete Kerley got me kitted out with the straps, hoops and belays with the ropes threaded through and around my waist. Fully briefed I made my way to the edge of the roof, turned around to face everyone else and felt my grip on the rope double its intensity. The butterflies in my stomach felt like they were wearing Dock Martin boots desperately trying to kick their way out of my body before I plunged to almost certain death. Pete Kerley did one last check of my kit before instructing me to commence my abseil. My feet stayed in position as I leant out slightly. The rope went tight as Pete Kerley told me to start lowering myself down by releasing my grip slightly and pushing my legs against the side of the building. I was now at 90 degrees to the wall some 60 feet above the ground but going no-where! My brain just wouldn't allow my hands to release their grip on the rope. I got shouted at several times before finally I did it and down I went 10 feet whilst letting out a sort of "Whoaahhh" noise. I went down in stages, still not trusting any of the things I needed to trust but within a minute or so I was back on solid ground and feeling rather proud of myself. I can't say I actually enjoyed the experience but I did it twice more that morning but on each occasion I crapped myself as I leant out over the edge.

CHAPTER 3

Brockenhurst Camp

We spent the rest of that Friday sorting out camping equipment like tents, water carriers, cooking equipment, food supplies etc in preparation for our weekend camp at Brockenhurst in the New Forest. As the guys from the other two houses prepared to go home for the weekend so Rowan and Fielding House helped load up the two Ford Transit mini buses and a battered Landrover with all the kit. I have to say that I was absolutely knackered. Our first week at CTS had been a very long and tiring one, both physically and mentally and I could have done with a rest but that wasn't going to happen. Having done plenty of camping in the Scouts and with my family over the years I secretly thought that I'd find this coming weekend relatively easy.

The journey to the New Forest took about an hour or so and we arrived late afternoon in a field on the outskirts of Brockenhurst village. The field was sort of triangular in shape and about 2 acres in size. On two sides was dense woodland whilst on the third a high hedge adjacent to the main road. We were instructed to pitch our tents near to the tree line and the first thing that struck me was how small they were. They were three-man tents but we were told that it would be five to each tent. This is going to be cosy then.

Our instructors were Sgt Gerry Todd, PC's Russ Parke and Pete Manns. They barked out their orders about putting up the tents, fetching water and preparing meals, all of it at the double with several Cadets receiving punishment press ups for being too slow, too noisy or just inept at something. Then suddenly we were

"Stand By Ya Beds"

all being called to form a squad and that meant lining up in height order in a block and standing to attention as if to be inspected. Except this was no inspection. Sgt Todd bellowed at us that we were a disgrace, that we were the worst intake Hampshire had ever had and that they were going to teach us some discipline and respect over the next couple of days.

"Squad, right turn" he ordered.

We turned as one.

"By the right quick march" and we set off as he called out the steps.

We headed along the tree line for 100 yards before turning left towards the hedge, then along the side of the road and then up a slight incline back towards the trees another 100 yards away, where we were halted. By the time we reached our starting point some of the lads were muttering under their breath about the pettiness of this little march but I had a bad feeling about it. We halted and obeyed the "left turn" order.

"Because some of you couldn't keep your mouths shut you can do it all again, only this time at the double, squad right turn, double march" bellowed Sgt Todd.

Jogging and trying to keep in step with your compatriots and keep the squad locked together is no easy thing I can tell you. By the time we'd run the first 100 yards we were getting out of shape and the muttering started again. This caused a lot of friction between us with the moaners being moaned at by the others because no-one wanted to do a third lap. But it was too late; Sgt Todd had already heard us and seemed to take great delight in telling us that we wouldn't be stopping and that we would be doing another lap. Apart from some grunting and whimpering our

56

Brockenhurst Camp

third lap was completed in silence. We arrived back at our starting point huffing and puffing and desperately trying to catch our breath. Sgt Todd kept us standing there at attention for ages. He had a smirk about him that indicated that he was enjoying this, certainly more than we were. At last we were stood at ease and I think we all let out a collective gasp followed by lots of long and deep intakes of air.

We were told to fall out and prepare our dinners which consisted of tinned stew cooked on little brass primus stoves. These single burners were basically a brass container that sat on three hinged legs. They were filled with paraffin with a cradle on top to hold a saucepan. You'd light the wick and then prime the thing using a pump embedded in the container. This would pump the paraffin up to the lighted wick and produce a flared flame like a standard gas cooker. They were grossly inefficient and heating a kettle of water would take nearly an hour. Our tinned strew was pretty tasteless and was washed down with luke warm tea made with powdered milk. By the time we'd finished tidying up it was starting to get dark and we were told to get our heads down because we would be having a busy day tomorrow.

For some reason we ended up with six in our three-man tent. Andy and I were joined by our next-door neighbours from CTS, Russ Bramley, Martin Gibson, Phil Mason and RD Smith. We actually had four Smiths on our intake; RD (whose first name was Richard) MH (Mick) CD (Colin) and M (Malcolm) and the instructors would just call them RD, MH, CD or M although sometimes M would just get called Smith as he only had one first name!

Despite the fact that we were knackered it has to be said that we were also in very high spirits. I'm not sure whether it was because we were under canvass or because trying to cram six bodies into a three-man space somehow made it funny or because

"Stand By Ya Beds"

Russ insisted that we have a fart lighting contest inside our tent! Maybe it was the stew or a weeks build up of CTS food but all of us it seemed were full of methane. Russ had an infectious laugh and even though we'd only known each other for a week it was clear that he was always going to be at the centre of everything that would go on at CTS and was one of those guys who everyone liked. Being his mate was a good thing.

I have to confess that I'd never heard of lighting farts before now and I was fascinated. So, there was Russ dressed in nothing but his under pants, laying on his back with his legs in the air and bent at the knees like a frozen chicken and holding a lighter close to his arse.

"Here it comes" he giggled "here it comes"

With that he let rip and struck the lighter at the same time and emitted a yellow and blue flame about 10 inches in length to howls of laughter from the rest of us. One by one we all tried it with varying degrees of success and at times I was close to wetting myself and could hardly breathe. Then Russ felt another one brewing and decided it was time to do this bollock naked, although I have no idea why. He got himself into position, giggling away to himself.

"This is gonna be a big one" he laughed.

Out it shot and bore a striking similarity to a flame thrower and from the scream that Russ let out it appeared to have had the same result because he'd somehow set fire to the hairs on his back side. His screams could be heard all over the camp site, as could our howls of laughter. Ah the future of British policing is safe in our hands!

58

Brockenhurst Camp

It wasn't long before Russ Parke came over and told us all to be quiet and to get our heads down because we had a busy day tomorrow which sounded ominous. Try as we might it just wasn't possible to come down from the high we were on and switch off. There just wasn't enough room to get comfortable with all sorts of inappropriate comments being made and of course every time one of us farted the giggling started up again. I doubt any of us got to sleep before midnight.

At one am all hell broke loose. The instructors were banging saucepans together, blowing whistles and screaming at us all to get up, get dressed into our walking gear and form a squad in front of our tents in five minutes. All of us were asking what the hell was going on. Most of us got in line within the five minutes having quickly learned over the last few days that it was definitely in our interests to do so. A few stragglers were threatened with press ups if they didn't make it. Once fully assembled there was no explanation, just an order to double across to the mini buses, to get on board and keep our heads down and eyes shut. If any of us were caught looking up then the entire bus would get punishment press ups. The mini bus was driven at break neck speed across the field and along the bumpy lane. After that we seemed to be driving on roads for about 10 or 15 minutes before we hit some bumpy area again. After a few minutes we came to a halt and were ordered out at the double and into squad formation again.

We were given an Ordnance Survey map, a compass, a torch and the coordinates of our base camp at Brockenhurst, told in no uncertain terms not to use the roads or railway lines because they would be patrolling the area to check that we didn't and to make our way back.

"Breakfast is at 0600. The sooner you get back the sooner you can get back to sleep. Good luck" smirked Russ Parke as he got back aboard the Transit and drove off.

"Stand By Ya Beds"

There was an eerie silence as we stood in the clearing of the woods that he'd dropped us at. It was pitch black. We all gathered around the map. We had absolutely no idea where we were so the first thing we needed to do was find a road. Despite what we'd been told we agreed that the quickest way back was to find a road sign or a proper land mark of some description as a starting point. We headed out along a muddy track hoping to find a road. We walked for about a mile and then saw some head lights way off in the distance through the trees. We headed straight for it and half an hour later, having tramped through the woods we arrived at a small country road. Do we turn left or right?

We turned right and in single file followed the lane for about a mile. At least the weather was decent with hardly a breath of wind, which is more than you could say about us; Bramley in particular was still full of it! At last we came to a T junction with a sign that said Brockenhurst left, 4 miles. We still couldn't quite work out where we were but did that really matter? If we follow this road then we'll be back inside an hour. Headlights. Shit. Everyone in the ditch. We dived to our right into the damp ditch and got caught up on some bramble. We kept our heads down until the car had passed, then untangled ourselves and climbed back onto the road. With renewed vigour we set off towards Brockenhurst.

We wondered how the other groups were getting on and speculated about whether or not they were cheating as well. We reckoned they probably were. We'd been walking for about half an hour when we saw headlights approaching. Into the ditch we went, only this one was several inches deep in water but that was still better than getting caught. A few minutes later we climbed out and continued our journey. We were starting to get tired. It was about 2.30 am and we'd been up since 5.30 that day anyway. We were now walking with our heads down in virtual silence which was lucky because someone called out "Quiet, quiet". We

Brockenhurst Camp

all stopped to listen. It was the sound of an engine. A Transit engine. There was no ditch this time, just a barbed wire fence to jump over and as we lay face down in the field so one of the CTS Transits drove slowly past us with no lights on. The crafty bastards!

"I am covered in fucking cow shit" whispered Phil Mason.

We all sniggered before getting back to our feet and climbed back over the fence and onto the road.

It wasn't long before we were approaching Brockenhurst village. The road was littered with New Forest ponies that are allowed to wander around the area freely. We were very conscious of getting caught so close to the campsite and had learned very quickly that there were no negotiations to be had if we were. We crept from parked car to tree, from garden wall to phone box, from bus shelter to hedgerow until finally we were opposite the lane that led to the campsite. When we were sure the coast was clear we dashed across the road and ran the last couple of hundred yards and into the field. We were the first team back which made us feel pretty good.

"So how many roads did you use then?" asked Sgt Todd with a wry smile.
"None Sir" we all replied as one.
"You're full of shit, all of you, now go and get your heads down" he snarled.

Before he changed his mind we legged it back to our tent. There were no fart lighting contests this time and within minutes we were out for the count.

At 0530 we were woken up by the whistles and the saucepan banging again. We were ordered to parade in five minutes in shorts and plimsolls only. It was a damp and chilly morning. The grass was heavily laden with dew as we stood in line wondering what the hell was coming next. It was morning run time., but with a twist.

We were ordered to right turn and double march towards the gate. Down the muddy lane we went and out onto the main road. After about half a mile we passed a milk float going the other way. The milkman's face was a picture. We entered the village, ran over the railway line, continued on down the main street before going over a bridge and then turning right into the grounds of the rather posh Balmer Lawn Hotel which has a small river running through the front grassed area. Here we were stopped and ordered to right turn, to face the river.

"Right in ya get" bellowed Sgt Todd.

We edged our way towards the embankment and then one by one we waded in. It was waist deep and bloody freezing. We had somehow got split into two groups with one lot close to the far bank and the rest of us closer to the near bank with Russ Bramley sort of stuck in the middle on his own for some reason.

"OK let's have you all getting right down, right under, get your hair wet, come on" shouted Russ Parke.

No-one moved, it was just too cold and there was some muttering going on.

"Come on we haven't got all day, get down" he shouted.

Again no-one moved.

"Right, all splash Bramley" shouted Mr Parke.

Brockenhurst Camp

And instantly Russ was covered in a tidal wave of murky river water which of course the rest of us all got covered in as well but Russ definitely came off the worse.

"Cheers fellas" he spluttered.

We were ordered out, reformed our squad and headed back through the village to the field. A hot shower would be nice right now followed by a full English breakfast I thought. As we had no showers at this place that was obviously a non-starter and I think I already knew the answer about breakfast. But I was very hungry so anything right now would be good.

No sooner had we got back and we were being ordered to split into two groups. In order to keep ourselves warm we were introduced to a game called Murder Ball. Basically, it was a mixture of football, rugby, wrestling, boxing and actually there was only one rule. Get the ball into the opposing team's goal. And the losing team would have to do a lap around the field at the double. It was quite an incentive. Whatever happened in between was all part of the fun. The ball though was a Medicine ball and if you don't know what that is allow me to explain. It's about three times the size of a standard football and covered in leather. It's not exactly round either and looks more like a Pumpkin than a ball so it doesn't actually roll. I have no idea what's inside it but it has to be the densest substance known to man because you can barely pick one up and if you kicked it you would almost certainly break your leg. Quite what their actual purpose in life is I'm not sure but right now all I know is my team has got to win. I cannot bare the thought of doing anymore running. The grass was still covered in dew as we literally fought each other for possession of the ball. We rugby tackled each other, kicked each other, wrestled one another to the ground, picked the ball up, dropped it again until eventually my team somehow scored the only goal necessary.

"Stand By Ya Beds"

It had taken about 15 minutes I suppose and we were dead on our feet.

We trudged slowly back to our tents where we were told to prepare our breakfast which consisted of something called London Grill. We were given tins of the stuff which consisted of chunks of hot dog type sausage, bits of beef burger, onions and baked beans. We heated it up on primus stoves and tucked into it as if we hadn't been fed in days. It had a strange taste it has to be said but right now I don't think we cared much. We baulked it out with slices of bread and washed the whole lot down with luke warm tea.

After breakfast it was time for map reading lessons. We were told that we would be undertaking a lot of expeditions on Dartmoor and the Brecon Beacons during our time as Cadets and that we all needed to know how to read an Ordnance Survey map. This would also come in handy once we went out to our stations next year as all police officers need to know how to map read. Well I shouldn't have too much trouble with this bit I thought, having done this plenty of times in the Scouts. Having said that the CTS method of camping wasn't what I was used to so maybe the map reading session won't be either. We got split up into small groups and just like our marching lessons some people could do it whilst others just couldn't grasp the idea at all.

After lunch we got taken to some disused airfield at Stoney Cross to practice what we'd learned so far. There were a lot of arguments going on about who was right or wrong with some of the groups getting hopelessly lost. By the time we got back to Brockenhurst it was starting to get dark. Our evening meal consisted of tinned stew that we boiled up on a primus stove again. There was barely enough for half a tin each and it felt like we were on half rations. That evening it was back to the map reading only this time with a torch and it was all kept fairly tame

Brockenhurst Camp

compared to the previous evening and by lights out we were all squeezed into our little tents like sardines. Someone farted and we giggled like the little boys we still were but no-one got the lighter out and within minutes we were asleep.

At 5.30am we were woken by the dawn chorus of whistles and saucepan lids again. We had two minutes to line up in our shorts and plim soles only. Any stragglers would get 25 press ups to start their day with. It cost some of them dearly. Then it was right turn, double march down through the village to the river and in we got. It seemed colder this morning and as I slowly waded in so my testicles took exception to the sudden temperature change and disappeared inwards. And Russ Bramley had secreted himself right in the centre of the largest group this time. It didn't work and the order came to all splash Bramley. It was bloody freezing.

The run back seemed to take forever and within seconds of entering the field we were split up into two groups to play murder ball again. Only this time we had a plan. It was quietly agreed that one team would pick up the ball and run with it whilst the other team made less than half-hearted attempts to stop them. The game was over in less than a minute!

"I suppose you think that's fuckin clever" bellowed Sgt Todd.

And he promptly made us get down and give him 30 press ups. It was cheap at half the price.

Breakfast was another tin of London Grill and slices of bread. We were now really hungry and at one point I saw two lads quite literally fighting over a tub of chocolate spread.

Some incidents take on legendary status and are always quoted by those who were there years later and sometimes even by those who weren't. As previously described the primus stoves we were issued with were a lot less efficient than the gas burners and could be a pain in the arse to light and keep lit. Andy Goward volunteered to get our groups primus stove up and running. He filled the base with paraffin, primed the wick, lit it and then started using the plunger to pump the fuel up the wick. He pumped and pumped and pumped and BANG……….there was a large explosion and his primus stove disintegrated and vanished, leaving just the three legs and the plunger. How no-one was injured remains a mystery but the words "Goward and the primus stove" are now immortalised into CTS folklore.

Our morning consisted of abseiling out of huge fir trees. Climbing up the rope ladder to the platform was more terrifying than the abseil back down but overall it was a much more relaxing affair than the previous day. But it didn't last of course. After lunch we were bussed out to some remote part of the New Forest, given a map and a compass each and introduced to the art of orienteering. This meant running cross country against the clock from our current location about five miles back to the camp site using only the map and compass. Although we were running as individuals there was a points system used to determine which House won overall. The losing House would have the pleasure of filling in the latrines at the end of the day so there was plenty of incentive.

So off I went running up hill, downhill, through thick wooded areas, wading through streams, climbing over fences, under fences, dodging ponies and the dog walkers and stopping every five minutes to check the map that yes, I was heading in the right direction. Despite getting covered in mud and gashing my right leg on some bracken I actually quite enjoyed it and Rowan House came first I'm relieved to say. Fielding House weren't quite so lucky!

Brockenhurst Camp

Returning to CTS felt like we were entering a five star hotel in comparison to that field. I think I stood in the shower for over half an hour without moving! Sunday evening was spent relaxing in the lounge, drinking pints of Coke and winding up the guys that would be going to Brockenhurst next weekend. I really don't think they believed us.

As we sat in the lounge watching TV so I saw Steve Mote, one of the Phase 3 Cadets lift up one of the cushions from a chair, unclip the rubber straps that formed the base and carefully put the cushion back in place. He then went and sat back down in his chair next to Nigel Niven. A few minutes later Pete LeGros returned from the tuck shop with a pint of Coke and a handful of chocolate bars. He slumped down onto the chair but went straight through it, his backside landing on the floor with half his Coke now splashed all over his chest just like the Martini advert with Leonard Rossitor and Joan Collins where he knocks the seat recliner back on the airplane and she poured a double Martini down her cleavage! Getting your head down dear, jolly good idea. It was more than funny to the rest of us but Pete LeGros wasn't laughing much.

By the start of week two we were starting to get used to the routines and getting to understand all about that self-discipline thing they mentioned on day one. If you didn't look after your kit or your time then nobody else would be doing it for you and you'd suffer the consequences. Our evenings were taken up with ironing uniform, bulling boots or lining up in the corridor to use one of the two phones. And commencing this week was Duty Squad. For one week each month each House had to undertake additional responsibilities in that we were tasked with the security of the school together with manning the front office in the evening and at the weekend to greet visitors and answer the switch board. Uniformed patrol was done in pairs armed with Pye two-piece radio sets which Sgt Middleton gave us instruction on using. The CTS grounds had to be patrolled every half an hour from 1800 until midnight, so at least we were excused the mandatory lights out regime. Doors and windows had to be checked together with the security of resident's vehicles and CTS equipment. Doing foot patrol was actually quite easy and made you feel like you were doing something more police like than training to become an Olympic athlete. But manning the office was much more of a challenge for me. I couldn't get the hang of the phone system at all and I think I cut off more calls than I actually put through.

There was a change of leadership at CTS with Chief Inspector Harrison leaving us for something possibly less challenging as Chief Inspector Jim Rowthorn moved in to take his place. I often wondered whether any or all of our instructors had volunteered to take up a position at CTS or whether it was in fact some kind of punishment placement. Over the next few months we had a number of temporary instructors come in with the likes of Sgt Roy Inskip who loved his rock climbing and abseiling, PC Jim Mowatt, a Scot with the broadest Glaswegian accent imaginable who Andy Goward took an instant dislike to after he bellowed out his name in the dining hall as Gowwaaarrrddd, PC Nigel Jones, PC Jim Hawkins, and PC Martin Nutbeam.

After Monday morning's parade and inspection, we were ordered to congregate in the car park for the course photograph. It took ages to organise but eventually all 68 of us plus our instructors and some of the Phase 3's all said 'cheese' and our place in Hampshire Constabulary history was captured forever.

Brockenhurst Camp

Chief Inspector Jim Rowthorn

"Stand By Ya Beds"

Hampshire Constabulary Cadet intake 1975

Then we spent a couple of hours in The Pavilion embarrassing ourselves with more impromptu lecturettes. It was excruciating to watch some guys just freeze in front of the rest of us when they couldn't think of anything to say. Even those who were generally quite gobby would just go completely blank, including myself. I had to talk for five minutes about the chair I'd been sitting on. After less than a minute I'd run out of material. Alan Dabbs was tasked with letter writing etiquette for gawds sake, whilst Russ Bramley had to talk about Police dogs. His opening line was;

"Police dogs smell" and that was the end of that because we all laughed for the next five minutes.

But then Ian 'Ted' Heath was called to the front. He was a big lad, very intelligent and leap years ahead of the rest of us intellectually. He hated the physical side of things and had a very,

Brockenhurst Camp

very dry sense of humour, but none of us were prepared for his lecturette.

"Right Cadet Heath, talk to us for five minutes about your name badge please" said Sgt Middleton.

Ted sighed heavily; this was way beneath him surely? He took his badge from his tunic and with a dead pan face akin to that of Jack Dee delivered the full life cycle of the plastic used, the pin it's fastened with, the history of Dyno tape and even the adhesive used to stick it to the badge. It was quite simply hilarious and after half an hours non-stop talking Sgt Middleton, himself crying with laughter thanked Ted very much and told him he was excused any further lecturettes for life. In that moment Ted became a legend.

In comparison to the previous week today had been relatively easy and we were all quite relaxed come evening time and by 9pm the lounge was packed because 9pm on a Monday meant just one thing; The Sweeney was on TV. As that thumping music blared out and the bronze coloured Ford Consul GT registration number NHK 295M headed towards us we all hankered after the idea that one day we'd be just like Reagan or DS Carter chasing villains through the back streets and calling them slags. Most of us had been brought up on a diet of Z Cars, Dixon of Dock Green and Softly Softly, so The Sweeney was a breath of fresh air. It was action packed with car chases, full on fist fights, some rather glamorous females and all of it intertwined with some typical police humour. It was compulsory viewing for us 16-year-old coppers in waiting and a great training tool! Shut it.

Wednesday arrived all too soon and after the morning run, room inspection and parade it was time for yet more physical. We got split up into Houses and Rowan House got sent down to the tennis courts where Clive Grace and Steve Mote, two of the Phase 3 Cadets had been given the authority to drill us in the art of lifting logs. We had learned early on that the Phase 3's were a bit pissed with power and in Clive Grace in particular we had the chief bully. He revelled in the role. The logs were actually telegraph poles about 10 or 12 feet in length and heavy, especially if they were wet. But before we got to play with the logs, we had to undertake some warm up exercises first. We got the usual squat thrusts, star jumps, press ups, running on the spot and sit ups before we were stood to attention but with our arms out stretched, sort of crucifix style. We then had to make small circular motions with our hands which got bigger and bigger until we resembled a line of wind mills, then gradually reduced them again back to hand movements and then without stopping went through the whole thing again and again. It was agony on the shoulders and the upper arms. It wasn't long before the grunting and the moaning started. If you stopped it cost you 50 press ups. This went on for about half an hour, the pain was incredible.

We all felt weakened by the experience and so by the time we'd been split into three groups of five our levels of strength and stamina were pretty low. We then had to pick up a log for each group. We were made to carry it at the double from one end of the tennis courts to the other several times, before stopping and holding it with our arms out stretched before lifting it above our heads for another five minutes. Then we had to put it down onto our feet, then lie on our backs and lift our feet six inches off the ground and hold it there for what seemed like forever. If anyone dropped it or failed in anyway the entire team got 20 or 30 press ups. It was the longest one hour session of physical I think any of us ever endured and we hated them for it.

Brockenhurst Camp

Logs! Feel the pain
Photo Hampshire Constabulary

After a break it was time for the assault course again followed by the cross-country course followed by a couple of hour's football in the afternoon. As knackering as it was I was actually starting to enjoy it all, apart from the cross country; even if I live to be 200 years old I will never enjoy long distance running, especially if it means wading through mud and having sloppy cow pats splash up the back of my legs.

"Stand By Ya Beds"

The CTS football team for 1975/6
Back row; Laurie Parsonage, Steve Dennis, Andy Guy, Andy Sewell, Kev Emblen, Kev Ackland, Paul Underwood
Front row; Tony Hastings, Russ Bramley, Tim Beazley, Stuart Montague and Neil Cheyne
Photo Hampshire Constabulary

In the evening we were herded into the old wooden classrooms where we commenced a First Aid course with Sgt Middleton. Over the coming weeks we would be taught CPR techniques, bandaging and other lifesaving practices with a view to us gaining our First Aid certificates from St. Johns Ambulance Association.

During breakfast the next morning about 20 of us were "specially selected" to take part in a major Police exercise. We were to be the dead and injured bodies in a major plane crash scenario where all the emergency services would be taking part. This sounded quite exciting and certainly better than doing

Brockenhurst Camp

anymore running. We were led down the road about half a mile to the Hampshire Ambulance Service head quarters. Behind their building were a lot of derelict buildings, mostly factory type units with tons of masonry and wood scattered about over an area the size of half a football pitch I suppose. We were briefed about the role we were to play, with some of us acting as dead bodies whilst a few were to be treated as injured. I was to be a dead body, so not much acting prowess required there then.

One by one we were shown to our respective points and to place ourselves under some wood or other debris. I was placed on the first floor of a building that had no frontage at all with most of it lying in a big pile on the ground. I gathered a few lumps of wood and what looked like an old curtain together and then lay down close to the open edge of the building, strategically covering myself in the aforementioned debris. And there we waited. After about an hour my side was aching so much I had to sit up. So far absolutely nothing had happened. No sirens, no noise, just complete silence. Have they got the right location I wondered? Or even the right day?

Then suddenly it all started to happen. There were more sirens than any American cop show I'd seen and within minutes there were coppers, firemen and ambulance staff crawling all over the site. There was a lot of noise with the injured shouting for help and emergency service personnel shouting to each other or receiving instructions over their radios. After about half an hour the top of a ladder appeared against the ledge I was lying on, followed by a fireman's yellow helmet.

"Are you dead or alive?" he asked.
"I'm dead" I replied.
"You can fucking stay there for a bit longer then can't you" and with that he disappeared back down again.

"Stand By Ya Beds"

Charming. Here I am covered in crap doing my very best dead body impersonation with no Equity card in sight and I'm treated like an amateur. Sir John Gielgud wouldn't have tolerated such behaviour I can tell you. After about an hour a whistle was sounded and those of us who hadn't been rescued were ordered to come out of hiding. About half a dozen of us clambered back down to the ground and were directed to the tent that had been set up as a mortuary and field hospital. A number of Cadets were swathed in bandages and laying on military style camp beds as the rest of us were given a nice cup of tea by the ladies from the WRVS. There was still a lot of noise going on but basically we'd done our bit, so after finishing our tea and a fag it was time to head back up to CTS.

Music defines an era and as teenagers most of us liked our music. The small lounge had a record player in it with some half decent speakers and so the likes of Tubular Bells (the first album I ever bought) could be heard on a regular basis together with the likes of Band on the Run from Wings, A Night at the Opera from Queen and 10cc. We were all pretty mainstream I suppose except for one lad; Geoff Weeks aka Chunky who did his best to convert us all to like some American R&B singer called Chubby Checker. He was obsessed by him and couldn't understand why the rest of us weren't.

Come Friday afternoon it was time to head back to the island for a weekend at home, but not before we got our last piss taking session in on the guys who were heading off to Brockenhurst. I don't envy them one little bit. I think I slept most of Saturday. But by 7pm on Sunday I was back on the ferry and my first big ride on my Puch bike. It was about 15 miles from Portsmouth to Bishops Waltham and I made it without any mishaps. We had to park our bikes behind the dining hall and as I was parking mine up another bike arrived. It was the strangest looking thing on two wheels I'd ever seen. It was an Aerial Leader ridden by one of the Phase 2

Cadets Steve Moore. We had a good old chat about bikes and it seemed we had a lot in common. Walking back into CTS was somehow quite comforting. Despite all the physical stuff and some of the bull shit it actually felt quite homely and it was good to see some of the new friends we'd made. Tomorrow was going to be another big day.

CHAPTER 4

Fareham Tech and the Oily's

Going back to school, for that's how I perceived it, was not to my liking. Although I enjoyed my time at school as far as I was concerned, I'd left all that behind me four months ago. I know college was sort of grown up school, but it still meant undertaking educational lessons on subjects like maths and French. And we would have to attend in full Police uniform.

CTS staff left to right;
Sgt Gerry Todd, PC Russ Parke, Sgt Keith Middleton,
Ch/Insp Jim Rowthorn, Insp Ray Chadwick
Photo Hampshire Telegraph

Sgt Middleton briefed us that some of the less desirable students would do their best to wind us up but that we were to rise above it. It was all part of our police education and experience and it wasn't something that was up for negotiation. The Hampshire Constabulary demanded the very highest of standards from its entire staff and this included us as we were now going out into public for the first time and wearing the uniform. The 'oily's' as he referred them as (those students with long hair, as was the 1970s fashion) would do their best to bait us and that we should deal with them in a mature and professional manner. Oh and if we needed to go into Fareham town at lunchtimes to the bank or somewhere else equally as important then we could do so just so long as we had written permission from the duty instructor for the day.

It wasn't all education though. As if we didn't get enough of the physical at CTS we'd all be pleased to learn that we would also be receiving judo and self-defence lessons together with some circuit training at Fareham Tech and we would also be travelling to HMS St. Vincent in Gosport for swimming and lifesaving lessons. Oh goody. That's on top of the morning run five days a week plus the all-day Wednesday sessions.

So, after breakfast on Monday morning we boarded the two brown and cream coloured Eassons Coaches and headed the 8 miles to Fareham. Our driver was old man Easson himself. He looked way too old to drive and it took him a full five minutes to change gear! This was of particular concern when negotiating the rather steep North Hill on the out skirts of Fareham where the coach needed to change down into first gear. It took him so long to do it that we actually started to roll backwards.

We arrived at Fareham Tech and made our way into the building. Everyone stared at us. It was a bit like being inside a gold fish bowl and made you feel very self-conscious. After all the usual admin type things we got the guided tour of the place and the hub of activity seemed to be the large refectory where the food looked a lot more appetising than CTS.

Turn the radio up driver!
Photo Steve Woodward

And so it proved although lining up at the serving hatch and having a thousand eyes gawping at us was actually quite unnerving. As if being in full uniform wasn't quite enough to identify each of us as Hampshire Police Cadets we had to hand over these little tickets, date stamped with the CTS name in exchange for our food. We all sat together obviously, safety in numbers and all that but I'm sure given time that might change.

After lunch it was time for our first lessons and our first proper interaction with our new oily friends. I have to say that all the ones I met seemed thoroughly decent and after their initial curiosity was satisfied that beneath the blue sage we were no different to the rest of the class, everyone seemed to get along just fine. Then horror of horrors we were given homework. Oh for Christ's sake, homework. Really? As if going back to school wasn't bad enough, to give us homework just rubbed salt into the wound.

No voucher, no lunch
Photo Ian Heath

Tuesday morning for half of us meant judo and circuit training whilst the rest went swimming and on Thursday we swapped over. On the first Tuesday Rowan and Fielding Houses reported to the gymnasium where we met the first of our two instructors Roy Scott. He was a slightly built man in his early 40's with bleached white hair and was wearing large framed glasses. He was dressed in a white vest and very short white shorts with legs that looked like he'd borrowed them from an Ostrich. He bore an uncanny resemblance to Jimmy Saville and spoke with a very broad Yorkshire accent.

He introduced us to his beloved gym equipment from the ropes to the wall bars, the pommel horse, the benches and the vaulting horse. He showed us which routines we were expected to do as we arrived at each item of kit as we did a complete circuit around the gym. In between each item we'd have to do 10 or 20 sit ups, press ups or squat thrusts. Oh great, I can't wait. But

"Stand By Ya Beds"

before we commence our circuit training   Mr Scott insisted on us doing some warm up exercises. We got all the usual running on the spot, sit ups and squat thrusts, followed by more running on the spot. Just when I thought I was warm enough thank you he lined us up in two rows, sat on the floor with our legs out front. He introduced us to relay races where you either went over or under the legs of each person ahead of you until you reached the end. He was very enthusiastic about this.

"Over legs relay GO" he shouted.

One by one we sprinted over the legs of the 15 or so people in each team before he then shouted out.

"Under legs relay GO"

And like Lemmings we crawled under the raised knees of those sat back down before returning to our respective places huffing and puffing like a class of asthmatics.

"I was told you lot were quite fit, clearly I was given duff information" he growled in his best Yorkshire bent "so I'll make it my mission to get you fit"

With that we started the circuit training as he bellowed out his encouragement with phrases like "There's noooo gain without paaain"

The whole torturous routine lasted for an hour before we got a 10 minute fag break. On returning to the gym we waited for another few minutes before a figure filled the entire entrance doorway. He was an enormous human being dressed in a judo suit complete with black belt. He went by the name of Big Johnny Elkington and he was to be our judo instructor every Tuesday for the next nine months. He must have been six feet five inches tall

82

with collar length brown hair and two days stubble on his face. He looked like Ogri (cartoon character from Bike magazine) and even rode a bright orange Laverda Jota as if to prove the point. He strutted into the gym as if he owned the place and stood in front of us with his thumbs tucked into the front of that rather intimidating black belt.

"There's only one thing I hate more than coppers" he growled "and that's fucking baby coppers"

Oh great, we're all gonna die.

He made us arrange a load of blue crash mats into a large square formation before telling us that we needed to do some warm up exercises first. Warm ups? We've spent the last hour warming up; in fact we are so warm most of us are running a bloody temperature. His version of warm ups had us doing bunny hops from one end of the gym to the other. It was agony but none of us complained loud enough for him to hear!

We then got paired off to start our lessons in the fine art of judo. I got Dave Brown who was already a green belt. Just my luck. Dave took it all very seriously and just like the boxing in week one my body got pulverised as it got slammed into the rubber matting time after time. And each time I tried to slam dunk Dave he just stood there like a fucking rock. The aim was to get us all to at least yellow belt standard and maybe higher. I don't think I'll live that long.

It had been a hard morning and as we trudged our way to the refectory some of us were starting to question the amount of physical we had to do, it seemed to be non-stop. And tomorrow is Wednesday.

Every Thursday morning we got bussed down to HMS St. Vincent in Gosport for swimming lessons with Roy Scott and Russ Parke. Let's just say that the pool and its facilities weren't what you might call luxurious. It was old, cold and depressing but the lessons were deadly serious because not only was our swimming ability being tested but we would also be examined for life saving awards through the RASA scheme. Some of the lads were fantastic swimmers, none more so than Al, who gained the nick name of Jaws, following that films recent release and Alan's ability to swim like a fish.

I was average at best I suppose and there were a few that could hardly swim at all. We were basically given instruction on breathing techniques, stroke techniques and a lot of stamina building just to get us up to a decent level before the lifesaving lessons commenced. This would involve us splitting up into pairs with one of us treading water in the middle of the pool whilst your partner then swam out, rolled you onto your back, put his hand under your chin and towed you back to the side of the pool. All fairly easy when just wearing swimming shorts. But it got decidedly more difficult and bloody scary when doing it fully clothed. Your body weight quadrupled as soon as you entered the water and the strength and stamina required was immense. As the months went on we had to undertake the RASA tests from bronze, silver and gold standards and were awarded badges if we passed.

Royal Amateur Swimming Association
Bronze and silver awards
Photo Steve Woodward

Back at CTS the standard of food and the quantities served up were starting to cause concern. It didn't help that Mrs Haysom wasn't exactly the friendliest of people to confront and she quickly gained the nick name of the Soup Dragon. Some of her staff were quite mischievous and revelled in stirring things up for her, in particular a lady called Ella. She was the sort of elder lady you'd have liked as a grandmother or great aunt, the sort who'd lead you astray with tips on how to wind up your parents or tricks to play on your teacher. She was great and we all loved her. In the evenings she'd always leave the key out for the door to the kitchen so we could fill up on peanut butter sandwiches, left over cake and coffee. One of the other kitchen assistants was a young lady called Mandy. She was probably a couple of years older than us, was very slim with frizzy blonde hair akin to the TV character Crystal Tips and her dog Alistair! A lot of the lads fancied her but the poor girl was incredibly shy and one or two of our instructors told us not to get our hopes up too high because the Soup Dragon had laced our tea with Bromide to keep our testosterone in check!

Maybe they should have given us a bit more because about half an hour after lights out one night we all got summoned down to the dining room where a couple of the instructors and Mr Chadwick were waiting for us. They didn't look happy either. Once everyone was accounted for Insp Chadwick held aloft a couple of porn magazines that had been found in a Cadets room. There had been rumours for a while that such magazines were in circulation.

He then said "I expect you've all seen these"
To which someone bravely shouted out "I haven't so can I borrow them when you're finished Sir".

Muffled sniggers went around the room. Mr Chadwick was clearly unhappy and gave us a lecture about the dangers of such

"Stand By Ya Beds"

items circulating an all-male establishment like CTS and then rather bizarrely declared.

"These magazines will turn you gay".

First Expedition

CHAPTER 5

First Expedition

On 24th September 1975 we got our very first pay cheques; the princely sum of £53.98p for the month. I think all of us at that time had been living off the money our parents probably gave us and so this felt great. One of the first things I did was to trot down to the corner shop in Albert Road to buy a packet of 20 Players No.6 fags for 30p. The tuck shop did a roaring trade in Coke and pints of limeade that evening.

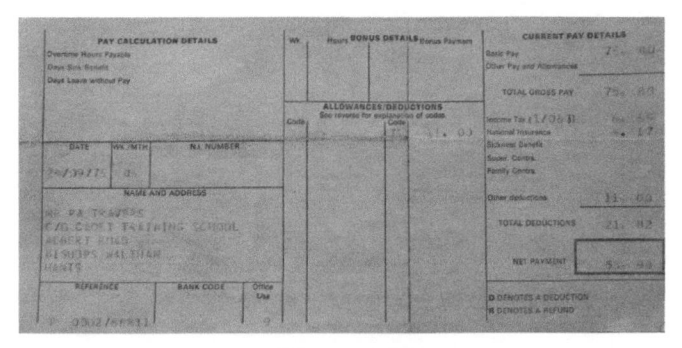

First pay slip
Photo Phil Travers

During the half term week in October we were getting prepared for our first proper walking expedition and we were all quite excited about it. The venue was the Dorset Coastal Walk which covers about 25 miles and it would take two days with one night under canvass. We had to take all of our kit like tents, food, cooking equipment, sleeping bags and personal kit in ruck sacks. We were given strict instructions about our feet. In order to avoid getting blisters we were instructed to wear two pairs of thick woollen socks and to ensure that our feet stayed dry we were instructed to rub Dubbin into the leather. This was a sort of water proof grease that had the texture of Vaseline. To aid the Dubbin we were also told to wear water proof spats over the top of the boots to prevent the ingress of water from above. With bright orange Heli Hansen water proof jackets and trousers plus a heavy ruck sack I could barely move.

We were all in high spirits as we boarded the Transit mini buses and headed south west towards the Dorset coast. It took almost two hours to get to Studland Bay where we stepped out of the cramped buses and onto the cliffs overlooking the sea. It was pleasantly warm and dry although there was a strong on-shore wind. We were split up into groups of five and sent off at ten-minute intervals. It was all very pleasant as we strolled along the footpath adjacent to a corn field where one or two Cadets tried eating the almost-but-not-quite-ripe cobs. It was all very casual.

Steve Woodward looks relaxed at the start of the little walk along the Dorset coast.

First Expedition

After a couple of miles the wide foot path started to narrow as it went downhill for about 100 feet. Under foot the smoothness of the original path gave way to lumps of white chalk, stones and loose gravel. And then the path started to go uphill. Steeply. It was hard graft and the talking and banter reduced somewhat. We reached the top and were treated to a fantastic view of Old Harry Rocks being caressed by a very blue sea. We carried on west wards occasionally getting glimpses of the other groups either ahead of us or behind. My feet were starting to hurt especially my heels which I knew were getting blistered; something I'd suffered with as a child every time I got new shoes. These multipurpose boots we'd been given were anything but comfortable. There was no 'give' in them at all and it was like having two planks of thick wood bolted to your soles.

The hills were getting steeper, the path ways less defined and the wind was now blowing straight into our faces. My energy levels were getting low so I ate a couple of Mars bars and half a packet of Dextrosol energy tablets. But it was a short lived spike as each hill seemed to get harder to get up. Even climbing over the stiles to navigate the multitude of dry-stone walls seemed to take more effort than was necessary.

By mid-afternoon we were absolutely exhausted. We reached the base of a hill and I looked up towards its summit. It wasn't a hill it was a cliff. My feet were on fire and I knew the blisters on my heels had burst open as I could now feel raw flesh and it was very painful. On top of that I think I also had blisters coming up between some of my toes. This cliff was a hands and knees job. It wasn't really possible to walk up it. I was in so much pain I started to cry but had to hold it in for fear of ridicule from the others, even though most of them were suffering the same way. Andy joined me at the base and we heaved our way up, digging our finger nails into the dirt and pushing up with our legs. It sapped the last of our energy and on reaching the top we collapsed in a heap unable to move.

After a five-minute break we all got back to our feet and trudged our way downhill again and as we did so all I could see was the next obstacle up ahead. A mile or so later and we started the next uphill climb although it wasn't as steep it was still knackering on the calves and feet. On reaching the summit we came across a pile of rocks which looked like a good resting place to us. As we sat down so one of the guys found an unopened can of cold lager placed between the crevices of two rocks. It was immediately opened and passed around for us all to take a gulp or two. It tasted great and seemed to give us all a much needed psychological boost. We were further encouraged by the news that according to the map we only had about two miles to go before we reached the base camp at Chapmans Pool.

Russ Bramley and his pet ruck sack take a break
Photo Steve Woodward

With renewed vigour we continued our walk until at last we saw the camp site situated on a nice looking grass plateau. The trouble was that nice grassy area was situated on the other side of a huge ravine. As the crow flies it was less than a hundred yards away but we couldn't even see the bottom of the ravine because of the trees and under growth far below us. Nothing for it but to head on down. It was incredibly steep and several times I lost my footing and was only saved from plunging all the way to the bottom by grabbing small trees or other vegetation. It must have been over a hundred feet to the base and immediately we hit the bottom so the climb back up the other side commenced. And it really was a climb, again almost cliff like, clinging onto vegetation, feet slipping away with lose dirt and stones raining down on us from those further up the hill. It must have taken us about ten minutes I suppose and sapped the last few drops of energy I had but at last we reached that grassy camp site and thoughts quickly turned to food and a restful evening in front of a camp fire.

We were greeted by Russ Parke and Gerry Todd who told us to dump our ruck sacks in the spot they had allocated for our tent and to then come over for a quick debrief. The two previous teams were putting up their tents and as I looked back across the ravine so I saw the group behind us starting their descent into the abyss. We sat down with Gerry Todd and a very informal chat about our expedition so far then took place. He asked us about the route, our map reading and any concerns we had over that, how were our feet holding up etc etc. Debrief over we all got back to our feet.

"Oh one last thing" said Toddy "Did you find a can of lager by the trig point rock? I accidentally left it behind when I sat there admiring the view"

We all sort of shuffled our feet and coughed a bit.
"It's OK I don't mind if you drank it" he continued "Wouldn't like to see it go to waste"

We intimated that yes; maybe we had found it and drunk it.

Sgt Todd smiled.

"What did you do with the can?" he asked.

We all looked at each other blankly.

"Oh, don't tell me you left it there?"

Which was met with more blank stares.

"Well we can't have the Hampshire Constabulary littering the lovely Dorset countryside now can we" he continued "So you'd best go and get it"

What? What now? No, I can't, I'm in so much pain I need to get these boots off. I was crushed.

"Off ya go then" said Toddy with *that* grin on his face. And he made us do it with our heavy ruck sacks on rather than leaving them behind.

We walked to the edge of the ravine just as the next group reached the top. We made our way down and then back up the other side in virtual silence except for the occasional expletive being muttered about Sgt Todd's parentage. It took us almost two hours to get there, grab the can and trudge back. I swear that ravine was twice as deep third time around.

We collapsed in a heap and the first thing I did was get those boots off. I then took off the top pair of socks and could literally feel my feet throbbing and begin to swell up now that they were no longer incarcerated inside their leather coffin. But getting the second layer of socks off was a different matter. Because my feet

First Expedition

were prone to blistering I'd taken the precaution of covering my heels in a three inch wide strip of elastoplasts. Unfortunately as the boots had rubbed so the plasters had moved and then partly peeled away from my skin and formed a sort of roll and were now stuck against the inside of my socks together with the large flap of skin that had pulled away from the raw flesh that had been a huge blister. I was left with no choice but to get my pen knife out and cut the skin away from the sock to release it. It was agony. After pulling the sock from my right foot I could then see that I had another huge blister on the ball of my foot and a third one between two of my toes. This one had also burst open and was very tender. I then set about pricking the big one under my foot and oozing out the liquid until it was dry. My left foot wasn't quite so bad apart from the rawness of the burst blister on my heel. I kept my feet exposed for the rest of the evening and hobbled around like a cripple and wondering just what state they'd be in by the time we finish tomorrow.

After sorting out our tents it was time to cook up another few tins of stew. We had a couple of primus stoves and a single burner Calor gas cooker which produced a much better flame. After a couple of minutes use the gas ran out and so I hobbled over to the instructor's tent to request a new canister. Russ Parke delved into the store tent and came out with a shiny new one and as he handed it to me he said;

"You do know how to change these don't you Woody?"
"Yes sir" I replied confidently.
"I should hope so, you were in the Scouts weren't you?" he asked.
"I was yes" I replied and with that I turned and headed back towards our tent.

I sat down on the grass and dismantled the gas cooker. This meant unclipping the two U shaped chrome legs that held the canister onto the main body of the cooker and then unscrewing the canister until it popped off. I then picked up the new one just as Russ Parke was heading towards our tent. For the life of me I've no idea why I did what I did next but instead of securing the canister with the U-shaped legs first and then screwing it on I just starting screwing the canister straight onto the main body. As soon as the canister was punctured by the main pin on the body so it shot off like a scud missile with high pressure gas spewing out of the hole and it missed Russ Parkes left ear by an inch and landed 20 feet behind him. He called me all the names under the sun and it cost me three laps around the field at the double whilst carrying a wooden tent pole above my head.

By the time I got back to the tent the others were already doing the cooking and we ate it as if it was our last ever meal. That evening we all sat around in a big group just chatting and laughing at the policing stories our instructors relayed to us. It was the first time since we arrived at CTS over a month ago that we'd been allowed to relax as a group, it was rather pleasant, although every time I moved my feet I winced with pain. It was an early night for all of us and the prospect of doing it all over again in the morning was the stuff of nightmares.

And the morning came all too soon. The first thing I had to do was swathe my heels in strips of plaster again and then pop on a fresh pair of those thick woollen socks, followed by a second pair. I sat there looking at my boots knowing they were going to crucify me for the rest of the day. My feet were so swollen that I had real difficulty getting them on and as I did so I could feel them gnawing away at the already exposed wounds. I stood up and took my first tentative steps. Jeeez Christ. I'm never going to make it. With every step it felt like I was being stabbed.

But I knew I had no choice but to continue. Wimping out now would get me labelled for life and I wasn't prepared to have

First Expedition

that no matter what. We set off once more, heads down and heading west. We told stories and jokes just to keep our minds off the hills and the pain. To be fair the morning wasn't too bad but towards midday the hills got steeper again and the footpaths seemed to vanish completely as we neared Lulworth Cove. As we climbed up a very steep incline I could see red flags ahead and then we reached a very high wire fence surmounted with barbed wire. The broken footpath ran adjacent to the fence and behind it we saw large wooden signs that read;

MOD Property
DANGER
Keep Out
Unexploded Shells

I'm pretty sure it was RD Smith who threw the first stone over the fence in the hope it may hit an unexploded shell and set it off. This seemed like a great idea and within seconds we'd found enough energy to launch a full scale mortar attack with stones raining down on the MOD land on the other side of the fence. Needless to say there was no 'Shock and Awe' in deepest Dorset and within a few minutes we'd come to our senses and moved on.

By mid-afternoon we were closing in on the finishing line at Ringstead Bay near Weymouth. I was in agony with my feet and every step was excruciating. I could feel the plasters had come away again and I was dreading the damage I might find come the time I could take those boots off. We reached Ringstead Bay about 3pm and those Transit vans were a glorious sight for they would be the chariots that whisked us back to civilisation and a hot shower. I couldn't take my boots off until long after we got back to CTS because we had equipment to unload, clean and put away before we were released to head upstairs to our rooms. My feet were in a state of shock and as I peeled the socks from the newly exposed flesh I cried out loud. Even walking bare foot was difficult and instead of a shower I sat in a warm bath to allow them to soak properly. It worked to a certain extent but they were going to take some nursing back to health. But I was content in the knowledge that I wasn't the only one in pain with plenty of the others suffering similar issues or had twisted ankles, various cuts and bruises and all of us ached from head to foot. And we all agreed on just one thing. We fucking hate Dorset.

The following morning I paid my first visit to D Block and met Snoddy, our resident Matron. As I entered the building I was struck by how modern it was in comparison to the rest of CTS and it had a very distinctive medical smell about it. There was no way I could partake in the morning run and I needed her permission to be excused. I wasn't the only casualty lining up in sick bay; there must have been a dozen of us, mostly with blistered feet. She slapped some antiseptic cream on the open wounds which smarted somewhat and told me to keep them covered as best I could.

A couple of days later Pete Kerley and Russ Parke took Rowan and Fielding House out for a little treat; canoeing in the sea! After an hours drive down to The Witterings on the Sussex coast we unloaded the trailer and walked across the stony beach towards a reasonably calm sea armed with an assortment of canoes. We lined them up on the beach and were told that this would be the first of several canoeing trips and before we entered the water we needed to know how to get out of one when it capsized. They emphasised the when and not if. I'd never done canoeing before and was quite looking forward to this.

The basic rule having capsized your canoe is to lean forward as far as possible and you pop out of the thing like a cork from a champagne bottle. As we sat in the canoes on the beach doing dry runs we got a lot of funny looks from other beach goers. And

First Expedition

then it was time to get wet. Although the sea was reasonably calm there were still a fair number of waves coming in which made getting into a canoe somewhat challenging especially if you thought you were a smart arse and tried doing it on your own. Cue an instant capsize. The secret therefore was to get someone else to hold one end of the fibre glass vessel whilst you clambered into it and slid your feet towards the front whilst pressing your knees hard up against the inside top of the canoe, whilst further balance was obtained by dipping the paddle into the water. Simple. And then the first wave hits you and over you go, rising quickly to the surface and spewing out a mouthful of salty water. Yuk.

There was a lot of laughter and piss taking going on and despite the relatively warm weather the sea was anything but warm and once you were wet you started to shiver uncontrollably. Heading into the waves was really quite exhilarating with the front of the canoe rising sharply upwards towards the sky before crashing down onto the water again. Then it was time to turn around and head back towards the shore. I'm not sure who started it but a new game of canoe surfing was started whereby we'd ride the waves as if on a surf board. It was great fun until the front of the canoe nosedived into the sand at the water's edge sending the rear of the canoe upwards until it was almost vertical. It was at this point that there seemed to be a moment of complete motionless as if the canoe had been planted by the hand of a giant, followed by the canoe falling to the left or the right with the occupant screaming like a girl as it crashed onto the beach. It was great fun but like everything else we were subjected to it was physically knackering.

Having now been at CTS for a few weeks and endured the likes of Brockenhurst camp, Dorset coastal walk and a multitude of other physical stuff we had definitely bonded as a group. Friendships were being formed and as in all walks of life a pecking order was also developing. But it was the banter and the general piss taking I liked the most, even if I was the victim (and I use the term very loosely) at times, I loved it. There were those who couldn't take it of course and accordingly they got targeted more often.

It had been a long and tiring day and I was fit for nothing except my bed. It was lights out in ten minutes time so after getting all my kit sorted for the morning I stripped off and jumped into my pit; except it didn't quite work out that way. My legs stopped half way down the bed by what felt like a brick wall. Although it wasn't painful it was certainly uncomfortable for a second or two. My bed had been 'apple pied' and I had a good idea who by. Andy laughed out loud and briefly checked his bed before getting in. He didn't check it thoroughly enough and as he shouted out the word "bastards" so we heard our neighbours laughing through the wafer thin wall.

The next morning we all lined up in the Games Area waiting to go out on our morning run. It was obvious that something comical had happened the previous evening because the lads from Fielding House were almost crying with laughter. It transpired that Paul Rowsell and Phil Travers had met on a stair well, sort of head on. Some banter was exchanged followed by some good humoured pushing and shoving as they tried to pass each other but Phil had pushed Rowse a little bit too hard and shoved him straight through the stud wall. After completing the morning ritual none of us could resist taking a look at the rather large, Paul Rowsell shaped hole in the wall. It was eventually patched up with a new piece of plaster board but will forever remain the hole that Rowse made.

CHAPTER 6

Dartmoor

It was late autumn and we were being briefed about our first visit to Dartmoor, a place we were told we'd get to know very well over the next couple of years. This four day expedition was just a taster and for the instructors to assess those who might qualify to be selected to represent Hampshire Police in the famous Ten Tors competition where teams from the armed forces and other organisations raced each other across the moors. I already knew within myself that I wouldn't qualify for that one but the likes of Wayne Colebrook, Tony Hastings, Andy Crawford and Paul Diaper were obvious candidates already. Part of the briefing concerned the armed forces who trained on Dartmoor all the time. We were to avoid contact with them if possible because some of their training consisted of living off the land and if that meant stealing our rations then to the average squaddie that was still living off the land! Oh and by the way if you see half a dead sheep up on the moors for God's sake don't go anywhere near it because there'll be an SAS man underneath it. Seriously. They use dead animals as doors to the shallow fox holes they've dug out of the earth to sleep in and if you blow their cover, trust me you could end up as their next meal. This all came from Gerry Todd and it was finished with one of his trade mark grins which you never knew when to take seriously.

Although I'd never seen the place Dartmoor held a bit of fascination for me because my father who was a prison officer was given a choice of Parkhurst or Dartmoor when he got promoted. Not much of a choice I'm sure you'll agree and I suppose if he'd chosen Dartmoor I'd have joined up with Devon

"Stand By Ya Beds"

and Cornwall Police instead of Hampshire and the path of my life would be completely different to how it panned out in the end.

The prospect of putting those bloody boots back on again filled me with dread. My feet had barely healed since Dorset and the wafer thin layer of new skin across my heels wouldn't last five minutes. I talked to Pete Kerley about the possibility of using training shoes instead but he said that wouldn't be possible because of the likelihood of me twisting an ankle on the very uneven surface of the moors and because it was invariably wet under foot and the boots would afford me some protection from both the ground and the weather. I couldn't give a shit about the possibility of twisting my ankle or getting wet it was the internal damage those things would do that worried me.

Situated between Exeter and Plymouth the Dartmoor National Park covers some 368 square miles of moor land, forest, rivers and streams with large rock formations called Tors. Its main town is a small place called Princetown which is where HMP Dartmoor is situated. We were bussed down to the south west corner of the moors to a place called Dewerstone where we pitched our little orange tents fairly close to the fast running River Plym. This river was to supply our drinking and washing water for the next few days and even though the instructors were constantly barking orders at us, overall it was a rather more relaxed atmosphere than the recent Brockenhurst and Dorset outings had been.

The next morning we were split into two groups with Rowan and Fielding Houses paired together whilst Peel and Mayne House got dragged off to start a two day hike. We were then marched a mile or two alongside the river to The Dewerstone itself. Set in some quite dense woodland adjacent to the river this cliff like rock towered above us like a New York sky scraper. And today we had to climb it. What? All of it? And once we'd reached the summit as an extra special treat, we could abseil back down it again. And we had to do it in our walking-skiing-climbing boots that weren't fit for any of the three disciplines they were alleged to have been good for.

The Dewerstone
Photo Steve Woodward

As a youngster I'd climbed a lot of trees and I do mean a lot. I'm not afraid of heights either unless I'm about to lean backwards over a cliff or tall building with abseiling in mind. Then its fill ya pants time. So, I was quite looking forward to the going up bit but not the coming down bit. I'd have preferred to have worn training shoes because you need to feel what you are holding onto and with these boots on I couldn't feel anything outside. It was like wearing a pair of boxing gloves to grip the rock climb with. The rock itself must have been about 80 feet in height with a sort of L shaped gulley running up the centre of it. Its granite surface was laden with cracks and small ledges to gain hand and foot holds although as you looked up towards the summit these seemed to become less obvious.

"Stand By Ya Beds"

Steve Woodward half way to the summit
Photo Steve Woodward

Pete Kerley donned all his climbing gear and set off, showing us the best places to get some grip or to place your lead-bound feet. He made it look easy and then it was time for volunteers. One by one we lined up to take our turn with the average climb taking about 20 to 30 minutes, so there was quite a lot of hanging around, taking the piss out of those who were screaming and laughing at those who made some pretty good comments as they struggled to find a crack big enough to get your thumb nail into.

And then it was my turn. With bright red cork helmet on and enough rope to anchor a small ship with I set off on my first date with The Dewerstone. As I took my first couple of upward steps I looked skyward and it looked a lot more than 80 feet high. It must be at least treble that? The first 20 feet actually wasn't that bad. But then I found myself desperately searching for the next foot hold and I couldn't see one. I found a couple of cracks to get my fingers into and now I needed to have some faith in my upper body strength to heave myself up to a half inch wide ledge which was just about big enough to place my right boot onto. There I sat for a minute or two trying to get my breath and some strength back. From there I had to lean a long way to the left to reach the next hand hold and then sort of swing across to the foot ledge I'd spotted. I have to admit that really was quite exhilarating and I found myself enjoying the experience more and more. Before I knew it I'd reached the summit and got a pat on the back from Pete Kerley. After taking in the quite magnificent view with a celebratory fag it was time to abseil back to Earth.

Roy Inskip gave me my instructions as he held onto the other end of the rope that would lower me down. I was desperately trying to remain calm about it but one look over the precipice towards that canopy of trees with no ground in sight had me doubting myself again. Roy Inskip was quite forceful but in a rather jovial way if that makes sense? So, there I was all belayed up, lifesaving cork helmet back on and my arse doing its half a crown and sixpence routine as I walked to the edge, turned 180 degrees, took a deep breath and commenced my descent. After a few feet I tried doing that bouncing off the wall thing that all competent abseilers seem to do. It would have worked had I remembered to actually lower myself at the same time. All I did was bounce of the same bit of granite a few times with Roy Inskip shouting obscenities at me from above. On reaching the ground I actually felt quite chuffed with myself and started to think that I really rather liked rock climbing and couldn't wait for my next turn.

In the meantime I sat on a nearby rock with Stef King whom I'd got to know quite well recently. He was a big lad who struggled with some of the physical stuff as a result but he had a hugely infectious laugh and the same sense of humour as me. He also had a great line in impersonations, in particular the PE teacher from Fareham Tech Roy Scott, in fact he was so good at it that it was impossible to tell them apart. We hit it off straight away and had a lot in common, doubly so because he was also from the island. As we sat there, we watched Andy Crawford getting kitted up to do his first climb. Andy was a bit of a character. He was of slight build but hard as nails. He was the sort of lad who'd walk through a wall of fire and probably not notice. His hair had a mind of its own and stuck out all over the place and he tendered to mumble a bit. I don't think he needed the ropes and all the safety gear, I half expected him to just shin up the rock like a lizard in 10 seconds flat. Well he didn't disappoint us. Not only did he do it in record time but climbed the whole thing with a fag in his mouth.

Over the next two days I climbed The Dewerstone another five or six times in various locations and I loved it, especially on day two when I wore training shoes instead. It was so much easier and with ten times the amount of feel and grip. Whilst doing some research for this book I looked up The Dewerstone on Wikapedia and this is what it said;

"Dewer" is an ancient Celtic word for the Devil, and Dartmoor tradition has it that the Devil, riding a gigantic black horse, gallops across the Moor each night and leads a phantom pack of black hounds to chase weary or foolish humans over the Dewerstone to their deaths.

I knew it.

On the third day I had no choice but to put those damned boots back on because we had our first introduction to walking the moors. OK so there were a few hillocks as we made our way from Little Mis Tor to Great Mis Tor and then Fox Tor with several others in between but the hills were nowhere near as steep as those in Dorset. It was actually quite pleasant apart from my fragile feet being ripped to shreds again. We camped overnight next to a small stream and the evening's weather helped as it was quite warm with hardly any wind.

Dartmoor

Great Mis Tor

*Here's a motley crew;
Left to right are Neil Cheyne, Kev Willis, Chris Lee,
Tony Hastings and George Barker*

"Stand By Ya Beds"

Back at CTS and our daily routines had now become second nature. Or had they? Bulling boots was still a pain in the arse, especially if you happened to damage the toe cap, usually when some clumsy git had trodden on your toes. But someone discovered a cheat and a lot of us latched onto it immediately. The average shine on your toe caps could be greatly enhanced by wiping on a layer of Klear Kote which was a liquid floor polish. It worked a treat although it had a tendency to dull down a bit after a few days but that wasn't a problem because a ten second wipe over with some fresh Klear Kote had your boots gleaming again. All of a sudden uniform inspections weren't quite so daunting.

Clothes brushes were another issue. Ever since we'd arrived at CTS most of us had used the mid-1970s invention called the Brush-O-Matic. This white plastic tool had a reversible Velcro like head finished in bright red that sort of lifted the debris from your uniform like a piece of selotape would have done. On the whole they were pretty good unless you had some stubborn dirt that the Brush-O-Matic would just glide over. It was a lifter rather than a remover of dirt. The new kid on the block was the brass wire brush. This was the Rottweiler of the brush world whilst the cheaper Woolworth's product was definitely the fluffy white kitten. There were arguments for and against both products and there was almost a daily competition between certain brush holders to see who could get the best brushed uniform. Then one morning it all went wrong for Andy Goward. He was an advocate of the wire brush and made sure that everyone knew that he was the proud owner of such a beast. It was final brush down time before the Wednesday morning parade. With less than two minutes to go Andy was furiously brushing the lower section of his left trouser leg when he screamed out loud.

"Fuck. No" as everyone turned to look.

The razor sharp creases on his trousers had resulted in a thinner and more fragile fabric along the crease line and as the

106

wire brush tore into the material so the crease split wide open from ankle to knee exposing Andy's lily white leg. There was a sort of pregnant pause before everyone burst out laughing as Andy was seen legging it through the Games Area and up to our room to quickly get changed into a new pair. He was back within two minutes and made the parade by the skin of his teeth.

Inspector Chadwick was the inspecting officer today and I don't think he was in a very good mood. Rowan House were the first to be inspected and my suspicions were right.

"Cadet French have you shaved today?" he enquired.

"Yes Sir, twice" replied Nigel who was the hairiest 16 year old I'd ever met.

"Well you need to do it again" growled Inspector Chadwick "and you can do an extra duty squad tonight".

"Hair cut Woodward" he snapped "See Mr Parke tonight and you can do duty squad with French"

Oh just great, thanks for that.

He stood in front of Andy, then walked around him once and spoke to him through gritted teeth.

"Did you sleep in those trousers Goward?" he growled.

"No Sir, I had a bit of an ...."

"I'm not interested in your fucking excuses boy; you're a disgrace to the uniform. Report to the officer of the day at 1800 tonight in your number one dress and after that you can join the others on duty squad".

In all he singled out another dozen or so Cadets for extra Duty Squad and then just walked back inside the building. So that evening Russ Parke was busy with his clippers and I got charged 50p for the privilege of having a grade 2 head shave whilst Andy

"Stand By Ya Beds"

and a couple of others got intimate with the iron. Come 1800 hours we all lined up in the Games Area, got inspected by Russ Parke who could hardly tell me to get my hair cut before he assigned us some extra patrols of the grounds until 2100 hours.

I needed to get to the bank and had to seek permission from the Officer of the Day. Come lunch time I donned my tunic and cap and stepped out of Fareham Tech to walk the mile or so down to Fareham town centre.

So, there I was at 16 years of age, all 9 stone of me, having barely started shaving and I'm in full Police uniform strutting my stuff in public for the very first time. I have to admit that I was crapping myself. What if I come across an accident or a bank robbery? What if someone asks for directions to somewhere? What if they ask me the time? That's OK I can do that one! And everyone is staring at me. I do mean everyone. I was still at school five months ago! As I entered the town centre and the High Street it was busy with pedestrians and I kept my fingers crossed that none of them wanted to talk to me. I got to Lloyds Bank unscathed, wrote out a cheque for £10 and handed it to the young lady cashier. As I didn't bank with Lloyds in Fareham she then had to phone my branch on the island to double check that I had sufficient funds in my account before handing me the cash which consisted of a crisp new £5 note and five £1 notes. It felt great.

En route back to Fareham Tech I came across Rafferty Newman's motorcycle dealership and couldn't resist having a look inside although I had no idea if I was allowed to or what kind of reception I might receive inside the shop itself. Although I'd only had my little bike for three months, I'd already decided that come my 17th birthday I'd be buying a 250 and that bikes were definitely for me. I entered this Aladdin's Cave on the High Street to be greeted by the sight of a brand new Honda Goldwing and a bright yellow CB750F1, a Suzuki GT750 triple in gold and a dark blue RE5. Over by the window was a black and red Moto Guzzi S3 and sat in the middle of the showroom was a Moto Guzzi 850 T3 California. Everywhere I looked there were superb looking machines and I just couldn't make up my mind which one I liked the most.

CHAPTER 7

Broccoli and Bromide

We'd been at CTS for several weeks now and the daily routine of morning run followed by Fareham Tech interspersed with judo, swimming, cross country and other physical pursuits was getting easier as we got fitter. Well mostly. The morning run was still a shit way to start the day with only the racing snakes of Andy Worship and Steve Matcham seemingly enjoying the apparent benefits of such torture.

There were those amongst us who started to find loop holes in the security of ensuring that everyone completed the run. For example, there were a couple of Cadets who were nearly always the first out of the door to the Games Area and then ran flat out towards D Block, took a sharp right, through the back door and back upstairs to bed. There were also two more who continued the run as far as the oil tank store on the corner of the car park, leapt over the wall and hid beneath the tank until it was time to run back inside some 10 minutes or so later. All very inventive and admired by the rest of us who hadn't thought of a similar escape plan.

Then one morning as we all stood there in our respective Houses with Pete Manns calling out the register it happened. A legend was born. Rowan House were always the first to be called and we stood nearest to the steps that led up towards the lounge area and dining room. Pete Manns was leant against the wall facing us, head buried towards his clip board.

"Gibson"
"Sir"

"Gosden"
"Sir"
"Goward"
"Sir"
"Howsego"
"Sir"

As he continued to call out the names, I saw Andy turn left and just casually walk up the stairs with his training shoes in his hands and disappear into the lounge. We all stood there, mouths wide open as Pete Mann's, completely oblivious, just carried on calling out the register. There were one or two sniggers as a result and Andy appeared to have got away with the most brazen of acts.

As the rest of us set off for the run a few Cadets asked me if I'd known in advance of Andy's plans to which the answer was a definite no, he hadn't said a word to me. I thought he might have been ill or something so when I eventually staggered back to our room and found him tucked up in bed it was the obvious question. But no, he wasn't ill, just sick of the morning run! Weren't we all? I have to confess I was somewhat jealous but also full of admiration for his daring. And he continued doing it every single morning for the next six months and didn't get caught once.

Mind you it came close once or twice. Doubly so when it became obvious that a good percentage of us had found alternative routes to the one we were supposed to be on and the instructors decided that it was time to put a halt to it. By now I'd joined the group that ran flat out to the rear of the main building where I bolted upstairs and back into my warm pit. It was bliss grabbing a few extra minutes especially if the weather was crap. But on this particular morning it all went wrong. Andy was already in bed when I came crashing through the door and jumped into my own bed. Within seconds we heard the familiar voice of Gerry Todd bellowing out the names Gosden and Warry from the end of our corridor. He'd caught them red handed.

"Stand By Ya Beds"

"Oh shit" we both cried.

Andy dived under his bed. It was right by the door, unlike mine which was under the window so anyone looking in through the door would see me straight away. Nothing else for it; I opened the wardrobe door and climbed in shutting the door just as our bedroom door came flying open. I held my breath. If they find us, we're dead. He must have stood there for all of ten seconds but it felt like ten minutes during which time I'd held my breath but could actually hear my heart pounding loud enough for Toddy to hear it. The door shut but I didn't trust him to not fling it open again a few seconds later. Like a frightened mouse hiding from a cat I stayed put.

But a second wave of fear then struck me. Without doubt they'll be counting all the runners back in this time; we have to rejoin the run. The coast seemed to be clear as we crept along the corridor and back down the stairs. As we peeped through the door so a few of the front runners were trotting past and it was time to make a break for it and dash out from our cover. Sure enough there was Sgt Todd and Pete Manns checking everyone back in by the Games Area door. We'd got away with it by the skin of our teeth but there were a few others who hadn't been so lucky and it cost them dearly with an evening run every night for a week. It didn't stop Andy creeping back up the stairs the very next morning though!

It has to be said that even though we'd only known each other for a few weeks we did all seem to get along well. Throwing 68 strangers together could have resulted in some of them clashing but actually, despite the odd skirmish, we had all bonded nicely. However, there were times when that entente cordiale was severely tested and none more so than when your room got 'jobbed' by your neighbours. Mathematically of course Andy and I were at a distinct disadvantage because all the other rooms housed

112

four inmates and not two. There were two danger times; five minutes before lights out or worst of all five minutes before Wednesday morning room inspection. The first time it happened was late one evening when our door came crashing open and in stormed Bramley, Gibson, Mason and RD Smith. Andy was dragged out of bed and sprayed all over with Brut 33 and shaving foam, whilst his bed got tipped onto its side and the contents of his wardrobe were scattered all over the room. Meanwhile my bed pack was completely destroyed after it was booted from one end of the room to the other and my cap and boots got launched out of the fucking window. Within seconds they'd left amid howls of laughter (from them not us) as we sat there stunned and feeling like we'd just been mugged. Dressed only in my under pants I had about two minutes to run downstairs, go out the back door, find my stuff and get back up to our room before lights out. I made it with about five seconds to spare. Revenge will be ours.

The other 'jobbing' exercise was having your bed apple pied. To do this the target bed had to be already made by the victim. When they were out of the room and the coast was clear the idea was to remove the blankets and top sheet and then undo the bottom sheet from the foot of the bed and fold it in half back up towards the pillows and tuck it back in at the sides, thus reducing the length of the bed by half. The top sheet and blankets were then replaced and made to look good. Cue the victim jumping into bed and shoving his feet towards the far end only to have their journey cut short by 50% followed by an "arrgghhh" and the words "you bastards" loud enough for the whole of CTS to hear.

You are probably aware of the saying "No honour amongst thieves" well the same could be applied to those who shared the room next door to us because two of them were A level students and two of them weren't. That meant that every Wednesday Gibby and RD Smith went off to Fareham Tech leaving Russ Bramley and Phil Mason to take all the crap during Wednesday mornings room inspection. Now Gibby and RD were immaculate residents and Russ and Phil, although not bad by any means, weren't quite up to the same standard. So, to ensure they received all the plaudits they would exchange their bed packs for the pristine and perfectly shaped bed packs belonging to their roommates. Now everyone, including Gibby and RD know the truth!

The fire alarm went off at 3am and down we all went to the Games Area and yes it was a drill. As we all stood there waiting for the register to be called so two lads came crashing in through the door carrying Andy Guy who was still fast asleep. They dumped him rather unceremoniously on the floor and left him there as Pete Kerley checked off all the names. If sleeping ever becomes an Olympic sport then Andy would definitely win gold.

When I was in junior school one of the things I absolutely hated was being forced to do country dancing. It was truly awful having to hold hands with girls and then 'dance' and skip around whilst some over enthusiastic teacher clapped her hands whilst calling out all the moves. I always seemed to get lumbered with the fat girl with body odour and smelly breath. So, imagine my disdain at learning that tonight a bus load of girls from a private school somewhere were being brought into CTS so that we could all have a go at country dancing. This has got to be some kind of wind up? But no, not only was it genuine but our attendance was compulsory. I wasn't the only one dreading it.

We filtered our way into the dining room and about 30 girls entered and sat on the other side, as far away from us as they could possibly get. They had the same look on their faces as we did; none of us wanted to be there. The silence was deafening and nobody moved. That is until Paul Forbes decided to break the ice by dragging Russ out to the middle of the floor where Forbsey commenced a Morcombe and Wise classic; The Arabian sand dance. Paul was very good at it, Russ died doing it. Whilst our side of the hall found it hilarious, the other side of the room stood there with dead pan faces. Russ said later that it was the most embarrassing silent audience he had ever played to and he would hate Paul Forbes to the grave for making him do it.

Rowan House had a day trip to Swanage to go abseiling with Pete Kerley and Russ Parke. Not from the side of the building this time or from a nearby tree but the cliffs above Dancers Ledge on the Dorset coast. After about an hour and a half travelling down to the coast in the back of the Transit it was good to get out and stretch the legs before grabbing all the gear from the roof rack and walking a mile or so to a large grass plateau atop the cliffs. It was a rather pleasant autumnal afternoon and the view from the cliffs out over the English Channel painted a picture of calm serenity.

We were ordered not to go anywhere near the cliff edge as Pete Kerley gave us a briefing about what to expect from this, our second proper stint of abseiling, not the pussy footing around we done from the roof of CTS. He further explained that when we went over the edge, as he so quaintly termed it, we wouldn't be able to see the ground below; just the sea……..Oh and some rocks. A lot of rocks! Our target was to abseil down the cliff until we reached the large cave entrance and then abseil free to the ledge at the bottom. Total height was about 150 feet. We all fell silent.

A huge metal stake was hammered into the ground about 20 feet from the edge to act as an anchor point and then Russ Parke got himself kitted up and was the first one to go over the edge and disappear out of sight. Once on the ledge below he would act as our guide as we made our way down. I have to confess that I was bricking it. Pete then asked for the first volunteer and without hesitation Phil Mason was the first to step forward. Phil was one of those rare characters who was both physically very fit and also incredibly intelligent and funny with it. Nothing seemed to faze him and he sought of shrugged his shoulders as he turned to face us all and then leant backwards and started to lower himself down towards the sea and those rocks. Once he was safely down Pete called for the next volunteer. No-one moved. So, he started picking us at random.

Dancers Ledge on the Swanage Coast

"Come on then Warry, your turn" he shouted.

Duncan didn't look too happy about it as he got kitted out with all the gear including that useless looking cork helmet. He moved slowly towards the cliff edge, gripping the rope as hard as he could. As he got to the edge he peered over as best he could.
"Fuuuck…..meee" he whimpered.

He turned to face us and he looked terrified. Pete Kerley gave him as much encouragement as he could, giving him step by step instructions as slowly but surely Duncan leant out over the cliff edge.

"Hands and feet Duncan, hands and feet" came the instruction, which meant you basically walked backwards with your feet pressed against the cliff face whilst simultaneously feeding the rope through your hands to lower yourself down. Except Duncan forgot to move his feet and as he fed the rope through his hands so his head and body were lower than his feet and within seconds he'd been tipped upside down and was now swinging in mid-air. He let out a blood curdling scream as Pete Kerley locked his grip onto the rope and hauled Duncan back up to the safety of the cliff top.

Unusually there was no piss taking from the rest of us. There certainly wasn't from me as I got called out next.

"Come on then Woody, your turn"

I still had Duncan's screams reverberating in my ears as I got trussed up like a Christmas turkey with all the harnesses, belays, gloves and that pointless helmet. My heart was pumping at twice its normal speed as I kept saying to myself "You can do this; c'mon you can do this" whilst the rest of me was shouting out "No fuckin way". With an audience of a dozen compatriots looking on, all mightily glad it was my turn and not theirs; I had little choice but to shut my eyes and hope. No, don't shut your eyes you idiot. I walked towards the edge and turned to face them. This was the worst bit, that first step backwards with the lean out towards certain oblivion when your brain is screaming at you not to do it. Hands and feet, hands and feet. As I leant out the noise from breaking waves on the rocks below grew louder. I moved down about five feet and stopped. My coordination had gone

"Stand By Ya Beds"

AWOL. I took a few really deep breaths and then started again; hands and feet, hands and feet as I inched my way down. As I looked up all I could see now was the sky and I dare not look down. By now I could hear Russ Parke below me bellowing his instructions. Then the cliff disappeared as I reached the entrance to the cave which meant I had nothing to push my feet against and now just had to use the rope and my hands to abseil free style down towards Dancers Ledge. It seemed to take forever as the sea breeze hit me and I started to swing from side to side. Finally, my feet reached the rock ledge and Russ Parke congratulated me and said something stupid like "There, that wasn't so bad was it?"

As I looked up, I was amazed at how high the cliff was. One by one, including Duncan, the others all made their way down before we walked a couple of hundred yards along the beach towards a set of old wooden steps and back up to the Transit buses. It had been quite a day. Would I do it again? Absolutely no way.

That evening we sat in the big lounge watching TV. As usual the lights had been switched off to aid television viewing which meant the only available light came from the TV itself. I was sat towards the rear of the seated area and I think there must have been about 20 of us in total watching Fawlty Towers. I'd just returned from the tuck shop armed with a pint of Coke and a Bounty bar. I put the Coke, which had been served to me in a traditional one pint beer mug on the floor to my left and settled down to watch Manuel being lambasted by Basil once again. I suddenly became aware of a slurping noise coming from my left. I looked down to see a dog with its head inside my mug, drinking my Coke. I sort of said "Oi" and pushed him away just as all the lights came on in the lounge.

"Who hit my dog?" bellowed Pete Manns who was standing by the door with his hand on the light switch.

"Woody did" came the collective reply together with some fingers pointed in my direction.

"I didn't hit him" I squealed.

"Thirty press ups Cadet Woodward, down you get, but be quick about it, because if you're down there too long Oscar here will try and shag you".

That got more laughs than Basil Fawlty, doubly so when Oscar, a fully grown male Bull Dog started sniffing around my arse as I did the quickest set of press ups in my life.

Oscar and Lucy were Pete Mann's pride and joy. He took great delight in telling us stories about the trials and tribulations of their enforced mating in order to produce litters of baby Bull Dogs that he then sold on. It was obviously a lucrative little business given the amount of times Oscar was expected to perform. I really didn't fancy being his next conquest and quickly took my seat again.

Twice a year CTS hosted Senior Officers Mess Night, based very much on military lines and was no doubt reciprocated by a number of military establishments within Hampshire. Mess Night was an opportunity for the rank of Superintendent and above to dress formally in dinner jackets and dicky bow ties, sit down to a five course meal (not cooked by the Soup Dragon) drink loads and partake in social intercourse, nowadays referred to as networking. High ranking military officers, Judges and the Lord Lieutenant of Hampshire were amongst the guests.

A number of Cadets were specially selected to act as waiters at this little soiree. I wasn't because I wasn't pretty enough obviously. They were dressed in uniform but instead of their tunics had to wear a white jacket and they were paid extra for doing so. Phil Travers was given the task of car park attendant which he wasn't happy about because all the others inside were

"Stand By Ya Beds"

having a good time and he wasn't. Anyway a rather nice blue Rover glided into the grounds and just as Phil was about to stop it so Russ Parke shouted out "Don't stop him Travers, that's the Chief Constable".

Those on waiter duties had to greet the guests with drinks, cigarettes and cigars which were all free. After serving them their meals they had to supervise the passing of the port and were given strict instructions to remove it from one officer who tended to hold onto it. RD Smith acted as the bar steward, which given the fact that all of us were only 16, maybe 17, serving senior coppers alcohol whilst under age was somehow lost in the clouds of cigar smoke.

As the alcohol flowed, so did the contraband of smuggled cigarettes that disappeared via a well organised supply chain that took packets of fags upstairs to our rooms.

As the guests moved from the dining room into the big lounge, they gathered in small groups swapping yarns no doubt. The Chief Constable Sir Douglas Osmond was a very heavy smoker and as he talked to Snoddy he flicked his fag ash onto the floor. She gave him a right old bollocking and he apologised to her for his behaviour. Only Snoddy could have got away with that.

As the evening wore on the Chief instructed Mick Dodds to go and rescue a certain Superintendent from the toilets because he had collapsed into a urinal. Mind you it wasn't long after that the Mick himself had to be carried upstairs to his room because he was shit faced (no pun intended!).

By the time Phil Travers was relieved of his car park duties the party was almost over and he was astonished to see so many drunken officers, one of whom couldn't even climb the half dozen steps from the Games Area up to the lounge.

Broccoli and Bromide

A few nights later news came in that a couple of Cadets who'd been on duty squad had seen a couple of youths in the grounds and when challenged they'd done a runner. Duty squad cover was therefore increased with particular attention being paid to the main building, the pavilion and the car park area. The rear of the main building had a public footpath adjacent to it and separated only by a fairly high hedge and some trees.

Over the next couple of nights a number of sightings were made with a few foot chases taking place but nothing to show for it at the end. About a week after that first incident a brick was thrown through the small lounge window, smashing the glass and landing in the middle of the lounge floor. It had a note taped to it with the word *Pigs* written on it.

The next evening a good number of us were ordered to dress in warm, dark clothing to undertake covert surveillance in and around the grounds of CTS in an effort to detain these insurgents. We were split into pairs and issued with radios. I was teamed up with Chris Cox and our position was a ditch behind the pavilion. It was cold, damp and very dark. From our position all we could see was the rugby pitches, the assault course and the back wall of the pavilion. We were told to maintain radio silence unless we spotted something. After a couple of hours the whole thing was called off because Rob Strong, who was sat in a tree at the bottom of the football pitches decided to light up a fag thus illuminating himself and most of the surrounding area.

By 11pm on the second night we'd been sat in our ditch for the best part of three hours. It was getting colder by the minute and if we had seen anything I doubt my legs could have moved quickly enough. Then the radio crackled into life. Two males in dark clothing were seen lurking behind the grounds man's hut. Then all hell broke loose as Cadets popped up from every nook and cranny and made a bee line for the hut. Then someone shouted they were chasing two around the back of the main building. This was quickly followed by someone else chasing a male around the front of the building, then another out the main gate and down Albert Road, before another one appeared by the tennis courts. This went on for a good five minutes and came straight from an episode of Keystone Cops. Then it got serious as reports came in that one of our number had sustained a nasty injury. We were then all ordered back to the Games Area for a debrief. The injury was to Dick 'Pigeon' Young who had basically garrotted himself on a washing line at the rear of the main building. Whilst running at full speed he was stopped in mid-flight by the washing line that was strategically placed at throat height. During our debrief with Sgt Middleton it was declared that most of those being chased were in fact Cadets being chased by other Cadets. As for the genuine intruders I had my suspicions that it was probably a couple of the instructors and that this was some kind of perverse exercise. All I really knew was that I was still very cold and needed a hot shower to warm me up.

We were all hungry too and it had been hours since we last ate anything. Thankfully the lovely Ella, our favourite dinner lady had left the kitchen door unlocked and so a few of us made our way into the kitchen where I made myself a large pile of peanut butter sandwiches and a mug of hot, steaming coffee. Lovely.

A couple of days later I felt dreadful and for the first time I had to report to sick bay with man flu and a chest infection. I've always suffered with these but this bout seemed particularly bad. Sick bay had a peculiar smell, a sort of mixture of disinfectant and new paint. Snoddy, our resident Matron greeted me like the caring nurse she was. Dressed in an immaculate, starched white medical coat which almost matched her white permed hair, she took my temperature and pulse, listened to my wheezing chest and then told me that she was admitting me and showed me to a side room and my temporary sick bed. She gave me a couple of paracetamol and a bottle of Lucozade and then told me to get some rest.

Broccoli and Bromide

Those were the best words I'd heard since walking through the doors of CTS almost four months ago. I'd been given permission to rest. I can't tell you how good that felt. Not just any old rest, but no morning run, no cross country, no Fareham Tech, no swimming, no ironing, no bulling boots, no room inspection, nothing, just sleep. Bliss. Sadly within 48 hours I was being kicked out and back into the fold of daily life at CTS.

Our daily routine at Fareham Tech still felt like we were back at school, although the staff were a little more relaxed than school teachers. And gradually we started to integrate a lot more with our student colleagues, well not so much the lads, more the girls, one or two of whom could be described as Cadet groupies! Actually, that's a rather unfair label but there were a small group of girls who did like to hang out with the boys in blue. There was Susie-Paul, a rather attractive blond with a set of teeth that rivalled Donny Osmond's and Dawn, who a lot of the lads really fancied, including Andy whose initial chat up line included looking at her across the classroom and giving her the wanker hand gesture! This caused a lot of hilarity and I doubt he will ever be able to explain just why he did it. Mind you not all of the relationships were quite so casual. On my first day in law class, which had a very laid back atmosphere, promoted by our ultra-cool lecturer who looked like Gilbert O'Sullivan's twin brother and who drove a bright yellow Triumph TR6, he insisted we arrange the tables in two rows so we could all sit opposite each other rather than in the traditional classroom manner. Anyway, I sat opposite Kev Mason and he in turn sat next to a very attractive young lady called Jill. From the moment they met it was obvious that they were made for each other. It was quite sweet really and a few years later they got married. I expect she was very impressed with Kevin's digital watch!

It was a Thursday which meant more physical jerks with Roy Scott followed by an hour's torture courtesy of Big Johnny Elkington. After doing a full hour's circuit training with the white

"Stand By Ya Beds"

vested Yorkshire man, including a round of under legs relay followed by that most futile of exercises "Top of the wall bars, gooooo" it was time for a five minute break before the man mountain that was our judo instructor arrived. He was quite often a few minutes late and on this particular day he was very late. So, we started mucking about in the gym having found some abandoned hockey sticks and a tennis ball. An impromptu game of hockey then took place with the ball ricocheting off the walls with lads whacking the ball at shoulder height as if playing baseball. I should have known better. I mean how stupid can you be? It was always going to go wrong. The ball came to Phil Mason. I ran up behind him in an effort to take the ball off him just as he swung his stick backwards straight into my face.

I woke up in the changing room about five minutes later and I was covered in blood. My nose had exploded on impact and it was obviously broken. I could hardly see out of my eyes because they were already swollen. I didn't know what day it was. As I sat up so the blood started to pour from my nostrils again. A toilet roll was thrust into my hands as Phil Mason and a few of the others did their best to convince me that I'd tripped over my own shoe laces and head butted the wall bars! Pissing about in the gym was a capital offence and would have cost us an hour's continuous press ups or worse…….bunny hops all the way into Fareham town centre! Big Johnny Elk came in and demanded to know what was going on. He took one look at me and said he'd arrange transport to get me back to CTS because he didn't want me bleeding all over his floor. Within minutes I'd been poured into a taxi and driven straight to CTS where I walked into Sick Bay to a chorus of sympathetic noises from Snoddy. Another dose of paracetamol followed, together with that magic word rest again, albeit in my own bed this time.

Thursday evening meant just one thing; Top of the Pops. It was compulsory viewing for us 16 year olds, all of whom had been brought up throughout the Glam Rock years on a diet of Slade,

Broccoli and Bromide

The Sweet, T-Rex, Mud, Mott the Hoople, The Glitter Band, Suzi Quattro, Wizzard and Alvin Stardust to name but a few. Queen were a relatively new act with a couple of hits during 1975 like Seven Seas of Rye and Killer Queen but tonight saw the debut showing of their latest single; Bohemian Rhapsody. We'd heard it a couple of times on the radio when travelling to and from Fareham Tech on Eassons coaches but only if old man Easson wasn't listening to Radio 4 instead of Radio 1. So, this was the first time we had seen it on Top of the Pops and it was greeted with a mixture of disdain and bemusement from us all. It'll never catch on.

Along with the music of course came the fashion which most of us were rather partial to. Oxford Bags with large button down side pockets and extra wide waist bands with eight buttons on them, huge butterfly collar shirts and Starsky and Hutch style wrap over cardigans with a matching belt, all finished in brown or cream were *the* clothes to be seen in, just so long as you also smelt of Brut 33.

A couple of weeks later and it was Christmas and we had two weeks off, so it was back to the island for me and a lot more of that rest thing.

But it was all over far too quick and before I knew it me and my Puch were back on the ferry and heading across The Solent to Portsmouth. It was pea soup fog out there and sub-zero temperatures made my 15 mile journey back to Bishops Waltham a somewhat hazardous one. My bike clobber at the time consisted of an open-face helmet, a faux leather flying jacket and a pair of gauntlets. Thankfully I'd recently bought a pair of Lewis Leathers bike boots that were fur lined so at least my feet were warm. Which is more than I can say for the rest of me. My knees were only protected by a pair of jeans so the cold went straight through them and the gauntlets were useless and my hands were so cold I could barely pull the clutch lever in. But it was my face that suffered the most as my nose, which was still somewhat painful from kissing that hockey stick, was running like a tap with snot which then froze to my top lip. I had to peel it all off when I got back to CTS.

As I walked through the door it was lovely and warm and for the first time it felt like a proper home and I was actually glad to be back. I went straight into the kitchen to make me some peanut butter sandwiches and a coffee only to find Ella had baked us a couple of large chocolate cakes and left a note saying help yourselves. She was like a grandmother to us all.

The warmth of CTS was short lived though because within a couple of days half of us were sorting out our walking kit because we were off to the Brecon Beacons in Wales for a few days walking, climbing and abseiling. Thankfully it didn't involve camping as it was deemed rather too cold and so we were being treated to a cottage in a remote place called Dolawyn. Luxury. Which is more than I can say for the long journey there in the back of that Transit, although this was always preferable to being cooped up in the old Landrover.

The Cottage was big enough to sleep 20 people, had decent cooking facilities, bunk beds, comfy old arm chairs and a log fire. That was the upside; the down side was the walking, albeit the distances involved weren't too bad, it just seemed that most of it was uphill. We were warned in advance that the Brecon Beacons was another training area for the SAS and not to approach them if we see them, although quite how we were supposed to recognise them wasn't forthcoming.

Broccoli and Bromide

The cottage in the Brecon Beacons with Chris Cox and Tim Payne

Cold and very windy. Steve Woodward holds onto his hat

"Stand By Ya Beds"

We were also given advice on the effects of hyperthermia and what to do if one of your team became that ill, plus what to do in the event of a white out. I'd never heard of this before but if it snowed and that snow became blizzard conditions then the visibility can become zero and you can very quickly lose your bearings and get lost. This all sounded like a lot of fun. But actually, it wasn't too bad. Although it was bitterly cold with incredibly strong winds as we walked across the Glyders and Carnyd ranges the really bad weather did hold off for us.

Loving the Brecon Beacons are:
Left to right Duncan Warry, Ian Heath, Chris Gosden, Steve Matcham, Paul Forbes and Sgt Gerry Todd with his dog Prince
Photo Dave Brown

The evenings in the cottage were very relaxed with no bull shit involved, especially as our instructors had popped down to a local pub most evenings and left us to our own devices, which probably wasn't a great idea! In their absence it was decided we'd have a fart lighting competition......again. Only this time we were split into two teams who had to nominate one individual to represent the team in the contest. Russ Bramley was chief organiser but ruled himself out of the running. Our two contestants were Al Robertson and Wayne Colebrook......who else. But before it could start we had to give them the right fuel and so several cans of baked beans were found and the two of them tucked into them before they were made to run on the spot and do other 'warm up' exercises in an effort to get their bodies to digest the beans quicker. That was the theory anyway. It wasn't long before the pair of them were stripped down to their underpants and sat on wooden chairs with their feet pressed against a big old pine table armed with a lighter, waiting for nature to run its course. Al's first effort was a bit weak but it still made the rest of us laugh. Then Wayne came in with his first and round one was declared a draw. Al's second effort wasn't much better but then Wayne got very excited as he could feel something brewing. He let rip, flicked the lighter and we watched in awe as a blue and yellow flame measuring a good 12 inches shot out of his arse to howls of laughter from the rest of us and Wayne was declared the winner. His prize was a tin of beans.

As we climbed into our bunks our spirits were still sky high and it wasn't long before someone started telling ghost stories, but not until all the lights had been turned off to help with the atmosphere. By now we'd fallen silent as the story reached its climax. Suddenly there was a knock at one of the windows which made us all jump but as Russ pulled back the curtains by his bed so he screamed like a girl because there was a face at the window. We all fell about laughing again as Russ was truly spooked but on closer inspection it transpired that the face had been sprayed on with shaving foam. No one owned up to doing it though.

"Stand By Ya Beds"

On one of the walks Gibby and RD Smith found something that they thought might assist them complete a section of the walk a lot faster than usual. At the top of a very steep hill they found an old motor bike with no engine, leaning against a fence post. They clambered aboard and then free wheeled it all the way down the track that led to the bottom of the hill almost half a mile away. Needless to say, they giggled all the way down. But we found out later that the bike actually had an owner; a farmer, who would push it up the hill each morning and leave it by a post so that come the evening, after a long day working in the fields he could just hop on the bike and cruise back down the hill and home. Except on this particular day.

RD and Gibby are still wanted for TWC
Photo Richard Smith

Back at CTS the daily grind of morning run, Fareham Tech, lots of physical mixed in with uniform inspections etc just became the norm, we were now so used to it that it was now second nature to everyone. But it wasn't all rosy in the Woodward/Goward suite. We'd been getting on each other's nerves for a while now, no idea why, but Andy irritated the shit out of me and vice versa. It all came to a head one Wednesday morning as we were preparing for the weekly room inspection. I'd just returned from the shower block and as I entered the room I accidentally brushed against Andy's bed pack and moved it slightly out of line.

"For fucks sake" he shouted out "How would you like it if I did that to yours?" and he strode across the room and turned mine 90 degrees.

That was like a red rag to a bull for me and a huge argument ensued during which I marched over to his bed and booted his bed pack half way up the wall. Andy then tried barging past me to get at mine again but I blocked his way and as we tussled in the middle of the room he managed to lash out with his leg and kicked my bed pack onto the floor where it split wide open. I had hold of his arm and sort of swung him around which resulted in us both falling to the floor where we wrestled each other for a good two minutes whilst wearing our best number one uniform. He got me into a head lock and my only means of attack now was to grab a handful of his inner thigh which I can assure you hurts like hell. As he let out a sort of muffled aarrggghhh our door opened and in marched Tony Astill and Inspector Chadwick. We'd obviously missed the shout of "Stand by'ya beds". We both lay there motionless on our backs looking up at the pair of them.

"When you two girls have finished romping on the floor with each other perhaps you'd be kind enough to get up and sort

"Stand By Ya Beds"

ya'selves out. Now move it you fucking wankers, you've got two minutes until we come back" bellowed Tony Astill.

With that the door slammed shut and Andy and I leapt to our feet, sorted our bed packs out as best we could, tucked our shirts in, brushed our uniforms down and were ready, stood to attention just as the door came flying open again. We hadn't said a word to each other and stood there huffing and puffing as if we'd just returned from doing two laps of the cross-country course.

"We are in deep, deep shit" I thought to myself.

Tony Astill and Mr Chadwick came in, walked around, looked us up and down, stood directly in front of us as if we were in some kind of staring competition to see who would blink first. I lost. I was waiting to be bellowed at in the face, but they just kept walking around us and said absolutely nothing, which was even more unnerving. Then the door opened and they left. Just as it shut it came flying open again and Astill popped his head back in and just said "You wankers" and left again.

We waited a couple of seconds until we knew they were next door and both burst out laughing but tried muting it as best we could. How the hell did we get away with that one? I wasn't entirely convinced that we had and reckoned they would punish us at some point in the future. But for now, Andy and I had cleared the air.

The day after my 17th birthday I walked into Bob Golners Kawasaki dealership in Denmead and traded in my 50cc Puch for a brand new Kawasaki KH250 triple in candy apple red. This was a proper motorcycle and not a sports moped and it felt great. I couldn't really afford it at £539 but that really didn't matter. I also bought a brand new Belstaff jacket and a full face crash helmet in metallic silver.....very 1970s. I wasn't the only Cadet to get hooked on bikes either. Chris Cox had a gold Honda CB250 G5, Malcolm 'Wolfie' Smith also had a Honda CB250, Andy Crawford and Paul Rowsell both had Honda XL125 trail bikes, Andy Goward arrived on a gold coloured Yamaha DT175 and Duncan Warry kept the embers of the British bike industry alight with his Triumph Tiger Cub and deplored the fact that we all rode "Jap crap" and should be supporting the British bike industry. Chris Gosden and Steve Matcham both rode Honda CD175's and Wayne Howsego chose a rather rare Harley Davidson SS250 trial bike in bright orange.

Steve Woodward and new Kawasaki

Meanwhile the likes of Steve Poselthwaite and Jim Humphries were the only two Cadets to have passed their car tests early enough and both purchased Minis.

"Stand By Ya Beds"

Andy had a bit of a problem with his Yamaha in that it would only tick over at 10,000 rpm and his mechanical knowledge, like the rest of us was sub-zero. But Larry Dwyer reckoned he could fix it. A small group of us had gathered in the pavilion car park basically taking the piss out of Andy's bike. Picture the scene. Andy is standing to the right of the bike whilst Larry is on the left. Larry instructs Andy to start the bike. Andy turns the ignition key which is situated in the usual place in between the two clocks on the handlebars, kicks it over and it immediately screams at 10,000 rpm. Larry then asks if the revs reduce if it's put into gear but Andy doesn't know as he hasn't tried it. So, Larry pulls the clutch lever in and pops the bike into first gear. The revs immediately go higher and straight through the red line. Fearing the engine is about to explode Larry stupidly took his hand off the clutch in order to make a grab for the ignition key and the bike literally took off and did a backwards summersault before crashing to the ground still screaming like a Banshee.

There were a couple of other minor incidents regarding bikes. A few of us went out for a ride one evening over towards Corhampton during which I completely misjudged a bend and ended up riding through a hedge and into a corn field. Meanwhile Paul Rowsell, who had RD Smith on the back of his bike got knocked off by a horse in Wickham and as if that wasn't funny enough picture this; Nigel French owned a Yamaha FS1E. Now Frenchie was a big lad and the Fizzy struggled a bit with him on it. So when Rowse hitched a lift from him one day the result was…….well, I'm sure you can imagine.

Music was still important to most of us and there were two songs in particular at this time in 1976 that had us singing to A Glass of Champagne from Sailor and best of all was I'm Mandy, Fly Me by 10cc. It seemed like these two songs were on the radio every time we were on the coach to or from Fareham Tech. Turn the radio up driver!

Broccoli and Bromide

It was just after lights out one night when there was an impromptu room inspection because someone had either lost or had a watch stolen. Each House instructor took on the responsibility of searching the rooms of their students. Tony Astill burst into the room occupied by Paul Williams and Colin Smith and shouted out "Stand by 'ya beds". They'd both been reading porn magazines that the mother of Pauls girlfriend had given him to distribute at CTS after she'd found them at the boarding school she worked at! They leapt out of their beds leaving the magazines behind which Tony Astill seized immediately.

No watch was ever found during our enforced cell shake down but the next day Paul Williams found himself stood in front of Mr Chadwick and we all know his thoughts on having such material at CTS. He gave Paul a right bollocking and then said he would be writing a letter to Pauls father about his behaviour and would enclose the magazines to make an example of him. So, Paul phoned his Dad to let him know. He laughed and said he'd pass them onto his work mates and that they would appreciate the gift. Apparently, no letter or magazines ever arrived at the William's household. I wonder who ended up with them then?

It didn't help that at Fareham Tech we had our very own soft porn star in Maria Eldridge, a very attractive tall blonde who John Gunner had to sit next to every time he attended his Social Studies class. She had appeared in a six-page centre spread in Penthouse magazine and it goes without saying that she was the talk of the college for a long time and it brought a whole new meaning to Johns Social Studies class.

John liked her for other reasons though because Maria introduced him to her best mate, a younger but equally gorgeous young lady who John dated for several months. He says dated, but actually they just went for walks during break time or had lunch together. One Friday evening she took John home to meet her

"Stand By Ya Beds"

parents and he obviously thought that the relationship was getting serious. To his horror it transpired that her father was a serving Chief Inspector! John was terrified. However, that evening, thinking he was onto a winner he kissed the girl and as he groped her, she slapped him hard across the face and said she wasn't that kind of girl and that was the end of that.

Football rivalry is usually fairly good natured amongst friends and colleagues but can sometimes be rather painful if the teams concerned are Portsmouth and Southampton, both of which were in the old second division at this time. In April they faced each other in the league and for our two resident Pompey fans in Duncan Warry and John Gunner it was agony because Southampton won, one nil. That was bad enough but within a couple of weeks Southampton faced the mighty Manchester United in the FA Cup final at Wembley which most of us watched live in the big lounge. All of a sudden it seemed that most of CTS had become Southampton supporters except Duncan and John of course. The result was hard for them to take and the piss taking was merciless.

Our neighbours next door were a constant source of amusement unless they were jobbing our room of course. I lost count of the number of times we could hear raucous laughter coming from them, in fact it was more unnerving if it was quiet because it usually meant they were plotting something. But if it was laughter, we would invariably get to hear about it at breakfast the next morning. On this particular morning Russ treated us to the details of Phil Masons latest escapade and was laughing before he'd even started. For reasons that no-one in the room could fathom Phil had decided to erect a two man tent in the middle of the room just before lights out. Just after 10.30 their door opened and in popped Tony Astill to be greeted by the sight of the tent with just Phils head sticking out with the zip pulled down across his throat. Tony Astill looked at Phil, said nothing, shut the door and left.

It was Friday evening and I was going home for the weekend. It was pleasantly warm and me and the Kawasaki flew down through Fareham and into Pompey where I stopped at the Sea Link ferry terminal to catch the 1800 car ferry to Fishbourne. The old terminal at the Camber Docks had seen better days. It was cramped and necessitated vehicles doing a sharp left turn from the car park and down the concrete ramp to the ferry once it had docked. To the side of the ramp was a deep water channel that usually had a couple of decent sized fishing trawlers moored up. Motorcycles were usually the first vehicles allowed onto the ferry and so we were always directed to park at the front of the car park.

There was at least another 15 minutes before the ferry came in and so I lay back on the seat with my feet dangling over the handlebars to have a little snooze. Well it had been a long week. I'd been there about five minutes I suppose when I thought I heard a cry for help. The docks area is busy with vehicle traffic, with additional noise from the harbour, the nearby train station and dozens of squawking sea gulls. I must be hearing things. But no, there it is again; very faint but definitely someone calling for help. I sat up and listened more intently. I heard it again and this time my senses said it was coming from one of the adjacent trawlers. I got off the bike and looked over the wall towards the water; nothing. Another cry for help but louder this time. It was definitely coming from the area of the trawler which was moored on the other side of the dock. I ran around the dock to the trawler and looked down onto its deck, but couldn't see anything. Then another cry for help. I looked down and there, in the water, trapped between the trawler and the wall was a young boy aged about 10. He was really struggling to stay afloat and I didn't have time to summon any help. There was a rusty metal ladder bolted to the side of the wall and I had no choice but to climb down it. I took my heavy bike jacket off and climbed down about six or seven feet but reached the bottom of the ladder. The water was at least another two feet further down I suppose and the boy was about five or six feet to my left. I told him that I was going to lower myself down a bit further and that he would have to jump across and grab my boots and then hang on as I climbed back up. There was no discussion about it, there wasn't time. I lowered myself down another couple of rungs and my feet were now in the water with me gripping the ladder as tightly as I could. I shouted at him to jump and thankfully he grabbed my left foot first time with both hands and I heaved myself back up the ladder. It brought a whole new meaning to the words "Top of the wall bars…GO". He clung on until I got to the top of the ladder but then I could feel him slipping. By now I'd been joined by another bloke and I asked him to grab my right hand to support me as I leant down and got hold of the boy's hand and heaved him up so he could put his feet on the ladder. I then pushed him up to the safety of the dock side before climbing back up myself. Maybe all the physical we'd been doing had paid off?

"Why were you down there?" I asked.

"I dropped me ball" and with that he produced a small rubber ball from his pocket.

I asked him where he lived and he pointed back up the High Street so I told him to get himself home and out of those wet clothes. With that he legged it. By now the ferry was coming in and if our ball boy was still down there I have little doubt that the wash from the ferry would have pushed the trawler hard against the wall with obvious consequences. I need a fag.

The following Thursday had been the usual daily routine, morning run, Fareham Tech, uniform prep in the evening mixed in with some homework before an hour's TV and a couple of snacks from the tuck shop. After watching about half of News at Ten I wondered upstairs to have a quick shower before I hit the hay. Duly scrubbed clean I came out of the shower cubicle and was busily drying myself when I heard someone calling for help. Bloody hell not again. I must be hearing things. Then I heard it again in conjunction with a knock at the window. But I'm on the first floor about 20 feet above the ground. Then I saw a figure outside the window sort of swinging from side to side. I went over and pushed the sash window upwards. I was greeted by Phil Mason, bollock naked, abseiling down the side of the building!

"Phil what the fuck are you doing?"

"I need the practice Woody" he replied with his trade mark grin.

"And the doing it naked thing, what's that all about?" I laughed.

"Oh I hadn't noticed" said Phil and with that he continued his abseil down to ground level. I watched him unclip himself from the harness and just shook my head in disbelief and then thought how lucky I'd been that no-one else had come into the shower block at the very moment I was stood at the window naked whilst looking outside at a naked Phil on the end of a rope.

So, I grabbed my stuff and was heading back to my room when I saw Russ Parke at the other end of the corridor.

"What are you doing up after lights out Mr Woodward?" he shouted.

"I was just taking a shower Sir" I replied. I could hardly tell him why I'd been delayed.

"You're duty squad this weekend aren't you?" he asked

"Yes Sir"

"I'll have some extra duties for you then. Now get to bed" he shouted.

Andy didn't come out to see what all the fuss was about this time and how the hell did Phil get back into his room before Russ Parke arrived?

"Stand By Ya Beds"

Come Friday evening Russ Parke wasn't around for some reason so I hoped he'd forgotten. How wrong was I? As I sat eating my breakfast Saturday morning in he came and plonked a pair of nail scissors on the table.

"The cricket pitch needs cutting" he said with a dead pan face.

This has got to be a wind up surely? Cut the grass on the cricket pitch with a pair of nail scissors?

"You can have an hour for your lunch and you can finish at 1600. I'll be checking on you from time to time so don't let me find you skiving off." With that he turned and walked off.

I must have really pissed him off somehow. It was a very warm day, the sky was blue and the sun was shining, just the sort of day you need when trimming a bloody cricket pitch……..with a pair of scissors! Off I trudged down to the playing fields where I sat down on the edge of the wicket, completely and utterly demoralised and started to snip a few blades of grass, which already looked like Mr Parke had given it a grade 1 with his hair cutting razor anyway. What is the point in this I kept saying to myself with a few choice expletives thrown in for good measure? By lunchtime I think I'd cut about an inch of grass, if that. It was getting hot now and I could feel the sun burning my neck. By mid-afternoon I was just sat there day dreaming. I moved my arms every now and then, just in case I was being watched from somewhere and at bang on 1600 I was off up that embankment and into the relative sanctuary of CTS to grab some shade. Utterly pointless…….but I'll never get caught out like that again.

A week or so later and we were on parade outside the Games Area. Mr Chadwick's weekly inspection was over and the extremely affable Sgt Middleton took over proceedings as the Inspector went back to his office.

"The following Cadets have been specially selected to represent the Hampshire Constabulary at an extremely prestigious event and the staff here have found it rather difficult in selecting suitable candidates, so without further ado, step forward the following; Cadets Goward, Woodward, Brown, Humphries, Dabbs, King, MH Smith, Howsego and Dwyer.

This sounds good I thought, I like the specially selected part.

Sgt Middleton continued "Congratulations, you will be taking part in the Regional Police Dog Trials in Winchester next Wednesday and Thursday. I believe they need volunteers to put those sleeves on and then try out running the dogs during their annual contests. You lot should be super fit by now so you shouldn't have too much difficulty getting away. And if you don't, well, it's been nice knowing you all" he said with a smirk as the rest of our colleagues burst out laughing.

We all looked at each other with pained expressions on our faces. I think we'd all gone from feeling rather elated to completely deflated in less than 30 seconds. The thought of being mauled by a hungry Alsatian was not something I was relishing to be honest. They wouldn't do that to us would they? Really? We had a whole week to worry about it.

So, the following Wednesday we got bussed up to some army barracks just outside Winchester where the air was rife with the sound of barking canines waiting in police vans from forces like Sussex, Kent, Dorset, Thames Valley, Devon and Cornwall, Hampshire of course and Essex. We were dressed in our oldest clothes which kind of had us believing that yes, we were that expendable. If we'd been ordered to wear uniform then we could have expected to be on some kind of security patrol or car park duties or something equally as 'important' but no, we were in scruff kit which could only mean one thing?

"Stand By Ya Beds"

We were eventually ushered into a room where we were briefed by an Inspector who seemed to be running the whole thing. Basically, over the next two days Police dog handlers from all over the south would be taking part in a competition, during which they would be judged on various aspects of their work, from following trails, to locating lost objects, obedience, agility tests and prisoner take downs. We all knew what that meant.

"Your job though," he continued. Here it comes I thought. "Will be to act as an unruly mob, which from what I've heard you'll be extremely good at" he laughed. "You will act as football hooligans whereby you will shout and scream at the handler and his dog whilst he attempts to control you for one minute. Once you have calmed down the handler will then be instructed to walk amongst you with his dog on a leash, the idea being that the dog should have enough self-control that it doesn't lash out and bite one of you"

"Oh great."

He went on that we would be required to undertake this mob behaviour about 20 times over the next two days. In between times we were at liberty to watch the other events.

Within the hour we were taken outside to face our first German Shepherd and his handler. We formed a tightly knit group and commenced our hollering, shouting and verbal abuse as the dog, straining at the leash with his front paws off the ground barked and snarled at us as if we were his next meal. This went on for one minute before we got the signal to stop. We were then ordered to spread out a little bit, leaving just enough room for the dog and his handler to walk through and around the group a couple of times. It's no lie, we were shitting ourselves.

And it didn't get any easier as the day went on. Not knowing the dog or the handler somehow made it worse. By day two it became apparent that some of the Hampshire dog handlers were very unhappy with one of their colleagues and his dog. Unusually it wasn't a German Shepherd but a Giant Schnauzer, which looked like a used Brillo pad that had just scrubbed a filthy black frying pan. For some reason they didn't like the handler or the dog, with one of the 'runners' accusing it of biting him in the arse and not the arm as it was trained to do. The others were warning us that during tomorrows mob exercise it was very likely that the Giant Schnauzer would take a lump or two out of our legs!

On day two we got to face this strange looking dog. It was a big powerful looking thing but its bark was no-where near as ferocious as many of its competitors. Come the time of the walk through I swear we were almost standing to attention, not daring to breathe, let alone move. To be fair the dog was as good as gold and we all let out a collective sigh of relief as they left the group. It had been an interesting couple of days and came as light relief from the daily routine at CTS.

It was nice to get away from CTS food at this time. Breakfast was always good but lunch on Wednesdays and most evening meals were stodge and often rather unpalatable. The complaints were getting louder and more frequent much to the disgust of the Soup Dragon, but always to the amusement of Ella. She was quite mischievous really. If we did get really hungry we could always pop down the road to the Little Chef and if we could afford it, treat ourselves to an Olympic breakfast or a mixed grill. It wasn't unusual, especially around pay day to find little groups of hungry Cadets indulging in such culinary delights.

On Wednesdays the likes of football, rugby and hockey gave way to field and track events with a sort of sports day being planned for the force's annual Families Day where a number of events would be show cased for the visitors to marvel at.

"Stand By Ya Beds"

The Cadet Life Saving Team consisted of the very best swimmers from our intake and we did have some that could swim like a fish including Al Robertson, Paul Forbes, Howard Marrs, Russ Bramley and MH Smith and they were entered into a number of competitions including one in Christchurch. Before they headed there Russ Parke shaved all their heads to make them more aerodynamic in the water apparently and they were all provided with matching black Speedos with yellow flashes on them. Very smart!

The scenario was that a helicopter had crashed some 30 yards off shore and the lifesaving teams had to run in and save the casualties from the wreck that had been placed just beneath the surface and they would be judged on speed of response and rescue, life saving techniques, mouth to mouth etc. Howard Marrs was the first CTS life saver into the water and came out of the wreck towing a body. He stopped when the water got shallower and gave mouth to mouth, showing great technique. He then dragged the body to the shore and continued to give mouth to mouth and it all looked very impressive. As Howard got the body onto the shore line so a judge came over with his clip board, said nothing to Howard and just pointed to the body's forehead that had the word …….DEAD written on it.

They were later entered into a rather prestigious inter-force competition hosted by the Met Police at an indoor pool somewhere in London. The teams were instructed that for the purposes of today's exercise the shore line would be the front edge of the pool with the far end and the two sides being classed as 'open sea' in other words all of your casualties are to be brought to the front of the pool.

First up for Hampshire was MH Smith who swam out, grabbed a body, tugged him and immediately dragged him to the side of the pool where he attempted to lift him out of the water. During the struggle the man was somehow turned over as Mick now continued to push him upwards but the small of the man's back was now stuck on the edge of the pool and he was screaming in agony. Meanwhile Paul Forbes dived in and swam out to a female who was treading water. Forbsey took his trouser belt off to use as a towing aid and as he got close to the girl he shouted out " Hello my love, I've got something here for you to get hold of". There were howls of laughter from the watching audience and Forbsey then realised what he'd said and couldn't help but laugh himself whilst spluttering water all over his casualty. Whilst all this was going on Micks victim was still screaming in pain and as the Hampshire effort was sinking faster than the Titantic Russ Bramley turned to Pete Kerley who just shrugged his shoulders and said "Hey ho, it's an away day………oh look at that (as a female walked past them in a swim suit) she's got some fluff coming out the sides; needs a shave that one".

After a weekend back on the island I picked up Adrian Prangnell on my bike to take him back to CTS. I wasn't used to taking passengers to be honest and the short journey from Newport to the ferry at Fishbourne had us wobble a little bit on the island's awful roads but nothing really untoward. But as we rode through Portsmouth, negotiating a couple of roundabouts and bends, the bike was all over the place. I thought I might have a puncture or the suspension settings were too soft but they all seemed fine. It wasn't too bad on the straight but as soon as I leant it left or right the handling went to pot. As we approached the village of Waltham Chase there's a decent double bend to get through. As I took the first left hander the bike wallowed and pitched like never before and as I took the right hander, I caught a glimpse of Praggers in my rear view mirror and he was leaning the wrong way! It transpired he'd never been pillion on a bike before and thought you had to lean in the opposite direction to the rider!

As we headed towards the summer things at CTS did seem to be getting slightly more relaxed. The discipline was still there and we'd all learned a thing or two about self-discipline that had been

"Stand By Ya Beds"

drummed into us from day one, so much of our behaviour was now second nature. The instructors often called us by our first names or nick names which was nice and the overall atmosphere was a bit more pleasant. So much so that Pete Kerley asked a few of us one evening if we'd like to join him in a little canoeing trip along the River Hamble. Don't mind if we do. Most of Rowan House tagged along and we hitched the trailer full of canoes onto the back of a Transit and headed down to the river a few miles away.

I'm not a great lover of canoeing to be honest, not for any particular reason, it's just not something I'd do off my own back. But at least the weather was on our side. It was one of those perfectly still, summer evenings and very warm. We clambered aboard our canoes and commenced a gentle paddle up stream, following Pete Kerley. It was perfect; the water was like a mirror, the sound of Mallard ducks and Moorhens could be heard everywhere as they darted in and out of the reeds along the embankments and every now and then one of our lot would crack a joke or take the piss out of someone which added to the atmosphere. About half a mile after travelling underneath the M27 motorway bridge Pete Kerley headed towards the far bank and a wooden jetty……by a pub. He'd told us to bring a couple of quid because we might need it but none of us were expecting this. He's not taking us for a drink surely? He certainly was.

After depositing the canoes on some grass we sat outside The Jolly Sailor overlooking the Hamble with pints of lager and lime in our hands, desperately trying to act like grown-ups! I said right from the beginning that Rowan House had fallen on its feet having Pete Kerley as our instructor and I was right. This was a real treat and meant that he trusted us not to cock it up by being stupid. He started telling us tales of his time in the job when he was more front line than he is now and each of his stories was interspersed with his trademark sayings of "F'kin arseholes" or "You will get this".

Broccoli and Bromide

After an hour or so and two pints, it was time to head on back. I have to confess I was feeling rather light headed and I wasn't the only one. By the time we got to the motorway bridge we were all over the place. My canoe kept veering to the left, no idea why! It was impossible to keep it in a straight line and all of us were giggling like little girls. When we eventually reached the relative safety of the shoreline from whence we had started, getting out of a canoe when half cut is no easy task let me tell you. Cue more giggling.

After any canoe trip you are obliged to turn it upside down to drain out any water and dependant on the size of your canoe it will dictate whether or not you require the help of a colleague. It's at this stage in the book that I have to tell you that it's taken Russ Bramley more than 40 years to confess to the following. Whilst paddling back down the Hamble Russ was caught short (no pun intended!) as it didn't take long for two pints to travel through him! Try as he might he couldn't hold onto it so just let it all go inside the canoe. The relief was palpable and rather warm and I think all of us can identify with that feeling. Anyway, once back on dry land it was Pete Kerley who came to aid Russ tip out the contents of his canoe. Only when they were lifting it up and down to get it all out, most of the 'water' landed on Pete Kerley! To this day he never knew. Until now.

For the last couple of years CTS had hosted what was to became known as the Force Families Day where the force would throw open its doors to the family and friends of serving and retired officers to treat them to all the usual summer fete type events like cake sales, morris dancers, throwing a wet sponge at some local bod in the stocks, all the usual classic old English attractions. Plus, for this year us Cadets would be putting on a number of displays including the sports day with full track and field events, gymnastics display and a display in the art of judo. Two of the judo team included Russ Bramley and Adrian

"Stand By Ya Beds"

Prangnell. You already know that if Brammers and Praggers are involved its going to go wrong somehow, especially as they had decided to completely ignore their brief and make their bit of the display a little more dramatic.

A good number of crash mats had been laid out and a large number of ladies with hats were sat on rickety old chairs around the outside whilst full commentary on the display was given to the watching spectators as they sipped their tea from china cups and saucers. Enter Cadet Bramley who ran and dived head first over the top of five other Cadets who were kneeling down and then did a neat forward roll and sprang back to his feet. It wasn't quite Evil Knievel but raised some serious applause. Then Russ and Praggers got together on the mat and demonstrated a couple of throws to more applause.

"Cadet Prangnell will now demonstrate a choke hold on Cadet Bramley" said the commentator as Praggers grabbed the judo suit lapels on Russ's jacket and twisted them across his throat. Russ struggled to breathe and slowly went down on his knees. The stirring of tea cups had now stopped. As Praggers pushed hard down onto Russ's neck, looking like a suicidal maniac so Russ was going a bright shade of red. As he held his breath his veins started to bulge and he was now making all manner of choking noises. There was total silence from the audience, their cups now frozen close to their mouths, which were wide open. Russ then collapsed to the side as if Praggers had literally strangled him, before leaping back to his feet. They got enthusiastic applause from a couple of 10 year old boys but complete silence from the Derby and Joans who looked rather shocked.

Towards the end of the day a number of presentations were made for various achievements on the sports field plus the Ten Tors team.

Broccoli and Bromide

Sports Day presentations made by ACC Wilkinson to Mick Dodds for 100m and 200m, Andy Worship Cross Country, Phil Travers 1500m walk, Andy Reed 400m and Steve Matcham, 1500m.
Photo Hampshire Constabulary

Presentation was also made to the Ten Tors Team, left to right; Paul Diaper, Tony Hastings, Wayne Colebrook, ACC Wilkinson, Steve Smale, Andy Crawford and Malcolm Smith

"Stand By Ya Beds"

Presentation of certificates for various sports, left to right;
Colin Smith, Paul Williams, Andy Worship, ACC Wilkinson, Kev Willis,
Tim Beazley and Chris Porter.

Presentation of walking cup to Phil Travers by ACC Wilkinson
Photo Hampshire Constabulary

Mick Dodds collected the overall athletics team trophy on behalf of Fielding House from the Chairman of the Hampshire Police Federation Taff Parry

There was one final award; Cadet of the Year 1975/76 which went to Malcolm 'Wolfie' Smith who was presented with the McCarthy Trophy by Chief Inspector Rowthorne. Wolfie was so proud of being a Hampshire Police Cadet and to prove the point he and I together with Chris Cox rode our bikes to the East End of London a few months later, to visit the pub where Coxy's brother was the landlord. It was a real spit and sawdust place in some back street with some very unsavoury looking clientele. As we entered, I noticed Wolfie was wearing his Belstaff bike jacket which had a large Hampshire Police Cadet badge sewn onto it. He refused point blank to hide it and Chris and I remained on edge throughout our visit, convinced we were going to get filled in.

Cadet of the Year Trophy
Photo Malcolm Smith

We were nearing the end of our residency at CTS when we were instructed to get into our best clobber because we were being taken out to a local disco. The shower blocks were kept extremely busy and the smell of Brut 33 filled the air as 17 year old lads, filled to the brim with testosterone, boarded two of Easson's finest coaches and headed out the gates of CTS for a wild night out. Where are we heading then? Southampton probably? Portsmouth maybe? Winchester? No, not Winchester there's nothing there. We were on our normal route towards Fareham Tech, so it could be Portsmouth then. But no, just before we entered Wickham the coaches slowed down and then turned right into the grounds of a Catholic Nunnery! This has got to be a wind up? There was a mixture of nervous laughter and incredulity that our big night out was to be held in a fucking nunnery!

Broccoli and Bromide

As the coaches drew up outside the front of the building, that bore an uncanny resemblance to CTS, so Sgt Middleton rose to his feet to address us.

"Gentlemen, don't look so despondent, I've been assured that you will receive a very warm welcome from the young ladies here, all of whom have been residents for as long as you have at Bishops Waltham. It goes without saying that as representatives of the Hampshire Constabulary you will be expected to be on your best behaviour throughout the evening. Relax, enjoy yourselves, the coaches leave here at exactly 2300, so don't be late, it's a long walk back to CTS".

We headed into the building and were ushered into the main hall that was rather dimly lit. There were a few tables and chairs scattered about and so most of us found somewhere to sit, still shaking our heads in disbelief. A few girls entered the hall, followed by a couple of dozen more, all of them wearing grey smock dresses, which made them look just like Julie Andrews! They all stood on the opposite side of the hall and just stared at us as we stared back. This was a scene straight out of the film The Dirty Dozen where on their last night before being parachuted behind enemy lines they were 'treated' to an evening's entertainment from some local good time girls. Except I don't think our girls were of the same calibre.

The music got going and it was nearly an hour before anyone moved. Eventually a few of them dared to venture out onto the dance floor. A few of our more confident lads went over to join them but most of us and most of them to be fair stayed put. It was excruciating. Its not like we weren't used to seeing females, as there were plenty of them at Fareham Tech, it was more the fact that two groups of complete strangers had been thrown together in a nunnery of all places and almost ordered to have a good time. We were also convinced that one or two of our instructors were probably in a back room somewhere getting pissed with Mother Theresa.

A few days later we were on parade outside the Games Area with Sgt Middleton doing the honours, so it was all quite relaxed. Once inspection was over he read out a few bits and pieces from his clip board before putting it down to one side and calling out.

"Cadet Humphries take two steps forward".

Jim Humphries jumped to attention and marched out the front.

"Cadet Humphries do you still own a white Mini?" enquired Sgt Middleton.

"Yes Sir" he replied.

"Could you explain why it's currently laying on its side down by the assault course?"

"Well......I was pissed Sir" replied Jim.

Now Jim was a strange lad with a rather weird sense of humour. In fact you never knew when he was being serious and when he was taking the piss. You could sometimes tell because of the glint in his eye. But today none of us was quite sure. Neither was Sgt Middleton who was rendered completely and utterly speechless by Jim's response.

Getting pissed of course is what most 17 year olds like to do but for us it was quite difficult. Bishops Waltham was a quiet village with only a couple of pubs. We couldn't use the Railway Inn because it was literally 200 yards from the gate and was the local watering hole for many of the staff so if we did venture out it was into the village itself where we found the White Swan, or the Mucky Duck as it got nick named, was more to our liking. It was a real spit and sawdust kind of place and even though the landlord probably knew we were under age he served us our lager and lime anyway. God forbid we ever got caught though.

It was around this time that we were getting ready for a Wednesday morning inspection down on the main car park by the pavilion. It was all very relaxed and we were in rather high spirits for some reason. Our inspecting officers were late arriving and so we decided that Nick Griggs would drill us whilst we waited. It was all very silly with him barking out orders which we either ignored or deliberately got wrong and there was a definite outbreak of morale. Then a car arrived and parked nearby. It was the Soup Dragon. Nick then brought us all to attention and gave the order that as soon as she stepped out of her car that we were to burst out laughing. It was a bit juvenile but incredibly funny at the same time. She didn't look too pleased, which made it all the funnier. God knows what we'll be getting for dinner tonight.

Our O Level and A Level exams at Fareham Tech were now over as was our full time residency at CTS. It was time to pack up and say goodbye to that little room and everything we regarded as home for the last 10 months. Although really tough at times I'd thoroughly enjoyed my time at CTS and I was quite sad to be leaving it all behind, although we would be returning every now and then for various courses in the future. After dumping all my stuff at home on the Friday I was back there first thing Monday morning because it was time for our one week summer camp on Dartmoor.

I think this was our fourth trip to Dartmoor and I have to say the thought of putting those boots back on again filled me with utter dread. After a four hour drive in the Transits we arrived at our base camp where we sorted out our kit ready for tomorrow's little walk; three nights and four days. Our base camp was a nice little grassed area with a sizeable stream running around the

"Stand By Ya Beds"

outside edge. In the evening sun in July 1976 it seemed rather idyllic as we sat around in various groups just chilling for a change.

The summer expedition was a big deal and rather than doing it with those from our own Houses we had been split into different groups because each house had a number of Cadets that were taking part in the gruelling Ten Tors expedition. I was put with Duncan Warry, Andy Worship, Paul Williams, Mick Streeter and Adrian Cleighton-Hills, so a good bunch of lads. What made this expedition slightly different was that we had homework to do en route. We were each given a topic to research on our travels. Mine was the different types of grass to be found on Dartmoor. Fascinating.

The first day was spent rock climbing, abseiling and orienteering, which was all very relaxed and good fun. But the fun had only just begun because that evening we all got bussed into Plymouth city centre where Pete Manns and Pete Kerley took us to the cinema to watch........Emmanuelle starring Sylvia Krystal as a nymphomaniac that most of us 17 year olds would be scared shitless with! It was an X rated film which had a very corny storyline, ie girl gets shagged everywhere she goes within five minutes of meeting someone, set to equally corny 1970s cinema music and which today is considered so tame that it wouldn't even get a daytime viewing on Channel 4 and yet back then was banned for a while. Being treated to an X film was a first for many of us and the testosterone levels went through the roof and of course there was lots of piss taking on exiting the cinema about who had or hadn't still got a huge erection.

The next morning I commenced my well-rehearsed routine to protect my feet. Armed with a box of broad elastoplasts, I cut large sections to place around my heels and smaller pieces to wrap around my big toes. Then I put on two pairs of thick woollen walking socks to protect them further. I was determined to look after them as best I could. So, with ruck sack packed it was time to head off across the moors in the early morning sun. We were advised to drink plenty of water and to ensure we had good supplies of Kendall mint cake and tubes of Dextrosol tablets, all of which were great energy boosters. I really liked the bars of mint cake, a sort of cross between a flap-jack and a stick of rock, they came in a variety of flavours. The Dextrosol were more like a packet of Refreshers sweets, just a bit bigger.

We set off in our respective groups and it wasn't long before I could feel the skin on my heels starting to pull but it wasn't too bad to be honest, so maybe the precautions I'd taken were working this time, or my feet had toughened up at long last. The first day's walk was not only rather pleasant but relatively easy. Shit, I'm actually enjoying it.

Out on the town; top left to right, Wayne Colebrook, Phil Travers and Al Robertson.
Centre row, left to right, Phil Mason, Trevor Murphy, Gary Keeble, Duncan Warry, Wayne Howsego, Andy Goward and Paul Sexton.
Front row crouching down, Nigel French and Steve Woodward

"Stand By Ya Beds"

We made camp next to a small river and set about cooking our evening meal which loosely resembled some kind of stew. I then set about making desert which tonight consisted of lime flavoured instant whip, made, not with milk, but with water straight from that river! It mixed up OK but there were a number of complaints that it contained a couple of small leaves, two insects that were still alive and a Water Boatman, that wasn't. Fussy bastards!

After cleaning up we sat around next to the river just relaxing in the warm summer air. It was close to midnight and we were on the point of getting into our tents when we heard what initially sounded like thunder. But it was a continuous noise and it was getting closer. Then out of the darkness came a stampede of Dartmoor ponies, about 30 of them galloping at full throttle. They raced past us and thankfully not through us and disappeared as quickly as they had arrived.

We were up early the next morning and set about our first full day tramping across the moor in blistering heat. We obviously didn't know it at the time but 1976, as everyone now knows, was one of the hottest summers on record with temperature in the high 80's to low 90's almost every day for months. And on Dartmoor there is little or no shade. A lot of the small streams that criss-crossed the moors had dried up completely and areas that were renowned for their peat bogs now crunched under our feet and made the going tougher than usual. The extreme heat was as dangerous as the cold and wet conditions often found on the moors during the winter. At one point we ended up in what was possibly the only woodland area on the moors and it was really nice to get some shade in the searing heat. But our enjoyment was short lived because we got attacked by a swarm of huge horse flies. All of us were swatting the things or slapping our own heads and arms as the cloud of flies just kept coming at us. We had no choice but to run flat out to the end of the woods and back out into the open. It didn't do my feet much good but the idea worked and as soon as we were clear of the shade the flies vanished.

Mind you that wasn't our last encounter with the local wildlife. As we trudged our way through some dense heather, I saw a large flat rock ahead, just above the tops of the heather. I stepped up onto the rock and instantly froze because there, right by my right foot was a good sized Adder. I'd startled it and its face was less than two inches from my foot. I used to catch Grass snakes as a teenager and certainly knew the difference between the two. I stayed perfectly still for a minute or so and allowed the snake to slither off into the under growth. We hadn't ever been warned about the dangers of Britain's only poisonous snake and wondered just how close we had all come to being bitten as we trekked across Dartmoor.

At the end of the second day I knew my feet were in a bad way again. After pitching our tents and sorting out our grub it was time to take the boots off. My feet were pulsating as I did so and no sooner had I taken them off I could feel them starting to swell. There was some blood coming through the outer layer of socks and as I tried to take them off the pain was unbearable and so I decided to leave them on. Paul Williams also suffered with blisters for the same reason. Those boots were lethal.

I could barely walk as we staggered back into the base camp on the last day. I'd been dragging my right foot sideways for most of the day now and couldn't put any weight on it at all. I knew I was in trouble and could feel both feet throbbing with pain. We all collapsed in a heap by the instructor's tent who welcomed us back with a few smiles, even Toddy. We got debriefed fairly quickly then got told to sort our gear out in readiness for our departure back to CTS once the other teams had come in. All I knew was I had to get my boots off. I sat on the grass and untied them. Slowly……..very slowly, I started to remove my right boot. It was agony and I winced as it came off. OMFG, my outer sock was soaked in blood from my toes to my heel. I took my left boot off and although not quite as bad there was still plenty of blood.

Taking a well-earned rest are left to right: Andy Worship, Mick Streeter, Duncan Warry, Adrian Cleighton-Hills and Paul Williams
Photo Steve Woodward

I tried to take the outer socks off but yesterday's blood had obviously congealed enough to bind the outer sock to the inner ones. I considered hobbling over to the river and dunking my feet in the water in an effort to reduce the swelling and the pain and maybe soak the socks off, but before I could stand up Duncan came over.

"Fuckin hell Woody you weren't kidding, wait there" and with that he shot off towards the instructor's tent, returning a few minutes later with Tony Astill. Within minutes I'd been carried to one of the Transit mini buses and Tony Astill then drove a few miles to the little cottage hospital in Princetown. I managed to sort of walk into the building on the backs of my heels with my toes pointing skywards, whilst leaving bloodied heel prints on the floor.

After being ushered into one of the two cubicles by the very attractive nurse I was told to sit sideways on a trolley whilst she attempted to remove the sock from my right foot. It refused to budge. She left the cubicle and returned a few minutes later with a sort of foot bath bowl that contained a solution of warm water and antiseptic. I placed both feet in the bowl and after the initial searing pain had reduced a bit I could actually feel it doing some good. I was left there for about half an hour before the nurse returned, all gowned up and with a trolley full of scissors, scalpels and other surgical instruments. She sat in front of me and put my right foot onto her lap as she got to work on my socks with a pair of scissors. The outer one came off fairly easily but the inner sock was a different story as it was partly stuck on with blood and partly by the mangled plasters I'd put on. Slowly but surely, she cut away the sock to reveal the damage underneath. I had no skin at all on my heel and blisters on every toe had burst open and the skin pulled back to reveal raw flesh. I had a similar issue on the ball of my foot with an exposed patch of flesh about two inches square. There was blood everywhere as she carefully lowered my foot back into the bowl. I squealed like a pig as the antiseptic met my uncovered foot for the first time. Then she did the same with

"Stand By Ya Beds"

my left foot which had near identical damage but didn't seem to hurt quite as much for some reason.

The nurse then replenished the bowl with a fresh solution and left me for another half an hour or so. She then beckoned Tony Astill out of the cubicle and took him a few feet down the corridor and gave him a huge bollocking for allowing me to get into such a state and told him that he was stupid and irresponsible and that people like him shouldn't be allowed to supervise youngsters on the moors! She left him no room to manoeuvre and he returned to the cubicle looking a bit sheepish. To be fair it wasn't his fault obviously but it was quite nice to hear a young nurse rip him up for arse paper.

She returned a while later, very carefully dried my feet before smothering them in some antiseptic cream and bandaging me up like an Egyptian mummy and somehow found me another pair of socks to wear. She then insisted that Tony Astill bring the Transit to the front door and she then wheeled me out in a wheel chair. The trip back to the camp site was conducted in virtual silence which was somewhat awkward although he did insist that I report to Snoddy as soon as we returned to CTS and finished that order off with "so no doubt I'll get a bollocking from her as well".

Meanwhile the super fit guys who loved all that walking over the moors stuff were busily racing other groups of like-minded teams in the annual Ten Tors competition. The CTS team for 1976 consisting of Paul Diaper, Wayne Colebrook, Tony Hastings, Steve Smale, Andy Crawford and Malcolm Smith. They must have done OK because they all got awarded certificates for their endeavours. Good on them, I certainly couldn't have done it.

At least I had three weeks annual leave to recover and I swore I'd never wear those boots again. Within days Coxy and I had made plans to ride our bikes down to Cornwall for a weeks camping holiday but we were skint. Somehow, via a friend of his father's we ended up moonlighting a second job in Alton for a few days. This was most definitely against the rules but we needed the money. Our job was to pack board games. Each game had a number of different coloured plastic counters that needed bagging up with a couple of dice plus the board itself all sealed inside its box. We did this every day for a week in a barn on the outskirts of Alton whilst listening to   Radio 1 as it blasted out the records from the summer of 76 from the likes of Abba with Dancing Queen, Elton John and Kiki Dee with Don't Go Breaking My Heart and The Starland Vocal Band with Afternoon Delight. It was years before I understood the meaning of that particular song!

I stayed at Chris's fathers house in Alton for the week. I'd stayed there a few times previously and I enjoyed going there because his Dad had an amazing collection of magazines from Penthouse, Mayfair and Playboy. He also smoked heavily and took the piss out of Chris constantly and when I joined in it made him laugh a lot. Mind you on the downside he never had any milk in the fridge and so I had to learn how to drink black coffee with about five sugars in it. In the evenings Chris and I would listen to a new album that had just been released called Mr Blue Sky. Fabulous.

With cash in our pockets Chris and I headed west to Penzance where we booked ourselves into a campsite right next to the air sea rescue heliport on the outskirts of the town. The field probably had grass on it once but due to the incredibly hot weather currently resembled a desert. We met up with three French lads who all had bikes like ours and we divided our time between dicking around on the bikes or visiting a pub down by the harbour each evening.

Upon our return to Hampshire things got serious for it was time to report to our local police stations and our introduction to front line policing proper. My local station was at Newport some

"Stand By Ya Beds"

five miles away. The plan was that over the next few weeks we would be assigned to a number of different departments to get a taste of what each of them did. This included station duty, admin duty, section patrol, traffic department, CID and the control room. There would also be attachments to the Force Control Room at Winchester, a two week stint at a Casualty Unit at a major hospital and a three month attachment doing community work under the Community Service Volunteers (CSV) Program which could be anywhere in the country. As if that wasn't enough, we would still get dragged back to CTS a couple of times to undertake yet more expeditions, including a three-week Outward-Bound course. All of this needed to be crammed in by the time we turned 18 years of age because then we were eligible to join up as regular police officers.

CHAPTER 8

Lima Papa

I reported to L Division, Newport Police Station (Lima Papa) and the first person I met was Sgt John Wavell, the man who had interviewed me at home 18 months ago although it felt like a life time to be honest. He was pleased I had survived CTS (so was I) and he gave me a quick tour of the fairly modern looking station, introducing me to a few people along the way. At the top of the stairs, towards the rear of the station was the kitchen where Sgt Wavell introduced me to the kettle and a large tea pot, which apparently I would become very familiar with as it was part of my 'job' to ensure that the tea was made for whichever department I might be working with. We'd been warned by Keith Middleton shortly before we left CTS that some officers might consider us as little more than uniformed tea boys but to rise above it with a smile, but make sure they don't take advantage and do your best to prove that you are worth more than that.

For the next three weeks I would be on station duty, answering the phones, ensuring the radio batteries were fully charged, helping the public at the front counter with whatever enquiries they were making, feeding any stray dogs in the kennel and prisoner welfare, although I got the distinct impression that a stray dogs welfare was far more important than any prisoners! Sgt Wavell was at pains to advise me about Chief Superintendent Fred Hodgson, the officer in charge of policing the entire island, whose office was just a few feet from the front counter. He wasn't called Fiery Fred for nothing and I was advised not to upset him - at all!

"Stand By Ya Beds"

I was then handed over to the Station Duty officer, Vic Newton, a retired Sgt, whose son Brian I already knew from my days at Scouts. Vic was a kindly gentleman who was rather slow and methodical in his approach to everything. He introduced me to the Lost and Found registers, the HORT/2 register, the Aliens Registration book, the G4 message pads, the Classified Occurrence file, the Unoccupied Houses register and a whole host of other official documents and files. Prisoners had to be checked on every half an hour and the details logged in yet another register.

Let's be honest here, Newport nick wasn't exactly busy. Don't get me wrong I enjoyed the interaction with the public and did my best to help where I could but station duty could be incredibly tedious, with long bouts of absolute nothing-ness. During the evenings sometimes the high light was listening to the incessant tick tocking of the station clock.

Occasionally I'd get despatched across the road to the Civic Offices where I had to make my way down to the basement to undertake vehicle taxation checks on behalf of an officer who had called up the station on the radio to ascertain whether or not a car was taxed. It was an antiquated Cardex system that could take forever to go through. Once I'd checked whether or not the car was taxed I had to run back to the station and call the officer up on the radio. On one particular day I recall undertaking this task more than six times!

On my third day though it was all change because there was a missing elderly male with serious concerns for his welfare. A large number of officers, including myself were bussed down to the south of the island to search the cliffs around Niton. We had all been ordered to wear wellington boots because the area above the cliffs and towards the lower area was covered in blue slipper mud.

166

The rendezvous point was a pub about half a mile from the cliff top. We were briefed that the elderly man was last seen the previous evening and suffered from dementia. He had no coat or other warm weather clothing and it had rained most of the night. We were to search the area thoroughly and it was likely that we would be looking for a body. We split up into various teams and set off in different directions to commence the search. The overnight rain had made the grass and surrounding area wet and slippery and welly boots aren't the most comfortable of foot wear, although still much kinder to my feet than those walking boots.

I was working with a group of three officers and we spread out across the slopes of the upper cliffs before heading down to a sort of wide ridge area that was covered in this thick, sticky blue slipper mud. It made walking really difficult as it tended to suck your boot down into the mud more than ankle deep in places. It squelched with every step and it was knackering even for a CTS trained super fit 17 year old like me. After about an hour trudging through this stuff the officer furthest away to my left found the old man sat down in the long grass. He was alive but very weak. He was soaked through and very confused. He'd been out all night picking flowers for his wife and he had a large bundle of weeds and grass clutched in his hands.

The trouble was he was far too weak to undertake the walk back to safety and so a decision was made to call in an air sea rescue helicopter to winch him and the rest of us off the cliffs. Within minutes a blue and red Wessex helicopter was hovering above us and the old boy got winched up by one of the crew. Then one by one the four of us had a harness wrapped around us and up we went. As I looked down all I could see were the waves crashing onto the beach far below us and it reminded me of that days abseiling at Dancers Ledge in Swanage.

"Stand By Ya Beds"

The helicopter landed in a field next to the pub and an ambulance took the old man off to hospital for a check-up. All the other officers returned and the landlord laid on drinks for everyone! Being 17 of course I was only permitted to have a Coke. It had been a really interesting exercise and thankfully had a happy ending. To get back to Newport I had to travel in the back of a Bedford HA van, which was the standard section vehicle for the island. There were no seats in the rear and I was thrown all over the place as the van hurtled along the island's awful roads. Health and safety didn't really exist back then.

Horrible Bedford HA van
Photo PM Photography

After three weeks manning the front desk, I started to work with a number of officers on either foot patrol or on mobile patrol. Unlike the mainland that ran three different types of vehicles to cover panda car duties, area car response work and topped off with the traffic division, the island only had a two vehicle system and combined the area car and traffic division roles into one. And unlike the mainland that was running Mini 850's as

Lima Papa

panda cars in the familiar blue and white colour scheme, the island had to rely on plain white Bedford HA vans, a truly awful vehicle, the bodywork of which was thinner than tin foil.

Over the next few weeks, I worked with the likes of John Troke, Graham Topliss, Ken Alp, Chris Warren, Stef West, Paul Mylnek, Graham Love, Stan Atkinson, Neil Pykett, Dave Watkins, Steve Sargeant, Pete Cobbett, Pete Hughes and Roger Poynter. There were also two traffic motorcyclists in Ken Ellcombe and Dave Gurd, who was a genuine legend on the island and feared by every single motorist over there. In truth he was a thoroughly nice guy and a bloody good copper.

One of the first officers I went out on foot patrol with was John Troke who was a slim but very tall 6 foot 5 inch young man but with his helmet on looked like he was over 7 feet tall. He was a brilliant communicator and it was quite an eye opener for the 17 year old me to see a local Bobby doing what local Bobby's were best at and that was interacting with their public. And I didn't have to make him tea or coffee either because he was a devout Mormon who didn't touch the stuff.

One officer I particularly liked going out on patrol with was Chris Warren. He was the archetypal 1970s man with a hair style that definitely wasn't regulation length, long sideburns and a Jason King moustache. He was great fun to be with, treated me in a decent way, possibly because he was a former Cadet himself and all the ladies loved him, so most of his tea stops were in hair salons, beauty parlours or at the reception desk of the local cinema. We popped into the lady's hair salon one afternoon and the rather attractive owner seemed particularly pleased to see him. She immediately put the 'closed' sign up on the door and invited Chris into the back of the salon. Chris told me to make myself comfortable whilst he conducted his enquiries out back and said

"Stand By Ya Beds"

he wouldn't be too long! It must have been a very thorough investigation because he was ages!

Newport town and the surrounding area was almost as quiet as the front desk and I soon became a little bored of constantly walking up and down the same old streets looking for something to do. By 9pm the place was completely dead. To relieve some of the boredom, a number of officers would sometimes venture into the Salon cinema just to check that the staff were OK and that there were no juveniles watching any X rated films you understand! On one occasion I was on patrol with PC Neil Pykett and he decided to check out the cinema. The big film at the time was The Exorcist and as we stood at the back of the half empty cinema, I was crapping myself watching the film. It was terrifying but of course I had to put on a brave face. However, after about half an hour Neil whispered in my ear that one of the local toe rags who'd been wanted on warrant for several weeks was sat about four rows in front of us. He was a big lad with a very distinctive large head and a big reputation for violence. Neil walked forward and very firmly placed his hand on the youth's shoulder just at a particularly tense moment in the film. It's true to say that despite his size and the fact that Neil was pressing down on his shoulder, he actually left his seat and screamed like a little girl. His hard-man of Newport reputation vanished forever at that moment.

I quickly decided that walking the beat wasn't for me and I was desperate to get mobile. I'd always liked my cars and bikes and so I asked if I could perhaps go out on patrol in the traffic car. My wish was granted and I double crewed the Vauxhall VX4/90 with PC Pete Cobbett or sometimes the brand new Volvo 244DL with PC Roger Poynter who was a real Caulkhead and called everybody under the age of 20 "nipper", me included.

My wish to get more involved was almost immediately granted by attending a couple of RTA's and pulling over a few errant motorists. Then late one evening we got a call to attend a very large country house near Wootton Bridge where the owner had detained a burglar. This was more like it; proper crime.

We arrived within a few minutes and were greeted at the door by a retired army Colonel complete with archetypal wing nut moustache, a tweed waist coat, polished brown brogues and a walking stick slung under his arm pit. He spoke with a full British Empire accent and was extremely authoritative. He explained that he and his lady wife had returned from an evening with friends and found the burglar rifling through the drawers in the bedroom and the Colonel had detained him.

"He's through here, this way gentleman" he said as he headed towards the kitchen.

I will never forget the sight that greeted us as we walked into that kitchen. In the middle of the huge room was one of those large pine kitchen tables and our burglar, a youth of about 17 years of age, was laying on his back on the table with his arms and legs tied to all four table legs! He was bleeding from the mouth and the nose and had a rather tasty looking black eye developing. He struggled a bit as he saw the Police had come to his rescue.

"Get me off, the blokes a nutter" he pleaded.
"Shut up you little bastard" bellowed the Colonel and he poked him hard in the ribs with his stick.
"It looks like you picked the wrong house nipper" Roger said with a smile.
"Can I offer you a cup of tea gentleman? My wife will make it and bring it through to the study".
It sounded more like an order than a gesture of good will and we duly followed him down the hallway to the study.

"What about me?" cried the burglar, whose plea fell on three pairs of deaf ears. As we sat in the rather grandiose study, surrounded by all manner of militaria on the walls I couldn't help but feel a bit sorry for the lad on the table. He was about my age and we probably knew some of the same people, as most island people do. I could hear him groaning and he was obviously in a fair bit of pain.

About 20 minutes later Roger stood up and said we'd better take the youth into custody. We untied his legs first, followed by his hands. Despite his ordeal he was still quite gobby, showed no remorse whatsoever and even had the audacity to threaten the Colonel that if he ever saw him out on the street he'd "sort him out". My sympathy for him evaporated at that point.

I was ready for more of that but within a couple of days it was back down to Earth with a huge bump as I was now on my two-week Admin attachment. What? Two weeks stuck in an office shuffling other people's paper. Ugh. I was introduced to the two Admin personnel, one of whom was a lovely, bubbly young lady called Karen. Her life would later be turned upside down when she married..........Stef King. Poor girl.

The work was mind numbing and involved me having an intimate relationship with the photo copier. The trouble is it kept breaking down with paper jams in one of three different areas within the bowels of its inner workings. I became the office expert at releasing wads of mangled A4 paper and sometimes had to do it six or seven times a day. One afternoon I got asked to unjam the infernal machine and after pulling out a handful of paper from the exit rollers it still wouldn't work. So, I opened the side door and looked in. There were a few more crumpled sheets right at the back. In went my hand to remove them and as I tugged on them so I flew six feet backwards across the room and was slammed against the wall in a sitting position. I was dazed and numb but clutching a wad of paper. I'd been electrocuted!! If Russ Parke had allowed me to have any hair it would have been stood on end. Karen made a fuss of me and for once someone else made me a cup of tea and I was allowed to go and sit in the bar and rest. Basically, that was the highlight of my two week Admin attachment.

Not to worry, as of next week I'm on my two-week attachment to CID. Thoughts of Reagan and Carter sprang to mind as no doubt I will be chasing villains and slags through the back streets of Newport, dragging them back to the factory, spinning their drums and shagging their Mrs.

The reality of course was somewhat different because the first thing I got told to do was make the tea. I'd arrived in my best tucker, in fact my only decent clothes really which consisted of brown flares and a cream blazer. I was pleased to find that Chris Warren was on his CID aid so at least I had a familiar face to talk to. The Criminal Investigation Department at this time was headed up by DC/I Alan Wheeler with D/I Arthur Mandry as his deputy. He knew my father quite well due to the close liaison between Newport CID and the prison staff, in particular C Wing at Parkhurst, which my father was in charge of and held the likes of Reggie Kray, one of the Richardson brothers, Ian Brady for a while and a number of IRA prisoners, although most of them had been moved next door to Albany prison during the riots of the previous couple of years.

I seemed to spend most of my time sat at a desk, occasionally given the odd job to do and on the whole, it was almost as mind numbing as doing the admin upstairs. If I did go out it was usually with Chris to undertake a minor enquiry, usually about a theft or maybe a burglary or two.

"Stand By Ya Beds"

Then one day DS Berry invited me to accompany him on a prison visit to Parkhurst and then Albany. I jumped at the opportunity, not so much because I was bored shitless but because of my lifetime connection with the prison service. Before moving to the island my father had been based at HMP Latchmere in Surrey which was a Borstal before becoming a Detention Centre. As a kid of about 7 or 8 I would play football with the Borstal boys on the pitch opposite our house or I'd stand on the roof of our rabbit hutch at the bottom of the garden and watch the prisoners doing various sports inside the wall. I thought they had a great life and it was my ambition to become a Borstal boy which must have sent a shudder down my father's spine!

As we drove towards the prison gate I couldn't help but smile and I was genuinely excited about seeing the inside of Parkhurst, a place I could see from my bedroom window. The huge wooden door opened slowly inwards and we drove into the holding area as the door slammed shut behind us. We signed in and were given our security passes and then drove through the inner gate and into the prison proper. After parking the Mini we walked up a set of stone steps to an office where we met the officer that DS Berry had come to see. He was investigating a serious prisoner on prisoner assault where the victim had been blinded in one eye after being hit with a lump of wood. We sat in an office talking through the circumstances when a prisoner came in. He was about 40 ish I suppose, quite plump but well presented.

"Cup of tea Sir?" he asked DS Berry.
"Yes please" he replied.

The prisoner then turned towards me.
"Cup of tea Sir?" he asked.
"Erm….yes please" I spluttered.

I actually felt embarrassed. Being called Sir by an older person just felt odd. Within a couple of minutes, he returned with three mugs of piping hot tea and placed them on the desk.

"Will there be anything else Sir?" he requested and was then gestured to leave. It was like a scene from Porridge with Fletcher acting as our tea boy. I looked around to see if he'd half inched anything before he left. I'm sure Mr Mackay would have called him back if anything was missing!

We were then taken to the Hospital Wing to interview the victim. Keys jangled, the clanging of steel barred gates and doors echoed everywhere. Almost every prisoner we passed called the officer Sir. Although cold and clinical the whole place seemed to have a positive vibe to it and I actually felt quite relaxed. We entered the Hospital Wing and were ushered into a side room. Within two minutes our victim, himself a convicted murderer was brought in and sat in front of us. He was in his early 30s I'd say and his face was heavily bandaged. Given the number of other bruises and abrasions he'd taken a right hammering.

DS Berry asked him a few simple questions. The man sat there in complete silence just staring at the floor. The questions continued as DS Berry took notes but the prisoner didn't utter a word. It clearly wasn't in his interests to do so. Whatever he'd done to receive such a battering is nothing compared to what would have happened if he'd squealed on his attackers.

Within minutes we were heading back to the car and en route to HMP Albany next door which was a follow up enquiry regarding an arson that had taken place a few months earlier. In previous years I'd seen Albany burning on a number of occasions during some of the riots they'd had there.

"Stand By Ya Beds"

As we approached the gates it was much the same routine, the obvious difference being that Albany was a much newer prison built in 1967 as opposed to the Victorian buildings of Parkhurst. After entering the neutral zone between the two gates, we booked in and then entered the inner part of the prison. We drove forward about 20 feet and stopped in a parking bay. As we stepped out of the car there was a huge bang as a large paper bag, full of nails landed on the bonnet. Nails flew in every direction as we both dived behind the security of the car doors. There were shouts of "Pigs" and a lot of laughter seemingly coming from every direction although I couldn't see anyone. I have no idea where that nail bomb came from but it scored a direct hit and scared the crap out of me.

We were quickly ushered into a nearby office where we met DS Berry's contact and he updated him on the enquiry, most of which went over my head. There was no offer of tea, no Norman Stanley Fletcher and not a hint of being called Sir. In fact, Albany just had a really hostile feel to it and I couldn't wait for us to leave. DS Berry explained on the way back to the office that Parkhurst was full of career criminals whilst Albany was just full of thugs; that was the difference.

A few days later Sgt Wavell came into the office to ask if I could be spared for a prisoner escort to HMP Haslar. Within minutes I'd met up with PC Ken Alp and we took a CID Mini up the road to Newport Crown Court to collect a 17 year old youth who'd just been sentenced to three months for burglary. Despite the fact that the island had three prisons less than a five minute drive from the Court, they couldn't house youths under 18. So, a trip across the Solent was required to take our boy to Haslar Detention Centre, a place with a truly notorious reputation for its strict discipline approach. Can't be as bad as CTS I thought.

I'd been out on patrol with Ken a few times so knew him quite well. He was a full blooded Caulkhead and loved the island.

He was a lovely chap and treated me as an equal. We arrived at the Crown Court and found our prisoner sat in a cell. Ken hand cuffed him to me and we somehow managed to squeeze into the rear of the Mini together. After boarding the car ferry at Fishbourne we got out of the car and sat in the lounge area. As we were both dressed in our respective suits, I reckon most of the public thought we were both prisoners. It was a weird feeling. Ken handed out the cigarettes followed by some very fatherly advice to our burglar.

"Is this your first time inside nipper?" asked Ken.
"Yeah," came the reply.
"Allow me to offer you one piece of advice young man. For your sake make sure you call all the officers Sir and you won't go far wrong" said Ken.
"Nah bollocks to that, I ain't calling no-one Sir" came the cocky response.
"This isn't a wind up; I'm telling you they'll make your life hell if you don't" came Kens advice.
"I can take it mush, you don't frighten me and nor will they" he said with a grin.
Ken put his hand on the lad's shoulder and said "Nipper, you'll be dead by morning".

That sent a shudder down my spine but Billy Burglar still thought he was tough enough to put up with anything that came his way. He was hard.

After docking at Portsmouth we drove a few miles around to Gosport and into HMP Haslar. My stomach was in knots as we got out of the Mini and still hand cuffed together, we entered the reception area where Ken handed over the necessary paperwork to a uniformed Prison Officer who was a small man in his late 50s, I'd say with very white hair. The prisoner and I were stood in a narrow corridor as Ken and the officer went through all the formalities. The officer then came out and stood in front of us.

"Stand By Ya Beds"

"How old are you son?" he asked.

"17," came the reply.

With that the officer punched him so hard in the face that it sent us both flying backwards and onto the floor. It was like being punched by Mick Dodds again but without the pain this time, at least for me anyway.

"From now on boy you call me Sir is that understood?" he bellowed, jabbing his finger towards the lad's face. I was crapping myself and it wasn't even directed at me but it felt like it.

"Yes….Sir" he quivered as the pair of us got to our feet.

"Cup of tea gentlemen?" the officer asked as the cuffs were removed and our prisoner was taken away to another room by two other officers. We sat in the office as Ken explained to the officer that he'd done his best to warn the lad but he didn't believe him. The officer sighed and said he'd learn one way or the other in here. After downing our brew and having yet another fag it was time for us to head back to the ferry. As we walked down the corridor, I looked into an adjacent room to see our boy stark bollock naked, standing to attention on the only black tile on the floor looking directly upwards at another black tile on the ceiling, whilst being shouted at by the other two officers.

As we walked towards our car so a group of about 20 prisoners in PT kit were marching past us at the double whilst being bawled out by another officer. I reckon they had it easy really; they didn't do Brockenhurst camp like we did and most of them were only in there for three months, we got the best part of a year doing that shit.

I had to leave the island and travel up to HQ at Winchester for my two week Force Control Room attachment. The accommodation rooms were on the fifth floor with the Control Room on the second floor. The dining room, the senior officers Mess, the bar and the all-important snooker room were on the fourth floor.

Lima Papa

I entered the Control Room for the first time and it looked like something from Cape Canaveral with four large console desks, one for each area in the force, with another couple of smaller units over to the right and a number of offices along the far wall. It was a hive of activity with plenty of radio chatter coming from everywhere. I was told that I was to observe proceedings for the first week in order to familiarise myself with various procedures and if I was confident enough, I might be allowed to get more involved in week two. In the meantime, the kettle is over there and no doubt everyone would appreciate a nice cup of tea. Of course they would.

I spent most of my time on the HS desk that covered the Portsmouth, Gosport and Fareham areas. It was quite busy although a lot of the time it was difficult to keep track of what was happening but the two guys I was sat with seemed very cool about things and took it all in their stride. Apart from the radio system there were the 999 phone lines, direct lines to the Ambulance Service and the Fire Brigade, plus several others. There were alarm panels for various high-risk premises including silent alarms for a number of Hampshire VIPs, MPs and other prominent people.

A Cadet in the Force Control Room with PC Chris Richards
Photo Hampshire Constabulary

"Stand By Ya Beds"

The mid 1970s of course meant that the IRA were at the height of their terrorist activities and Hampshire had already seen the bombing of the Aldershot army barracks in 1972 that resulted in seven deaths, shootings in Southampton when Police unearthed an IRA cell, the hunger strikes in the island prisons and other IRA activity within the county.

My first week had been on day shifts but by week two I had been put on 6-2 earlies. I'm not good at mornings. Getting up at 0500 when on shift at Newport was hard for me. I'd have to leave home by 0530 for the five mile ride from Northwood (my parents had moved house whilst we'd been at CTS and I often wondered if they'd done it on purpose so I wouldn't know where they were!) to Newport. So, being at HQ and only three floors above where I was to start work surely meant I could have some kind of a lay in? Just so long as I was there by 0600.

Tuesday morning I woke up at 0610. For the first time ever I'd over slept. Oh shit, I'm in serious trouble now. By the time I'd got dressed and legged it down the stairs to the second floor I was 25 minutes late and I looked like a bag of shit too. My obvious punishment centred around the kettle and no sooner had I filled everyone's mugs I was tasked with taking a large cardboard box full of paperwork down to uniform stores in the basement. The stairs at headquarters were two tiers for each floor and circumnavigated the lift shaft, in other words there was a semi landing for each flight of stairs. The box I was carrying was large, flimsy and rather heavy. I couldn't really see where I was going and as I got the semi landing between the ground floor and the first floor, I lost my footing and plunged head first onto my knees, spewing the contents of the box all over the floor.

"Oh for fucks sake" I growled "could my day get any worse?"

It was just about to because as I swore out loud so a pair of polished brown brogues appeared by my hands, standing on the

180

papers. I looked up and there was the Chief Constable Sir Douglas Osmond.

"Do mind your language young man, you never know who might hear it" he said with a stern look on his face.

"Yes Sir.......sorry Sir" I grovelled.

He then continued his trudge up the stairs. Oh my God, what the hell is the Chief doing here before 7am I asked myself? I quickly swept all the paperwork into the box just in case the DCC Headley Phillips comes in early as well. I doubt I'd get away with saying the same thing in front of him. I ran down to the basement, dumped the box and ran back up to the relative safety of FCR.

The day did improve and by the end of the week I was taking 999 calls, writing all the details down on G4 messages and passing them to my two controllers. When it came to officers booking on and off via the radio system, I was allowed to answer the radio and log their status. It made me feel useful and I thoroughly enjoyed the experience.

The following week we were back at CTS for interviews with Insp Chadwick on a range of things including the results of our exams from Fareham Tech. I got another B in technical drawing and a B in law, which I was reasonably happy with. But my maths and French results were poor and I got quite a bollocking from him over that. However, on the plus side the reports he had on my performance at Newport were glowing, so at least I wasn't a complete failure.

During the day we were interviewed by Sgt Middleton and a woman from the Community Service Volunteers (CSV) organisation to assess where they would place each of us on our three month attachment next year. It was made clear that we could be sent anywhere in the UK to help out at a range of worthwhile community projects, many of which were with charitable organisations. We would be informed by post of our respective date and locations by next Spring at the earliest.

There were also a number of places up for grabs to work abroad on the Project Trust program, which for some reason passed me by but five of our intake got chosen; Al Robertson went to St. Martins Children's Home in Durban whilst Tim Beazley attended the YMCA also in Durban, both for 12 months. Martin Gibson went to an agricultural centre in Nairobi whilst Gerry Hutchings spent a year at St. Nicolas' Home for Coloured Boys in Johannesburg. Mick Dodds meanwhile got shipped out to Hong Kong for 15 months, first teaching English to refugees and then as an Outward Bound instructor.

Cadet Martin Gibson just before he set off for his 12 month stint in Nairobi

Shortly before we'd left CTS in the summer Sgt Middleton announced that the next intake of Cadets in September would include females for the very first time. He looked quite dismayed at the prospect and said that a number of changes would have to be made to accommodate them and that we were to behave ourselves when returning to CTS in the future, which was said more tongue in cheek than anything else.

He was right, there seemed to be a different atmosphere to the place. Maybe it was because it wasn't 'our home' anymore or maybe it was because the instructors didn't seem to swear quite as much. There were 10 girls altogether with Theresa Bartlett, Sue Parker, Madeline Casey, Tina Nash, Heather Summersgill, Dawn Murfitt, Julia Lake, Mandy Cole, Helen Smith and Elizabeth Holah and they were all billeted in the rooms above the main reception area with the only access via that creaking wooden staircase.

Back at Newport I was doing another stint on the front desk the week before Christmas, when Sgt Wavell came over and said that Ch/Supt Hodgson wanted to see me immediately. Why? What have I done? I daren't even look at the man when he enters the building let alone engage in conversation with him. He wasn't called Fiery Fred for nothing. I must be in the shit. Oh no, maybe the Chief has spoken to him about my little trip down the stairs a few weeks ago. Nervously I walked down the corridor to his office. I quickly brushed down the front of my tunic with my hands, took a deep breath and knocked on his door.

"Enter" came the command.

Sgt Wavell had already instructed me not to salute but to stand to attention in front of his desk. My stomach was churning like a washing machine.

"Stand By Ya Beds"

"I need you to go up to Timothy Whites in the High Street and collect my wife's Christmas present. They are expecting you. Here's £10, make sure I get the change" he said with a half smile.

I came out of his office and informed Sgt Wavell that I was just popping up the road on my errand. I put my hat on and took the five minute walk up to Timothy Whites. No sooner had I entered the shop I was acknowledged by a lady who presented me with a box containing a hair dryer.

"That's £12.50p please my dear" she said, holding out her hand.
"What? £12.50, but he only gave me a tenner" I squealed.
"Best you go back and ask him for the rest of it then" she laughed "I'll keep this under the counter until you come back".

So many thoughts went through my head on the way back to the nick. He's going to kill me. At the very least he's going to chew my face off. How am I even going to tell him? Maybe I'll ask Sgt Wavell to do the dirty deed. No that's a bit cowardly of me. But right now, I'm feeling cowardly. This is the end of my career surely.

My heart was pounding so hard I could visibly see it through my tunic. I stood outside his door, took the biggest intake of breath possible and knocked.

"Enter" came the command.

I stood to attention in front of his desk and just blurted it out.

"HOW MUCH?" he bellowed. I felt like Oliver Twist holding out the bowl and asking for more. The entire station must have heard him shouting at me. He begrudgingly gave me another fiver from his wallet and just wafted his hand for me to leave, which I did as quickly as my legs would carry me.

So off I trudged back up to Timothy Whites where I handed the lady the extra cash before heading back again with a Timothy Whites carrier bag containing Mrs Hodgson's new hair dryer. I felt a little more relaxed entering his office this time and he merely beckoned me to put the bag on his desk and didn't even lift his head to acknowledge me.

CHAPTER 9

Our Final Year

Nineteen Seventy Seven was going to be a very busy year for us and it got off to a flying start because midway through January I found myself armed with a travel warrant from CTS and boarding a train to head north to the Lake District to undertake my three week Outward Bound Course. Oh goody, more walking, more rock climbing, more abseiling, more bullshit. I was joined by Andy Guy, Chris Cox, Tony Hastings, Steve Matcham, Paul Forbes, Paul Williams and Dave Brown, who arrived late. Our base was a huge old manor house at Eskdale that bore an uncanny resemblance to Hogwarts. There was a large lake in front of the main building and the rest of the place was surrounded by thick woodland.

Outward Bound Centre, Eskdale

Our Final Year

It wasn't just us Cadets that were there though. We were joined by dozens of other youths from a variety of organisations and backgrounds. There was a pretty large contingent of lads from an agricultural college in the North West, with most of them coming from either Manchester or Liverpool. There were a few army cadets and one or two private individuals who had paid for the privilege. We got split up into various groups of ten and taken to our respective accommodation which was basically a large room with a load of wooden bunk beds in it. Thankfully I got Andy Guy for company and we seemed to have got the bulk of the Scousers and the Mancs with us and the banter between them started almost straight away. I have to say the quick fire piss taking they did was hilarious, so maybe this three weeks won't be so bad after all.

After our evening meal that took place in the great hall, we were briefed by the head of the college who introduced us to the rest of the staff and outlined all the rules. It was very similar to our introduction to CTS. To reinforce the comparisons we were then told that there would be a morning run every day, only this one had a slight twist, in that it consisted of one lap of the lake, but half way around there is a wooden jetty that we had to run to the end of and then jump into the water, swim back to shore and then continue the run back to the main building. Oh shit.

After our welcome introduction we retired to our rooms where Andy and I got all manner of questions thrown at us about our chosen careers. They all had stories to tell about their own dealings with the Police especially the two lads from Liverpool. They were funny though.

The next morning we assembled outside in shorts, tee shirts and plimsoles. It was bloody freezing. The run commenced downhill on a sort of gravel track for about half a mile I suppose until we arrived at the jetty. One of the instructors directed us along the jetty to where another was waiting at the end to ensure we went in. Standing there waiting for your turn was purgatory and worse than that dip in the river at Brockenhurst. I jumped in and the shock of cold almost paralysed my body. I've never swum so fast in my life but as I climbed out at the shoreline the cold air temperature we'd experienced before getting wet was now much warmer than before. I mean it wasn't Barbados warm but the air was definitely warmer than the water.

After breakfast it was time for a spot of team building on the assault course. Our instructor was joined by a rather keen trainee instructor who was very 'jolly hockey sticks' and irritated the crap out of me every time she opened her mouth. It was a good exercise I suppose and I quickly learned who to depend on or otherwise within our little group. The only one I knew I could trust 100% was Andy Guy.

Over the next few days we did a fair amount of rock climbing, abseiling, map reading and walking. For us Cadets it was pretty tame stuff in comparison to what we'd been used to but for some of our new found friends it was all new. One thing that was new to me though was the parachute jump. OK not from a plane but from a tree. We had to climb a rope ladder attached to the tallest Pine tree I'd ever seen. There was a platform at the top and once they had tucked your body into a harness with two ropes above you that acted like the strings on a parachute, you quite literally just stepped off the platform and a series of weights and pulleys would slow your decent. That was the theory anyway. I think it was about 80 feet to the ground, which when you are looking at it from the platform is a long way down. It was a bit like the initial approach to abseiling, you know, that first lean out backwards. I found myself consciously fighting my natural instincts not to do it. But do it I must. I stepped out expecting to drop like a stone but instead I floated down. It was a bizarre sensation and I did it again twice more. The most dangerous part of the entire exercise was climbing up the tree to get to the platform!

By the beginning of week two the weather had got even colder with sub-zero temperatures during the day. We woke one morning and were overjoyed at seeing the lake had completely frozen over. No morning dip for us then we cheered. How wrong were we. On arriving at the jetty we were ordered to run to the far end and then given a couple of large poles and told to break the ice before diving in. I think a collective "You must be fucking joking" could be heard from everyone but no, they weren't joking. The ice was less than half an inch thick and broke easily enough but that was only at the jetty. Our bodies would have to break the rest of the ice as we swam back to shore. It was not a pleasant experience.

By mid-morning much of the ice had melted which was a blessing because today we were canoeing. Dressed only in swimming shorts, a tee shirt and a life vest we were blue with cold and shivering like I'd never shivered before. The instructor, who sported a full ginger beard, was dressed in a full wet suit. As we froze on the shore line he gave us instruction on how to escape from your canoe in the event that it overturned. This was something we'd done a thousand times before at CTS. Once he was satisfied that we all understood the basics it was time to get in the water. One or two capsized as soon as their arses touched the seat which was funny of course and one by one we paddled out about 20 feet before being told to manoeuvre our canoes into a straight line. With each movement of the paddle or a neighbour's paddle, droplets of ice cold water would land on your arms or your face making us squeal like little girls. In a line-up of ten canoes I was number seven in line. I was horrified to see the instructor enter the water and grab the front of the first canoe and turn it over, forcing the lad to escape from it whilst under water. Then he did the same to number two, then number three and he slowly made his way towards me.

"Stand By Ya Beds"

He went to grab my canoe and I shouted at him.
"NO, don't touch that" I bellowed.
"Why not?" he asked.
"Because I've done this dozens of times and really don't need to do it today thank you" I replied.
With that he made a lunge for my canoe but missed. I raised my oar to head height and shouted at him again.
"Touch my canoe and I'll wrap this oar around your ears" but I knew as soon as I'd said it that I shouldn't have done.

He walked away glaring at me and tipped the next canoe over. The rest of the session had us paddling around the lake for an hour or so, doing various exercises, which was reasonably pleasant but still incredibly cold.

Immediately after breakfast the next morning I was summoned to the Principles office and carpeted. He wouldn't tolerate such behaviour or threats towards his staff and that if there was a repeat, he would have no hesitation in sending me straight back to Hampshire for them to deal with me. I apologised to him and said I would apologise to the instructor which I did later that day.

A couple of days later and we were preparing for what they grandly labelled as our "solo expedition" which I rather liked the sound of. Except it wasn't an expedition at all; more a test of character, initiative, self-sufficiency and resolve. We were each given a sheet of thick polythene about 10 feet square, several lengths of string, some tin foil, a box of matches, a water carrier, a saucepan, two cans of London Grill, two cans of stew, several tea bags and some powdered milk and sugar, a tin opener, a mug and a set of camping cutlery. We had to pack all of this plus our sleeping bag, spare clothes and water proofs into our ruck sack. We were not permitted to take the following items; Cigarettes, a watch, sweets and chocolate, writing material or transistor radios.

Our Final Year

We would be thoroughly searched before setting off. It goes without saying that I smuggled out 20 JPS, a bar of Dairy Milk, 3 bars of Kendall mint cake (loved that stuff) my camera and a note pad and pen. I didn't own a radio so that wasn't an issue and I wasn't really bothered about the watch. They didn't mention knives on the forbidden list so I took my trusty sheath knife too. Guess who I got searched by? Yep our ginger bearded canoeing maestro. Oh how he hoped he would find some contraband on me. He failed and I felt very smug.

So, we piled into one of the mini buses and as we headed out the gate we were told to shut our eyes and keep our heads low. Shades of Brockenhurst again. We seemed to be driving for ages before we stopped and one of our group got told to get out of the bus. Five minutes later we were on the move again, then stopped and dropped another one off. Then it was my turn to get out. Mrs jolly hockey sticks took me over a gate and across a grassed area about 200 yards from the road. We were high up on what was basically a small mountain and we stopped at a large rock.

"This is your spot" she said "There's a stream at the bottom of the hill so you can collect water. Make yourself comfortable, do not leave here at all and we'll pick you up in three days' time".

With that she disappeared back towards the mini bus.

So, there was no expedition as such, just three days' rest. I had a cracking view across the valley with the Eskdale miniature railway just about in view far below. The sun was shining, the weather had warmed up nicely and I was as happy as a piglet in shite. No morning run, no swim, no bullshit, I'm gonna love this. The first thing I decided to do was dump the ruck sack and head on down to the stream and fill the carrier with water. It was really steep and a lot further down than I imagined and the climb back up reminded me of Dorset. Yes, it was that steep.

"Stand By Ya Beds"

Back at my rock, which was about the size of an armchair I suppose, I had to sort out a shelter. About six feet to the left of the rock was a small sapling tree and so I decided I would use the area in between those two permanent items to anchor my shelter to. I hunted around for some decent sized boulders and once I had enough I spread the polythene sheet on the ground, used the string to tie it to the trees, the boulders and my rock to form a sort of tent like structure with my upturned ruck sack acting as a door. Once inside it felt very snug and actually quite warm.

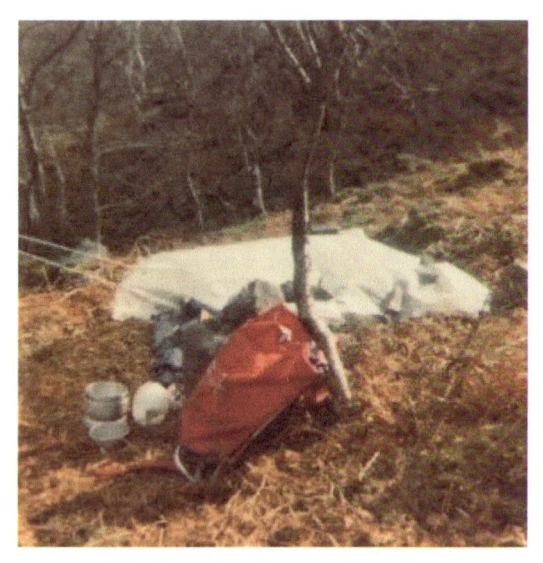

My home for the next three days

After that I went and found a decent supply of wood and within minutes I had a good little fire going on the other side of my rock. I boiled some water and made myself a cuppa and then just sat back, lit a fag, took in the view and enjoyed the peace and solitude. After an hour or so I stoked up the fire and heated up a can of stew and for afters took a few bites from my choccy bar. However, by about 5pm it was just about dark and the temperature had plummeted, so it was time to get into my shelter and get my head down. It had been a long day and within minutes I was asleep.

I've no idea what time it was but it was still dark, the wind was howling and it was pissing down with rain. My shelter was flapping about like a country dancers dress and then whoosh.......... it was gone! Fuck, no. I leapt out of my sleeping bag and dressed in just a tee shirt and my underpants went running up the hill chasing my sheet of polythene. Thankfully it got stuck against another tree and as I grabbed it so I fell over into a load of mud and water. I ran back down the hill and did my best to build myself another shelter, in the dark, in strong wind and heavy rain. My sleeping bag and all my gear was soaked through and I was freezing my nuts off. I managed to tie it all down and used a load more rocks to weigh the edges down with. I got back into my sleeping bag which was somehow still dry on the inside. I pulled the ruck sack across the doorway and prayed it would all stay intact. I dozed on and off but every time that polythene flapped I shit myself that it was going to happen again.

By the time it got light the wind and rain had eased off and eventually the sun came out. I wouldn't say it was warm but it was a lot more pleasant than the inclement weather during the night. I had real trouble trying to light a fire though. The grass I'd used as tinder the previous day was now soaking wet and so I tore out a few pages from the notebook I'd smuggled out, then tied half a dozen matches together, placed some twigs on top of it all and set the match bundle alight. The resulting flare up was enough to ignite the paper and the twigs at the same time and within minutes I had a decent fire going. I had a very welcome cup of tea and a tin of London Grill and after breakfast I set about drying out all my kit and making the necessary repairs to my abode. As I did so I suddenly noticed that I was actually talking to myself, giving myself instructions and calling myself a twat when things didn't go right. Its only been 24 hours and I'm losing it already!

"Stand By Ya Beds"

I spent the rest of the day laid out on the grass as if I was at the beach. I felt relaxed and the rest was doing me the world of good. My thoughts then turned towards my evening meal which tonight would be stew (again) with a couple of baked spuds. I knew these would take some considerable time to cook so I stoked up the fire and placed the potatoes, wrapped in foil on top of the stones I'd laid as a base and which I knew would retain their heat even if the fire went out. After about an hour it was starting to get chilly again so I went and sat close to the fire that was now just a glow of smouldering logs and ash. As I sat there, I thought I saw one of the potatoes move. I must be losing it I laughed to myself. Then it moved again. No, I really did see it. A few seconds later it moved again, this time completely out of the embers. I jumped back but then saw underneath the potato was a large toad and the tin foil was welded to its back. I grabbed the water carrier and poured water over it to cool it down. Once cool enough I picked it up and tore the foil from the potatoes and then tried very carefully to remove the foil from the toad's skin. It wouldn't budge, so I doused more water over it and very carefully peeled the foil away without damaging the toad's delicate skin. I felt terribly guilty and kept apologising to him. He seemed to be alright in the end and I found another decent rock for him to hide under and poured a load more water over him and the immediate area to help keep him cool.

Thankfully my second night under the stars was a lot more pleasant weather wise and I managed to get a full night's kip. After breakfast the next morning I took down my shelter, made good the area I'd been using, packed my ruck sack and just sat and waited......and waited......and waited. I think it was about mid-afternoon before the mini bus returned and one by one we all got collected and returned to the manor house. We all regaled stories of talking to sheep, hallucinating, laughing about the contraband we'd smuggled out and a whole host of other misdemeanours. It transpired that one of the lads from our room bottled out half way through the first night and managed to find his way back to the manor house and was found asleep in our room the following day! I personally really enjoyed the solo expedition and would have cheerfully done it for an entire week.

Our third week in the Lake District meant just one thing; the final expedition, consisting of four days and three nights away traipsing over the hills and down the dales of this rather beautiful landscape. But us Cadets weren't happy. Although Andy and I didn't have too many issues with the lads in our group the same couldn't be said for some of the others, plus we wanted to extend the mileage on our expedition to cover the brief required for the Duke of Edinburgh's Gold Award scheme. So, the eight of us made representations to the staff that we be allowed to undertake the D of E expedition together which they granted. Truth be told we trusted each other implicitly and that was important to us.

So, on the Monday morning we set off from the manor house to trek our way over 60 miles of a pre-planned set route with a number of check points along the way. As soon as we got outside the gate we stopped so that I could remove my walking boots and put my training shoes on. There was no way I was going to suffer as I had done previously and hold everyone up. They felt so much more comfortable.

The first day was brilliant with decent weather and fantastic company with Paul Forbes keeping everyone entertained; there was a lot of laughter. As a result, the first 15 miles seemed to fly by and before we knew it we were at our first overnight stop, pitching tents and preparing our evening meal. We'd all done it so many times before that we were on auto pilot and everyone just knuckled down to the tasks at hand. And I didn't have a hint of a blister.

"Stand By Ya Beds"

Scafell bound, left to right; Steve Woodward, Andy Guy, Dave Brown, Tony Hastings, Paul Forbes and Chris Cox

We set off early the next morning with at least another 15 miles to cover and we knew the terrain was going to be a lot tougher this time. By mid-morning it had started to rain and it was obvious the weather was really closing in. By about lunch time it was torrential, I mean huge amounts of water tumbled from the sky, which meant our footings were becoming increasingly difficult. By early afternoon we were all completely soaked through, I mean down to our underpants kind of wet. The streams were now fast moving torrents and it got to the stage where it didn't matter about finding a dry area to cross them, we just waded through, sometimes almost waist deep. With the rain hitting us full in the face and getting in our eyes it made it difficult to see and visibility was now reduced even further because the low cloud had enveloped the hills. The laughter had stopped a long time ago and tempers became a little frayed when it transpired that we were completely and utterly lost. We were in trouble.

We got to the crest of a hill and as we looked down the other side it looked like we'd stumbled across a slate quarry. As we descended down the steep hill all of us lost our footing on the millions of slate chippings that were made even more slippery by the rain. About half way down we stumbled upon a single story prefab building that had metal shutters bolted to the windows. We quickly decided that we would get in somehow and use it as shelter. Out came the Swiss army knives as a couple of us set about trying to unscrew the bolts. But they wouldn't budge. Our initial excitement soon evaporated and we decided to carry on down into the valley because it was safer lower down than being stuck up on one of the hills. We slid down the slate slope to the bottom and waded through yet another stream; we didn't care anymore.

We had to find somewhere reasonably sheltered for the night but were concerned that our tents, sleeping bags and spare clothing would be wet inside our ruck sacks. As the light and our hopes were fading fast we came across a barn in the middle of nowhere. We ran towards it, found an open entrance and dived in. It was a two-storey wooden building and we decided to use the upper floor as our place of rest. There were quite a few straw bales scattered around with even more lose straw on the floor. It felt warm and cosy and it was quickly decided that this would be our home for the night.

As we unpacked our ruck sacks our suspicions about everything being soaked through were confirmed and so we hung a lot of it up on the rafters to dry out. Although our spirits had been lifted by having somewhere safe to sleep over night it was tempered with the knowledge that we would have to do it all over again tomorrow. And although my feet were saturated, I didn't have a single blister.

We woke the next morning and the weather hadn't changed at all. In fact, looking out of the barn you couldn't see more than about 50 feet and the rain was still lashing down. We decided it just wasn't safe for us to continue the walk in such conditions and wandered how the others were getting along. Not continuing caused a few arguments amongst us but Dave Brown came up with a solution. Whilst we'd been bickering about it, he'd been studying the map and worked out where we had been and more importantly where we were now. It transpired that we had only been a mile or two off course the previous day but that coming down through the quarry had effectively chopped the walk in half and that we would get disqualified now regardless because we hadn't done the miles required. Dave knew the area really well and said he could probably bull shit his way through our debrief with the instructors! It sounded like a great plan to us. So, we sat back in the barn whilst the weather continued to deteriorate outside.

On the final day we had about ten miles to do to get back to the manor house although it was suggested that we just get the miniature railway back to Eskdale instead. Needless to say we didn't, although it was very tempting just for the laughs it would have given us. By lunchtime we were trudging back into the grounds of the manor house to discover that two of the other three groups had been rescued by the instructors the previous day because of the weather. The other group had somehow toughed it out. We obviously didn't let on about our five-star accommodation and within a couple of hours we were sat in a classroom with one of the senior instructors talking through our expedition in fine detail. We all chipped in about the first couple of days and then Dave just sort of took over and gave details of places we had never seen. Did it work? Yeah of course it did. Do you know why? Because we all remembered what Sgt Middleton had said to us 18 months ago that Police work is 10% knowledge and 90% bull shit and there's your proof.

The next day we packed our gear, said goodbye to all the Mancs and the Scousers and got bussed down to the railway station and headed south towards London and then onwards towards home. I enjoyed most of my Outward Bound course I suppose especially as I'd come away with no blisters.

After three days off it was back to Newport nick for my Traffic attachment, which I was really looking forward to. I was crewed up with PC Pete Hughes who was from Sheffield and spoke with a very broad South Yorkshire accent. He wasn't that keen on being banished to the island and as a consequence a lot of his Relief weren't that keen on working with him. But I was, in fact we got on really well and it just so happened that he lived less than half a mile from me and therefore picked me up for work each day.

Our patrol car was a brand new Volvo 244DL, which looked space age in comparison to my father's old Morris Traveller. Pete drove to 'The System' and I was in awe of the style and the control he showed at speed. And he was allocated a Belstaff jacket with a red lining which was like a badge of honour to me. The combination of the car, the Police style of driving, that jacket and the work itself had me hooked. We attended a number of RTA's and other motor related incidents and with Pete's permission I got granted an indefinite extension to crew the car with him. I was in my element.

"Stand By Ya Beds"

LP-11 Newport's Volvo 244DL (left) and interior shot as it bombs down the Military Road towards Freshwater.
Photos; Stef King

We picked up a Suzuki GT750 motorcycle heading down Newport High Street one afternoon and Pete wanted to talk to the owner about an incident the bike had been involved in a few weeks before. The bike failed to stop for us and before I knew it we were doing over 60 mph along Fairlee Road with the two-tone horns blaring away. As we hit the national speed limit the speeds increased to over 100 mph for a couple of miles before the bike braked really hard and swung left onto the Whippingham Road. It accelerated away hard and at the left hand bend outside Osborne House the rider overcooked it and was on the wrong side of the road for most of the bend and if there had been anything else coming the other way there would have been a nasty head on collision. We were now in a 30 limit and as we headed down York Avenue into East Cowes the bike was still doing 70 mph. At the bottom of the hill the bike turned right onto Castle Street and just stopped. The rider put his hands in the air as if to surrender. Pete was pretty cool about it all really whereas I was shaking like a leaf, not out of fright, just a huge adrenalin rush. Our biker only had a provisional licence and no insurance and so got reported for all the offences.

Our Final Year

We were on late turn and had to collect the car from the brand new workshops at Fairlee. They were so new that the surrounding area was still a building site with other units in the process of being built. The local wildlife hadn't quite got used to being evicted yet either.

We collected the Volvo and commenced our patrol for the day. By early evening it was raining heavily and the streets were virtually deserted. As we neared the end of our shift we drove down Newport High Street and stopped at the lights. We'd been there a few seconds when the engine died. Pete tried to restart it but we had no ignition, no lights, nothing. We popped the bonnet and armed with a torch we started tugging at cables and prodding all the usual bits and bobs like people do in the vain hope that it might provoke the engine back into life. It didn't obviously and then Pete called out "What the fu……….?" And he pointed his torch towards the battery tray where there was a rabbit staring back at us and it would appear that he had chewed through the live cable from the battery. We carefully closed the bonnet and called for another unit to come to our rescue armed with a tow rope and a cardboard box with a lid. Once help arrived Pete picked up the rabbit and dropped him into the box and after being towed back to the nick we took another car back up to the industrial estate, released our furry friend from custody to re-join his mates.

As I was back on the island for a solid three months I'd often meet up with Wayne Colebrook and spend the evening at The Globe pub on Cowes seafront. It was a small pub with a few tables, a juke box and a pool table. It was run by his Uncle and most of the time we seemed to be the only customers. We played a lot of pool and drank a lot of lager and then staggered about a mile and a half back to Wayne's caravan that was parked in his parent's garden. Out there we could smoke, drink more alcohol, play music and generally have a good laugh without interruption.

"Stand By Ya Beds"

Then one night whilst playing pool at The Globe we got into a conversation about alcohol and I coughed to never having tasted whisky. Wayne was incredulous that I was a whisky virgin and with that two whisky shots appeared on the bar. I couldn't drink it neat so Wayne poured some orange juice into it. I downed it in one but really wasn't that keen. He said it was an acquired taste and so we had a couple more followed by another couple of pints and we were well on our way to getting completely shit faced. After that I don't recall much other than throwing up on the walk back home and how much whisky and orange burnt your throat on re-entry.

Getting pissed at this time was a fairly common occurrence and if we could afford it Wayne, Al Robertson and me would often find ourselves aboard the Medway Queen, an old paddle steamer moored on the River Medina, midway between Newport and Ryde. At the time it was just about the only disco in the area and was therefore frequented by just about every teenager on the island at weekends. The music was loud, the beer reasonably priced and it was always packed. We'd had a few it has to be said and Al had disappeared somewhere with some female as usual and Wayne had gone to the bar to get more drinks so I was sat there on my own in a slightly drunken stupor. Suddenly out of the dark came a large male armed with a knife and he pressed it hard against my throat and pushed me backwards against the wall.

"You and your fucking mate got me banned" he growled.

"What are you talking about?" I said, sobering up almost immediately.

"You fuckers chased me down into East Cowes and now I'm fucking banned" he growled again.

Then as quickly as he'd arrived, he was gone but only because Al had seen what was happening and grabbed him by the throat

Our Final Year

and virtually lifted him off the ground and promptly frog marched him off the boat. Thanks Al, I owe you one.

1977 was Her Majesty Queen Elizabeth's Silver Jubilee year and to help celebrate her 25 years on the throne a large number of events were planned culminating in the big one with the Fleet Review in The Solent on Wednesday 28th June. From a Police point of view this was a huge operation with massive crowds expected in the Portsmouth and Gosport areas. As part of that operation Police officers would be drafted in from all over the county and from a number of neighbouring forces and as such they needed to be accommodated and fed somewhere for a few days. Part of the former army barracks on Thorney Island was therefore requisitioned but needed recommissioning as the huge three storey accommodation blocks were completely empty.

Who better to do all the donkey work than a few of Hampshire's expendable Cadets? So, a couple of mini busloads of us were transported to Thorney Island where we unloaded lorry's full of metal bed frames, mattresses, tables and chairs etc. It was knackering work even for super fit lads like us, dragging these things up two flights of stairs and then slotting the beds together and positioning them in dormitory fashion. Midway through the first afternoon I was standing at the back of the truck waiting for a bed frame to be passed to me when one of them fell from the stack and timbered like a fallen tree straight onto my left hand, breaking one of my fingers. The pain was excruciating and I got carted off to the first aid post and was their first ever patient. My hand got bandaged up and within half an hour I was back out there helping to unload more furniture. In all it took us three days.

We were then assigned various duties either on Thorney Island itself or elsewhere in Portsmouth and Gosport for the rest of the week. Chris Cox and I got given night shift security patrols at the barracks. Oh great, Duty Squad but in a different location.

"Stand By Ya Beds"

To make matters worse I now had a dose of man flu and its always worse at night. By Monday night the place was filled with 150 coppers and a large number of airmen for the fly past. There was a lot of noise and laughter coming from the accommodation block but by about 0100 it had gone quiet as Chris and I did our hourly security checks. By day we slept in a side room and weren't required back on duty until 1800 each day. In between each patrol we'd drink coffee, play darts in the office and talk bikes, because the week after this shit was over, we were heading west back down to Penzance for a week's holiday again.

On the Tuesday night into Wednesday morning it started to rain. This wasn't in the plan at all. By all accounts it was a thoroughly miserable day weather wise and that helped reduce the expected crowds somewhat but Chris and I didn't care because we slept through it all. On the Wednesday night however, because the operation was effectively over it seemed to be an excuse for a huge piss up for those who were still on the site. As Chris and I were doing our rounds at about 0400 we came across one of the airmen lying face down on the narrow concrete path that led to the accommodation block. He was incredibly drunk and had both his hands and his feet gripping the edges of the path as he snored in his drunken sleep. Despite shaking him, prodding him, shouting in his ear we just couldn't wake him, let alone move him. So, we left him there and on our next round he'd gone.

A couple of days later Coxy and I were bombing back down to Cornwall. He was on his brand new Honda 400/4 and at times I struggled to keep up with him on my 250 Kawasaki, but I would never tell him that obviously. But I had the last laugh because a few days after we got back I collected my brand new Honda 750F2 from Ryes Motorcycles in Southampton.

I only had a week or so to get used to it because I'd recently received the joining instructions for my Community Service Volunteer assignment and before I knew it I was heading north towards Farnborough Hospital near Bromley on the Kent London border. I reported to the CSV coordinator at the hospital and she told me what my job would be for the next three months and I was somewhat taken aback. I was to report to the Children's Ward each day because my role was to be a Play Therapist for the kids on the Ward. A what? A Play Therapist? Oh, she added, you will also be required morning and afternoon to accompany one of the Ambulance staff to collect a number of day patients and bring them back to the Ward and return them home each evening.

Chris Cox and Honda 400/4
Photo Steve Woodward

"Stand By Ya Beds"

Farnborough Hospital

The hospital itself was very old and was built on the site of an old workhouse and backed onto the village of Locksbottom. After finding my accommodation I set about finding the Children's Ward which was on the first floor of the main building. I spoke to the Ward Sister who had absolutely no idea who I was, why I was there or even what CSV was. Not the best of starts. Anyway, she did know that the Ambulance driver was Phil and that he usually arrived on the Ward around 8.30 am each morning so that would be a good place to start.

The next morning I teamed up with Phil who was mid 30s I suppose with shoulder length fair hair and a closely cropped beard. He was pleased to have some help because some of the kids were quite challenging. The area he covered seemed rather large and we picked up kids from Bromley, Beckenham, Croydon and Crystal Palace. In Croydon we stopped at a large block of flats to collect 6 year old Paul. He had severe learning difficulties and a mental age of a one year old. He couldn't talk and was still wearing nappies.

He had recently undergone a major hip operation and both his legs were in plaster and splayed outwards with a steel bar set between his ankles to prevent any movement. As we climbed the stairs to the third floor Phil warned me that both parents were smack heads and could often be quite threatening so best not let on that I'm a Police Cadet. I was so naïve back then that I didn't even know what a smack head was!

The stairwell stunk of piss and vomit. There was graffiti everywhere and the constant noise of shouting and banging doors came from everywhere. It was a pretty grim place to live. Phil knocked on the door and after about a minute it opened and as it did so I saw a woman walking away from us down the hallway. She didn't say a word to us and then I saw Paul on the floor and she'd just stepped over him and gone into the kitchen. Phil and I went in and between us we picked the little lad up and carried him down to the ambulance. Phil was very gentle with him and even though he wasn't getting a response he did talk to him constantly which I thought was really nice because I'd already guessed that there probably wasn't much in the way of stimulus or love at home. We then collected a five year old girl from Beckenham and a 13 year lad from Orpington and returned them to the hospital for the day.

The Ward which consisted of five side rooms, each with four beds in was only half full. There were two single rooms, both of which were occupied; one by a 16 year old anorexic girl who was the thinnest human being I'd ever seen and who spent her entire day pacing up and down the room like a caged Lion. I was told in no uncertain terms that I wasn't to engage with her at all, although I have no idea why. At the far end of the corridor was the second single room with a young lad called Norman who was slumped in a wheel chair. I think he was about 18 or 19 and was obviously severely disabled both physically and mentally. He couldn't talk and just made a few grunting noises now and again. He was a

"Stand By Ya Beds"

permanent resident on the Ward and it was suggested that if possible, I spend a lot of time with Norman in an effort to get some interaction going. The Ward Sister left me with him and as I sat on the window sill I thought "I'm not trained for this; I don't have the faintest idea what I'm doing". I told Norman who I was and why I was there and that if he needed anything all he had to do was ask. I felt embarrassed even though I was the only person in the room and how the hell can Norman ask me for anything, he can't talk.

I found the toy cupboard which was a bit sparse to say the least; a few old jigsaw puzzles, some well read books, half used colouring books, a lot of old toy cars, some very sorry looking dolls complete with a badly broken dolls house and best of all, three boxes full of Scalextric sets. I decided to pull the whole lot out, tidy it all and commenced a repair regime on things like the doll's house and some of the cars. But overall, it was a pretty crap selection and over the next couple of weeks I made a number of posters and pinned them up throughout the hospital requesting donations of suitable toys. I was inundated with boxes and boxes of toys, some of it brand new, including new dolls, cars, Airfix kits, puzzles, books, painting materials, two brand new Spirograph sets and a decent train set. In fact, I had so much that the cupboard wasn't big enough to store it all.

Once Phil and I had collected the kids and brought them back to the Ward the rest of my day, until about 4pm consisted of me trying to keep the children on the Ward occupied either collectively or individually, depending on their age, their medical condition and whether or not they were interested. I'd visit Norman as often as I could and depending on what else was going on I'd wheel him down to where all the action was; I couldn't bear the thought of him just sitting in that room all by himself, I thought that was a terrible way for him to be treated. It took a while but I'm pretty sure Norman started to recognise me and I got a sort of smile when I entered his room, which was quite satisfying and boosted my confidence a bit in that I might actually be doing things right.

On the 16th August the world awoke to the news that Elvis Presley had died and the radio was filled with Elvis music for days on end, especially the song Way Down which stayed at number one for weeks. Other music of the period included The Stranglers with No More Heroes, The Jackson Five with Show You The Way To Go, Hot Chocolate with So You Win Again and Abba with The Name of the Game.

I came in one Monday morning to find the Ward virtually empty other than Norman and the anorexic teenager. During the morning handover with the staff I was told that they only had one new admission over the weekend and that was a ten year old lad who had recently been diagnosed with diabetes and was having to learn how to inject himself with insulin; so could I look after him? I found Charlie sat on his bed. He had a huge mop of ginger hair and he was as miserable as sin. I tried talking to him but he just wasn't interested. Then one of the nurses came to test his blood and it was decided that he needed more insulin. I watched in horror as the syringe was drawn up and handed to him. The needle looked like a javelin and he just sat on the edge of his bed with tears streaming down his face. He had to inject himself into his upper thigh and he was understandably terrified. It was awful to watch and as calm as the nurse was, he just wasn't going to do it. In the end Charlie agreed to let her do it and he hardly felt a thing. It was a psychological thing I suppose, not wishing to inflict pain upon yourself.

Once he'd calmed down a bit I introduced him to the Scalextric set, which he'd always wanted to play with. Truth be told, so had I. There was so much of it that we built a straight piece of track that ran half way down the corridor, did a sharp U turn and came racing back to the start again. His tears soon turned to laughter as we raced each other for the rest of the day. Every now and then the staff would take him away to test his blood sugar levels and eventually he plucked up the courage to inject himself. I was actually really proud of him. In 1998 I was diagnosed with diabetes and in 2008 had to go onto insulin. When I was learning how to inject myself, I thought about Charlie quite a lot.

Collecting and depositing young Paul was a rather harrowing experience for Phil and myself. His parents were scum bags and taking him home each day and leaving him with them was just awful. The flat stunk, there was no carpet anywhere and their entire life seemed to revolve around heroin. Phil taught me a lot about drugs and their various effects and it seemed like the area we were driving to and from was rife with the stuff, especially in Croydon.

We carried Paul up the stairs to the flat. The front door was wide open but despite us knocking and calling out we got no reply. We took Paul in and sat him on the settee. Phil then found the father spread eagled on the filthy bed with a syringe hanging out of his arm. He was off his face on heroin again and there was no sign of the mother. There were needles on the floor of every room, there was no food in the fridge or the cupboards and Pauls cot looked like it had never been changed, it was disgusting. Phil took the decision that we take Paul back to the Ward as a place of safety and so we carried him back down the stairs to the ambulance. As I was strapping Paul into his seat Phil said he had something to do and wouldn't be long. With that he disappeared back up the stairs and I saw him walking along the balcony and going back into the flat. He emerged less than two minutes later rubbing his right fist with his other hand. I didn't need to ask what had happened, I knew full well and endorsed it completely. Paul was kept on the Ward for a week before he was placed with foster parents. We didn't see him again but hopefully he was safe and well cared for.

I came onto the Ward one morning to be told that Norman had died in his sleep that night. I was really quite upset, not just that he had passed away but more because of the poor hand he had been dealt with in life.

After three months it was time to leave. I'd learned a lot of invaluable life lessons both on the ambulance escorts and up on the Ward and although I was somewhat sceptical about doing it at first, in the end I was grateful for the experience.

Other CSV assignments included the following examples;

Mick Streeter and Malcolm Collins

Malcolm Collins and I went to an overnight shelter in Wolverhampton. It was run by a group of American Monks called ' The Little Brothers of the Good Shepherd', they were an amazing group of guys. The homeless had to be in before 5pm, where they would have soup (made by us) with bread, a shower, fresh clothes and a bed. We stayed in the halfway house and whilst there we helped to decorate the shelter, passed our driving tests, learnt all about horse racing and betting with regular visits to the bookies for some of the permanent residents. Enlightening times for a 17 year old and fond memories.

Chris Gosden

I also went to work in the overnight shelter in Wolverhampton run by monks (the Little Brothers of the Good Shepherd). It was definitely an eye opener; it was half of an old cinema. The other half was a night club. This led to some amusing incidents. Definitely an eye-opening experience.

Kev Emblen and Nick Griggs

Nick and I were dispatched to St. James psychiatric hospital in Southsea. We saw some very sick people and strange ones to boot. We also witnessed ECT treatments. Some patients were very manic before treatment but very subdued almost zombified for days afterwards. We also spent quite a bit of downtime in The Good Companion pub. Soft drinks only of course.

Duncan Warry

Best part of my Cadet time. I did my CSV at the Katherine Low centre which was a youth centre in Battersea High Street, which had accommodation attached. Besides the happy memories, what did I get from it? Became good at table tennis, playing one particular young black lad, got to know the real London, met a lot of really nice people.

Laurie Parsonage

I was a 'direct entry' phase 3 but still did my 'community service' volunteering at St Ebba's hospital in Epsom, Surrey. That was a hospital for adults with learning difficulties. I found myself working in the recreational facility, basically three (became four) months of playing games and arranging day trips away with about thirty or more adults with Down's syndrome.

Now remember I'm 17 years old, nearly 18, I've recently passed my driving test and on the form asking what I like to do, I write driving.

Somehow that is interpreted as I'm a coach driver (very apt for incidents later in my police career at Stonehenge). A week into my placement I find myself taking a test to drive their 52 seater coach, to take the 'Kid's' down to the seaside at Brighton. On the test, I'd been driving quite well, I thought, for about twenty minutes when the instructor says to me, "you are over 21 aren't you" whoops! The thing is he let me carry on driving to take the coach back to the hospital.

Our Final Year

I was at the hospital on my own, no other Cadets or anyone I knew so when I was in the workers canteen I decided to sit with a very pretty blonde nurse. She didn't speak much English so I guessed she might not know how to say no if I asked her out for a drink. She didn't say no and we ended up being 'good friends' for the whole 4 months. I was a 17 year old from Southampton thinking I knew a bit... she was 21 and I knew nothing!

When she returned to France she wrote me a letter saying that if she'd spoken English better things may have been different but, 'body has a way of expression and we seemed to understand each other'

I enjoyed my CSV experience! So much so, I nearly packed in the police force. Now I've been retired nearly 13 years I'm glad I didn't!

Matt Coumbe and Steve Norcross

We landed up at the Spoon Lane Adventure Playground in Smethwick, Birmingham. It was good, in as much as I had a town house to myself. Had feature in the Star newspaper with kids hanging from length of rope climbing up a tree. It was an interesting area where the IRA collected money in the local pubs. I used to meet up with Steve Norcross and we visited a couple of girls who worked for CSV in Wolverhampton running a woman's refuge. Steve had a motor cycle at the time. One day Steve came down to the playground and was messing about on the climbing frame and pulled a muscle in his back. I ended up calling an ambulance as he was in severe pain. I was also socialising with another girl (not in police) who was doing CSV but she was staying at a nunnery in Birmingham. I think she wanted to be a nun.

Dave Brown

I ended up at the same place at Matt Coumbe but a year later, a great place, multi-racial and many great experiences, a lot not to be published for public eyes.

Stef King

I went to a children's home in Lambeth and learnt that there was a lot to do in the Smoke but you needed money! Learnt that kids could be horrid to the extreme and that I didn't want a job in childcare.

Phil Travers

I had my interview for CSV after a nightshift of my weeks' stint at the Cadet School as Night Warden. They kept us hanging around so by the time I had my interview I was tired and grumpy. Made my preferences pretty clear. Whether it made a difference I don't know but I was sent to a children's Day Nursery in I think Grove Park Road, in Chiswick not long after Chris Lee had gone there. Had a room in the house. The women running it were a couple of hooray Henrietta's. There was also a girl about our age there but she was doing a Community Service sentence so wasn't keen on the Police, refused to tell me about any good pubs or nightclubs to go to. Found a pub down the road (City Barge) pop group Hot Chocolate would hang out there, played darts, before going onto a club. Some would turn up in a huge American car and one in his Morris Minor! Did great sandwiches, would sit out by the Thames with a beer. Met up with Ian Heath who was at a doss house in Battersea, went to the Red Cow in Hammersmith to see the Tom Robinson Band. Really stuck out as the only two with short hair. Learnt that unless you know people London can be a lonely place. With so many women there dropping off their children, my life lesson learnt was that my chatting up technique was crap.

Alan Dabbs

Glasgow Night Shelter just off St. Georges Square, looking after homeless alcoholics, druggies and mental welfare. I had never seen anything like it before. One lad was my age addicted to hair lacquer in lemonade, you could buy it ready mixed from some of the local shops. Life expectancy one year, we managed to get him dry, into accommodation and then he vanished, turning up a month later worse than before. That was hard to deal with. I learnt everyone had a story and reasons for being there. They were all individuals. After that I was always polite to the homeless, even if they had to be moved on.

Andy Williams
I went to Liberton Assessment Centre (secure school) in Edinburgh. Ended up doing nearly 6 months and loved almost every minute of it. The most serious under 18 offenders were housed there including two who were there for murder/manslaughter. Almost all of the kids were great a lot of the time, the 12 year old murderer had ADHD although it wasn't called that then. He was a wonderful young boy who should not have been there. He would literally climb the walls at night in frustration - incredibly sad to watch and almost impossible to calm him down. Learnt how to deal with violent young offenders' intent on stabbing me and why one should never first foot in Scotland in a block of flats. Amazing and life changing experience without a doubt. Before I went I envied those going on Project Trust overseas. After I had done it I didn't.

John Gunner
I got sent to the YMCA in Norwich and took over from Lee Hunt. The YWCA next door was closed so there were a number of females also living in our building. Now, aged 17 and a bit naïve, I was still a virgin (come on…most of us were) and somehow some of the ladies could tell. During my first week I was seduced by an 18 year old girl who introduced me to naked female flesh and the art of losing one's cherry in her room, whilst her boyfriend was out!!! To make matters worse and to illustrate how desperate I was, not only was this lady in a steady relationship, she was also 7 months pregnant!!! My recollection of her is constantly telling me to SLOW DOWN. Then there was a very mature Thai lady in her 30's who was employed as a cleaner.

"Stand By Ya Beds"

She seduced me whilst I was trying to watch the FA Cup final in my room. She was insatiable and wanted sex all the time. I remember walking around Norwich city centre just to get a break from her and limping like John Wayne because my nether regions were so tender!! The Thai woman, by the way, wrote a letter to me about five years later via Hants police who forwarded it to me. She was struggling for money and wanted to move in with me!! OMG imagine that? Obviously I didn't respond. I think my role was to sit on reception but that memory escapes me because of my sexual coming of age.

Chris Cox

I was at Napsbury Hospital, London Colney near St. Albans. Basically, I was assisting in activities for the patients within the hospital and in the community. Napsbury was one of a number of large Victorian institutions in the area. There was a lady I visited on a secure ward. She was bedridden having suffered a broken hip some years before. As far as I could tell there was nothing mentally wrong with her. I kept on asking why she was in Napsbury but never got an answer. She would tell me that she had been there for 25 years and that she had no family to look after her. Never could get my head around why she was locked away. That is why they closed these institutions down. We would take a group of men into St. Albans for a walk around the town ending up in the pub. Some would have a beer and one man would drink as much as he could in the time we were there, downing pint after pint. As a result, we wouldn't stay long and so headed back walking down a busy St Albans High Street the man in question stopped abruptly. As I went back for him, I saw a river of urine coming from his foot and pedestrians were politely circumventing the flow as it sped down the hill. Very embarrassing for him and me but funny to see everyone avoiding the flow. There were many people in this hospital that would now be looked after in the community. I enjoyed my time there and it was totally worthwhile as it opened my naive eyes on one part of the community.

Our Final Year

Richard Smith

Myself, Howard Marrs, Malcolm Smith and Paul Rowsell stayed on for a second year at CTS as Phase 3 Cadets to mentor the new intake so we didn't get the chance to do CSV. However, I do remember that we went to an Acorn Camp at a place called Noss Mayo (near Plymouth). It was linked to the National Trust and we were to work on clearing paths and hedges etc. We were joined by other young people from different backgrounds. I will always remember a guy called Sam from Cambridge. He was posh but had no common sense. We got him pissed on drinking Cider/Guinness through a straw. He also wore an old-fashioned raincoat and when we were walking one day, we got him to open his raincoat in front of a family and say "I've got something to show you". He was clothed underneath. We slept in the village hall and most nights the sleeping bags would be full of stinging nettles. The village hall had a clock above it and on our last night we managed to break it. As we left the next day, we heard an old local say "I've never seen that clock stop before". Instead of helping the village, I think we nearly destroyed it! An award must go to Paul as he rode his Honda 175 all the way from the Isle of Wight to Plymouth while Howard and I let the train take the strain.

One of the first things I had to do upon returning to Hampshire was to get my hair cut. It hadn't been this long since I was at school. Within days I was back at Newport nick where I teamed up with Pete Hughes again but I knew it was only for a couple of weeks. On my first day off I went out for a blatt on my bike and stopped off at Dave Death bike dealers in Carisbrooke to take a look at the new bikes in the show room, something most bikers tend to do. I'd only been there a few minutes when another Honda 750F2 arrived outside. I thought I had the only one on the island (there was no Honda dealer then) and so I was intrigued to see who the other biker was. He'd parked his bike next to mine and he and I swapped notes about them as his lovely girlfriend grabbed a cup of tea from the nearby burger van. After 15 minutes or so I left.

The next afternoon I was on late turn and discovered that there had been a double fatal on Forest Road the previous day involving a Honda 750F2. Both the lad and his girlfriend had died instantly when a car pulled out in front of them less than half an hour after I'd been talking to them. It was quite a shock and it transpired that I was possibly the last person to see them alive and therefore had to provide a witness statement to that effect.

The officer dealing with it all was none other than Dave Gurd. He wanted to borrow my bike to assist with the accident investigation and said he wanted to carry out certain brake tests, stopping distances and handling issues. I reluctantly agreed to let him have the keys and off he went on my pride and joy. Its at this point that you need to understand that Gurdy was a Brit bike fan and loved his Norton Interpol. Several hours later he returned with my bike, that had now gained another 60 miles and lost a tank of fuel. As he threw the keys at me I asked;

"Well, what did you think of it then?
"Fucking rubbish nipper" he laughed "go out and get yourself a proper bike".

Second week of November and I was on my final attachment as a Cadet; three weeks night shift on the Casualty Department at the Royal Hospital in Portsmouth. I was teamed up with MH Smith. Mick was a Gosport boy and quite loud and extrovert, who tended to swear a lot. Our accommodation was at HMS Nelson and our rooms were on the 10th floor of Saumarez Block, which bore an uncanny resemblance to that shit hole in Croydon. The two lifts were out of order and there were take away cartons, chip wrappers, empty beer cans and vomit on just about every stair well.

218

After sorting out our rooms we decided to go and sample some Royal Navy food in the canteen. As we walked across the large parade square I heard what sounded like a bugle call over the tannoy but didn't take any notice of it because Mick and I were talking about something or other. I then heard a bellowing voice behind us.

"YOU TWO, STAND STILL"

We turned to look and saw a Naval officer in full uniform with scrambled egg on the peak of his cap marching towards us. He looked really angry.

"WHAT THE FUCK ARE YOU TWO DOING?" he shouted in our faces "DON'T YOU KNOW WHAT TIME IT IS?"

We both looked at our watches. It was exactly 1600.

"IT'S SUNSET" he yelled.

We looked at him blankly, yeah OK its almost dark. We very quickly explained that we weren't RN personnel and that we were Hampshire Police Cadets and had no idea we were causing an upset.

He sort of back peddled a bit, not much, but enough to explain that at 1600 each day, at sunset, all personnel were to face the main mast, stand to attention and salute, as the White Ensign was lowered. Not doing so was a serious disciplinary offence. We had little choice but to apologise and he begrudgingly let us go.

We found the canteen and it was packed with Navy ratings and the place had a real buzz about it. The food looked fantastic and we doubted that The Soup Dragon was in charge here. We both tucked into a large portion of sausage, egg and chips and very nice it was too. Except for some of the chips, you know the sort, the really hard, impossible to eat bits that you tend to get sometimes. Anyway, like the well trained lads we were we took our trays up to the serving hatch area that we had observed the local staff had used to deposit their plates and cutlery. To the left of the counter was a very shiny slop bucket and as Mick scraped the remaining chips from his plate into the bucket another bellowing voice came from the kitchen.

"Oi, WHAT THE FUCK ARE YOU DOING?" said the chef in his best whites, looking into the bucket, which only contained the left overs that Mick had scraped in and nothing else.

"Oh sorry mate" said Mick "I thought this was the slop bucket"

"It is" growled the chef "but that doesn't mean you can use it"

With that he poured Micks left overs back onto his plate and snarled "You take it son, you fucking eat it" and with that he stomped off with the bucket under his arm.

It was rather embarrassing as we both sat back down to eat our little bits of chip whilst the entire canteen glared at us. Two major bollockings in our first hour at HMS Nelson was probably a record.

The Royal was a ten minute walk from HMS Nelson and we arrived at 1800 in time for our first 12 hour shift. It was an old Victorian building that had seen better days. The staff were quite used to having Police Cadets around as they had been going there for a number of years now and so at least we didn't have to explain too much about who we were and why we were there. We were given white coats to wear which immediately made us look like junior Doctors but in fact we were to act as porters when needed or to assist staff in other ways when requested. The whole department was run by the fearsome Dr McDonagh, a Scottish lady who didn't suffer fools.

Our Final Year

The entrance to A&E at the old Royal Hospital in Portsmouth

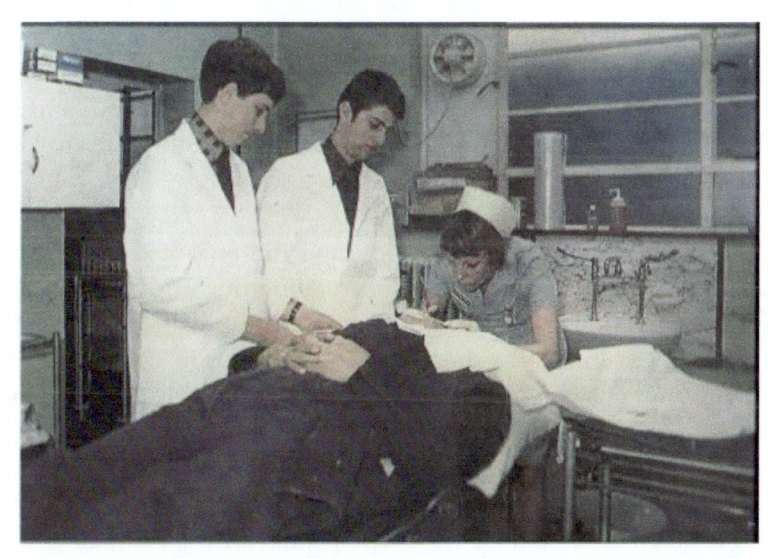

Cadets Laurie Parsonage and Clive Grace on their attachment at the Royal

"Stand By Ya Beds"

We'd only been there a couple of hours when a man in his 30s came in clutching his left elbow and said he'd done something rather silly. He said he had been laying on the lounge floor at home, had rolled over onto his left side and as his elbow hit the carpet a stray sewing needle had pierced his skin and was now completely embedded inside his arm. The only tell-tale sign was a small amount of blood and a couple of inches of black cotton sticking out of his elbow. I took him around to reception, got him booked in and then sat with him in a cubicle.

A young Doctor entered and after a brief examination sent him off to be x-rayed. The results came back showing that the needle had hit a bone and then bent double. No wonder it hurt. So, after a couple of local anaesthetic injections the Doctor got to work by making a small incision in the man's arm. As he did so the cotton fell out onto the floor. Sadly, this meant that the only real clue as to the needle's location was now lost. He made the incision a bit longer. Then a bit longer still. Then a bit longer again. He couldn't find it. By now the cut to his arm was more than an inch long. After almost an hour and a number of further injections the wound was more than four inches in length and the needle was finally removed. The patient declined the offer to keep it as a souvenir.

It was an interesting start although the rest of the night was quiet and by 6am Mick and I were trudging our way back to HMS Nelson and then had to climb ten flights of stairs, dodging the puddles of vomit and other bodily fluids before collapsing into our pits. When we got up, we decided that we would stay inside until after 1600; it was safer that way.

On our third night ambulance brought in a young woman who'd taken an overdose of sleeping pills all washed down with half a bottle of vodka. She was unconscious. She was taken into a special room just inside the main door and lifted onto the only bed in the room. I was somewhat taken aback at the rough handling by the staff who seemed unusually indifferent to her condition. A nurse pulled back the woman's eye lids and shone a torch in her eyes whilst shouting at her to wake up, but got no response.

"She's faking it" said the nurse to a colleague.

With that they dragged a trolley across to the bed that had a length of what looked like a rubber hose with a plastic funnel attached to one end and a large metal jug filled with water. A metal bowl was placed on the floor next to the bed.

"This is your last chance to open your eyes and talk to us or we'll have no choice but to pump your stomach out" the nurse shouted. There was no response.

The rubber hose was then thrust down the woman's throat and into her stomach. She gagged but it was too late because the water jug was then poured into the funnel and the gagging suddenly got much worse. The funnel was held aloft until all the water had gone down and then it was lowered below the height of the body as the contents of her stomach then came gushing out with the water. The smell was putrefying and made me gag somewhat. Within seconds the procedure was repeated twice more and by now our patient was very definitely awake. The hose was removed and the woman was left spitting bile and flehm into the bowl. It was an extremely unpleasant thing to watch.

One of the nurses explained afterwards that they had little sympathy or patience with those who take an alleged overdose of drugs. They often feigned unconsciousness and are little more than attention seekers and the staff here have enough to contend with without pandering to any drama queens. The one thing she couldn't understand was that some of them are repeat offenders who know full well the horrors of the stomach pump and yet they still go through with it. Over the next couple of weeks, we helped out with another half a dozen such cases and I had no idea until then just how common an occurrence it was.

By mid-November the country was on full alert because for the first time ever the Fire Brigade were on strike. HMS Nelson was turned into a temporary fire station with a number of 'green goddess' fire appliances, hurriedly commandeered from the militaries Auxiliary Fire Service and put back into service, all manned by military personnel and escorted to any incident by a Police motorcyclist.

One afternoon ambulance brought in a motorcyclist who'd fallen from his bike and smashed his elbow. We got to look at the x-rays and the bones in his elbow and lower arm were smashed into several pieces. Within an hour or so he was being carted off to the operating theatre and we were asked if we'd like to watch a proper operation. Within minutes we were scrubbed up, gowned up and stood less than five feet from the operating table. The patient's arm was cut wide open and several fragments of bone were removed and placed on the trolley. There were two surgeons who examined the x-rays and the pieces they had removed to ensure they had them all and then set about drilling holes in the bone and literally screwing it all back together again with a couple of metal plates attached to help keep it altogether. Within an hour or so the gaping hole in the arm was being stitched up before he was wheeled out of theatre and into the recovery room. The surgeons were confident that given time the man would regain the full use of his arm. It was fascinating to watch.

Within minutes we were being asked if we'd like to observe a full hip replacement operation? We readily agreed and after getting prepared with new gowns, masks and gloves we walked into the theatre next door. The patient was a huge woman in her 50s I think and we were told that her operation was necessary because her hip bones had basically worn out due to her weight.

The two surgeons, the anaesthetist and three nurses then set about slicing the woman open and I use that term deliberately because it was like watching Japanese fishermen slice open a whale with one of those huge knives. As both her legs seemed to have been almost completely separated from the rest of her body so the smell hit us. Nobody warned us about the smell. Then the old hip bone was removed and we were allowed to take a closer look. By now both Mick and I were feeling a bit queasy but we persevered, not wishing to wimp out at this stage. The new plastic hip was inserted and then out came the electric drills, a saw and a sort of metal grinding tool that was used to remove surplus bone from the hip joints. The noise and the smell of burning bone and flesh was a smell I won't ever forget. With the new hip in place they somehow pulled all her fleshy bits back together and spent another hour or so stitching her back together again. It was amazing to watch the medical team perform, what for them was a routine operation, but to us two was something to marvel at.

Midway through our final week ambulance brought in a 15 year old lad who'd crashed the stolen motor bike he'd been riding, head on into a car up in Cowplain. It was obvious he was in a bad way. He was rushed straight into the emergency room and I went in with them. Dr McDonagh was in charge and she and her nursing staff were doing their best to save his life. The room was frantic with drips and life lines being inserted, oxygen being administered and heart monitors attached. Then he started fitting, with his whole body thrashing about. One of the nurses told me to hold his legs down, which was easier said than done and in the end I laid across his lower legs to keep my weight on him. As his legs moved I could hear the sound of broken bones grinding together. And then it stopped.

"Stand By Ya Beds"

"You can let go now," said the nurse "he's dead".

I stood back and looked at him. What a waste of a young life I thought. He looked very small and very battered. As we filed out of the room, one of the nurses told the police officer waiting outside. No doubt he will end up having to tell the boys parents I thought. That will be me one day.

Our three-week stint had come to a close and I had learned an awful lot about life, death and about myself. It was probably the most beneficial attachment I'd done.

The following week I was back at HQ in Winchester for my interview with the Chief Constable to determine whether or not he would take me on as a Constable. I met Coxy, Andy Goward, Howard Marrs, Ian Heath and several others from our intake, all of us reasonably confident that we would get through, even though we had been told in no uncertain terms that it wasn't guaranteed. But we did all get through and within days had received our joining instructions dated January 4th 1978.

So, our Cadet days were over, it was time to do *'the job'* for real. Had being a Police Cadet for the last two and a half years been worth it? Absolutely. Had I learned anything? Yes, some real-life skills and experiences. Would I do it again? In a heartbeat, just so long as it was with the exact same group of lads whom I had come to regard as real friends and colleagues. We had experienced so much together and as a result formed a bond that is completely different to anything else I've ever known. Would a similar scheme work today? I very much doubt it but only because the instructors would probably end up being disciplined or maybe even in court for what today would be classed as bullying. But to us, back then, it was anything but, it was genuine character building, it worked and we loved it.

Our Final Year

I did have one ceremony to undertake as my parting gesture to my life as a Hampshire Police Cadet; I filled those walking boots with petrol and set fire to them. It was a cathartic moment.

"Stand By Ya Beds"

HOUSE NAMES

ROWAN HOUSE

PC Pete Kerley
Alan Spiers – Phase 3
Steve Woodward
Andy Goward
Russ Bramley
Martin Gibson
Phil Mason
Richard Smith
Duncan Warry
Chris Gosden
Gary Keable
Gary O'Flaherty
Wayne Howsego
Nigel French
Paul Sexton
Wayne Colebrook
Alan Robertson
Trevor Murphy
Andy Sewell

FIELDING HOUSE

PC Russ Parke
Steve Mote – Phase 3
Trevor Bucket -Phase 3
Paul Forbes
Stef King
Phil Travers
Chris Cox
Mick Streeter

House names

Andy Reed
Mick Dodds
Kev Mason
Andy Crawford
Chris Porter
Kev Willis
Terry Clarke
Nathan Johnson
Paul Downey
Andy Worship
Mick Smith
Pete LeGros
Ian Robinson

PEEL HOUSE

PC Pete Manns
Paul Underwood – Phase 3
Nigel Niven - Phase 3
John Gunner
Dave Brown
Adrian Cleighton-Hills
Shaun Terry
Alan Dabbs
Kevin Emblen
Nick Griggs
Paul Rowsell
Malcolm Smith
Steve Postlethwaite
Bob Strong
Jim Humphries
Ian Heath
Neil Cheyne
George Barker
Andy Williams

"Stand By Ya Beds"

Howard Marrs
Stuart Montague

MAYNE HOUSE

PC Tony Astill
Clive Grace – Phase 3
Steve Smale – Phase 3
Paul Diaper
Chris Lee
Andy Guy
Tim Beazley
Larry Dwyer
Paul Williams
Colin Smith
Malcolm Collins
Gerry Hutchings
Geoff Weeks
Lee Hunt
Jeff England
Adrian Prangnell
Steve Matcham
John Fraser
Tim Payne
Richard Young
Barry Howard

Phase 2 Cadets

Steve Moore
Steve Norcross
Bill Channing
Laurie Parsonage
Matt Coumbe
Brian Foley

BOOKS BY STEVE WOODWARD

Steve Woodward was a Police officer with the Hampshire Constabulary from 1975 to 2008 and has written four books so far about his experiences whilst in *'the job'*. His first book **'From T Ford to T5'** is the definitive reference book on the history of the vehicles used by Hampshire Police. The second book **'Kilo Sierra Five One'** charts his first 10 years in the Police and how he nearly got thrown out because he didn't measure up. It will make you laugh and cry out loud as he deals with the locals of his adopted city of Portsmouth. His third book **'The Long Short Walk'** dealt with his role as a Traffic Police Family Liaison Officer and is a hard-hitting diary looking at 16 real life cases and the harrowing journey that each family has to contend with following the death of a loved one in a road incident.

His latest book **'Stand By Ya Beds' (Life as a 1970s Police Cadet)** takes us way back to the mid-1970s when Steve joined the Police Cadets at the tender age of 16 during which he spent the first 12 months at a residential training school where physical training and self-discipline were drummed into him by instructors, who by today's more enlightened standards would probably see them being accused of bullying. But Steve and his 65 colleagues loved every minute of it.......except for the morning run, the constant uniform inspections, the walks across Dartmoor, punishment press-ups, bulling boots, the food, the blisters and making bed packs.

The book delves into the history of the Police Cadet scheme both nationally and within Hampshire before it morphs into Steve's own experiences whilst based at the training school followed by a further 12 months at his local police station seeing at first-hand how each department within the service worked. It's hard to imagine in this day and age that teenagers once patrolled our streets in full police uniform, from the 1950s through to the 1980s.

'The Long Short Walk'

'The Long Short Walk' was Steve's third book. It's something we all dread; the knock at the door from a Traffic Cop and sadly for 3000 families a year in the UK that becomes a reality. The Police officer has come to deliver the news that their loved one has died in a road incident. This diary of 16 real life cases takes us through what these families had to contend with and some of it is truly awful (although there are some light hearted moments in it too). Steve describes the journey these families embark upon as the biggest roller coaster ride of their lives with more highs and lows than you could ever possibly imagine.

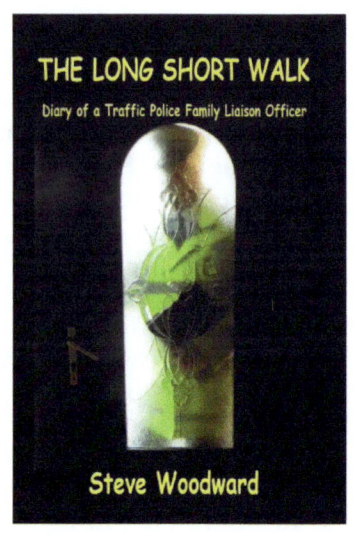

Reviews

Mick Panormo.

We will always be thankful. You supported myself and my family through the worst time of our lives. I am not sure if we would have made it without your support, you were there for us 24 - 7. I just hope others will read your book and maybe it will help them to be a little more thoughtful when they are out there on the road and appreciate what you guys do. This is a very emotional book that you won't be able to put down. It is very personal to me because my family is unfortunate enough to be featured in it. This guy had a tough job, read it and find out why.

John Clelford

A book crammed with the emotional and little seen effects of the unsung Family Liaison officers. A superb read, and highly recommended.

Keith Mitchell

This book is superbly written in every way. I took it on holiday with me and there was no way that I could put it down. It really is an insight into the role of a Police Family Liaison Officer and all of the trauma that goes with it, both for the author and all of the families involved in the tragedies of road traffic collisions. I thoroughly recommend this book.

PLA Portsmouth (5 stars – Thoroughly recommended)

An excellent book from start to finish - I just couldn't put it down. Such an honest insight into the role of a Police Family Liaison Officer.

Tina (5 stars – Excellent read)

Excellent book, I've never finished a book so quickly, couldn't put it down, made me laugh and also cry, absolutely fabulous.

Mick Smith (5 stars – Irrespective of whether you served in the EMS or just want a good read, and which will grip you from the beginning)

As I read the book, I shed tears for the stories as they obviously stirred memories of traumatic times I experienced whilst serving in the EMS. The memories never leave you and as Steve says in the book, the emotional sponge overflows on occasions. Steve

"Stand By Ya Beds"

Woodward, yet again has produced a book which hits home to the reader, irrespective of whether you served in the EMS or just want a good read, and which will grip you from beginning to end. I picked it up and couldn't put it down. He has written it with mountains of empathy for the victims and their families who have to mentally deal with the aftermath and the book is a must read.

'Kilo Sierra Five One'

'Kilo Sierra Five One' is part auto-biography, part history book on policing one of Britain's toughest cities; Portsmouth. Written by a Police officer who experienced at first hand a turbulent and violent decade, it takes us through his very first days at training school in 1978 right through to the late 1980s and includes national events like the year-long miners' strike, the Falklands conflict, New Age Travellers, the Greenham Common Peace Camp and the 1987 hurricane. But it is perhaps the local incidents he attended that will make you either laugh, cry or shout out loud as he deals with human beings and all their failings, from horrific car accidents to football hooligans, he gives us a candid view of what it's like to be involved in such incidents and how it can affect the lives of those that do. This book tells the story of his first years in *'the job'* and how he very nearly got thrown out because he didn't measure up. It's a warts-an-all personal account, a real-life Ashes to Ashes.

Reviews

Afficionado (5 stars - A gripping read)

From the first opportunity I had to start on this book, all other reading was pushed aside! Woodward's writing is just totally honest; -there is certainly nothing pretentious in his style. He is nevertheless a natural writer, able to convey in compelling manner -from cover-to-cover of this 350+ page read- a vivid and gripping account of the incidents which form the raw daily life of a city police officer.

All the daily frustrations, the traumas, the disappointments and successes of a policeman in Portsmouth during the late 70's, running through to the 80's, are recounted in a simple but grippingly vivid style.

For anyone even half-familiar enough with the area to envisage the nightmarish car-chases or areas of danger (if not, log on to 'Google-Maps'!) this book is not only a gripping read, but opens the civilian eyes and mind to another world happening around us daily, of which we would otherwise most probably be totally unaware.

I have lost some of my cynicism regarding the police through reading this book, in the hope that at least the majority may just be as sincere and dedicated as Woodward evidently was throughout his career.

Paul240480 (5 stars - KS51 a great read)

Great book, which arrived 'early'. Have you ever wondered why you rarely see a bobby on the street? Have you ever thought, on seeing a Police car drive past with a 'subdued' looking officer onboard, that he may have just left the scene of something 'we' hope never to witness? Have you ever wondered why Police don't just 'sort out' the 2000 strong gang of away fans at the local match. Well read this 'eye opener' from one who experienced it 'first hand' and see that they really do have an uphill battle. Funny sometimes, serious others. Truthful & to the point. Excellent.

John A. Antonelli (5 stars - OK Steve Woodward where's the promised sequel?)

If you like Mike Pannett you will also like edgier Steve Woodward. A great read and well written stories about the good, the bad and the ugly of policing Portsmouth. It is also a historical review of the 80s from a policing perspective. My only problem is this book came out in 2010 and we were promised a sequel about policing Portsmouth in the 90s and needless to say after reading this one I am chomping at the bit for the next one. So Steve W get writing!!

Jimmy Page (5 stars - Totally gripping – I couldn't put it down)

After I took delivery of the book, I opened it up intending to have a quick dip into it. From the outset I found it so gripping and the characters so involving that I really couldn't put it down. Only the necessity for sleep interrupted my reading and the next morning I picked it up again and couldn't put it down until I had finished it. This is a brilliant expose of what Policing in Portsmouth in the 1980's was like. Often funny, sometimes tragic and occasionally dangerous and frightening but always gripping. I highly recommend this book - it is a damned good read.

From T Ford to T5
(100 Years of Hampshire Constabulary Transport)

The definitive reference book for anyone interested in the vehicles used by the Police.

Reviews

Jim Whatley (5 stars - Record of police transport)

This book will obviously appeal to a niche audience of readers interested in transport and particularly the emergency services. It has been meticulously researched and will serve as an historical record of knowledge that would otherwise be lost. I thoroughly enjoyed it and found it could be dipped into when one had the inclination. I look forward to future books by Steve Woodward.

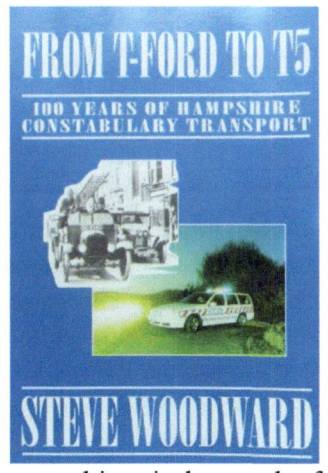

Pat the Trucker (5 stars)

For petrol heads and law breakers alike, this shows how the Police source and test their cars. As a 'star' of the television show 'Traffic Cops' the author tells it how it is on the front line for the boys in blue as they protect and defend the law-abiding people and put fear into those who are not.

D. Pimbblett (5 stars – Fantastic summary of Police transport)

Superb book ideal for anyone with an interest in Police vehicles. The amount of research Steve Woodward has carried out to produce this impressive book is fantastic, what dedication! Great book with lots of images of some of the more interesting experiments in Police Transport. Steve, now retired from Hampshire Constabulary, can frequently be seen on old runs of the TV series ' Traffic Cops'.

Natterjack (5 stars – History of police vehicle use in Hampshire and I.O.W)

For anyone like myself interested in the subject, this book is a 'Must Have' A former Hants police constable, the author has researched his subject well. An excellent read and so informative.